The Bear Almanac

A Comprehensive Guide to the Bears of the World

SECOND EDITION

GARY BROWN

THE LYONS PRESS

Guilford, Connecticut

AN IMPRINT OF THE GLOBE PEQUOT PRESS

The Lyons Press is an imprint of The Globe Pequot Press.

Text design by Diana Nuhn
Layout by Melissa Evarts

This book was previously published as *The Great Bear Almanac* (1993).

Library of Congress Cataloging-in-Publication Data

Brown, Gary.
  The bear almanac : a comprehensive guide to the bears of the world / Gary Brown. — 2nd ed.
      p. cm.
  Includes bibliographical references and index.
  ISBN 978-1-59921-331-6 (alk. paper)
  1. Bears—Miscellanea. I. Title.
  QL737.C27B765 2009
  599.78—dc22

                                                        2008042726

Printed in China

10 9 8 7 6 5 4 3 2 1

To Pat
My friend and wife of a wonderful half century,
for the support and many sacrifices

What is man without the beasts? If all the beasts were gone, man would die from great loneliness of spirit, for whatever happens to the beasts also happens to man. All things are connected.

Chief Seattle

Contents

Foreword

BEARS COMMAND OUR INTEREST and attention as do few other animals. They are as individual and entertaining—and sometimes almost as dangerous—as humans, and their appeal is only heightened by their scarcity. Most of us can't begin to recall all the deer we've seen, but we never forget a bear.

Gary Brown's immensely informative and entertaining *The Bear Almanac, Second Edition,* proves that it's been this way between people and bears for a long time. The bear's capacity to amaze and enchant us only grows as we learn more about these extraordinary animals. Gary's splendid book will tell you all about that, so I will tell you a little about Gary.

First, you should know that you couldn't find a better guide to the world of the bear. I've known Gary for more than twenty-seven years. I have worked closely with him on some of modern conservation's most controversial issues, and I admire him not only for his remarkable bear savvy but for his calm good sense about pretty much everything else. Gary was something of a legend in the world of bears long before he started writing his outstanding bear books. In a long, productive career in the National Park Service, he was known as one of the *real* bear experts—and one of the nation's foremost professional champions of smart bear management—and he played a pivotal role in the development of modern bear management in Yosemite, Alaska, and Yellowstone (I'm entirely neglecting his similar stature as a mountain-rescue ranger in the Sierras, but that's another story).

So read this wonderful book confidently. Your guide not only has a deep and lifelong personal acquaintance with his subjects but has a well-deserved reputation for putting his wisdom to work on behalf of the bears.

I've published half a dozen books about bears myself, so I fancy I know something about them, too. But as I cruised through Gary's manuscript, I kept stumbling over things that made me think, "Where in the world did he find *that?*" There have been many bear books, but there's never been anything like this. You, I, and the bears are all in debt to Gary Brown for *The Bear Almanac*.

Paul Schullery

Acknowledgments

MANY HAVE BEEN EXTREMELY SUPPORTIVE of me in this endeavor (revision and initial publication), researching and providing information and graphics, allowing me to present the bears in as complete a manner as the almanac will allow. Distinct appreciation is owed to Diana Doan-Crider, bear biologist (for the Mexican black bear); Kerry Gunther, bear biologist, Yellowstone National Park; Mark Haroldson, wildlife biologist, Grizzly Bear Study Team, Bozeman, Montana; Treven Hembree, grandson, translator (of "bear-names"); Johnny Johnson, photographer, Alaska; Dick Knight, Interagency Grizzly Bear Study Team (retired); Kellie McNelis, architect (for graphics); Jack Reneau, Boone and Crockett Club; Harry Reynolds III, Alaska Department of Fish and Game (retired), now working to save the Gobi brown bear in Mongolia; Dr. Christopher Servheen, Grizzly Bear Recovery Coordinator (USFWS), Missoula, Montana; Paul Schullery, historian, author, and editor, for his knowledge and guidance; the many state, territorial, and provincial wildlife managers and biologists (for the multitude of bear natural history/management/research information); and a special appreciation to Pat, my patient wife, for her computer genius—the charts—and especially for bailing me out of my computer "goofs."

Introduction

. . . The sight of the bear stirred me like nothing else the country could contain. . . . He implied a world. He was an affirmation to the rest of the earth that his kind of place was extant.

—John McPhee
Coming into the Country

THIS IS A FAMILY BOOK for all ages, meant for the reader to digest alone or read to another person. It is for the "arctophile" (a "bear fancier," a "lover of bears") or someone just becoming interested in these great animals. This is not a technical publication, though students of all ages and disciplines may utilize it as a reference. An almanac is a publication composed of lists, charts, and tables of information in many related and unrelated fields, and this almanac is just that, *except* that it has a single focus—*bears*.

The many "fields" of bears are related and intertwined, not only within the world of the bears but within the human world as well.

This revision addresses the important bear information of the past as well as the multitude of changes in the bear world during the past fifteen years (original publication, 1993).

Time alone has provided additional investigation and new technology for improved research, adding historical data as well as contemporary information. We know more about bear evolution, foods, movements, enemies, population trends, the status of each species, human/bear relationships, and much more.

DNA testing has importantly enhanced research and management of bear species, better defining subspecies and species, population numbers and distribution, bear evolution, and the habitats and health of bears.

Possibly the most important change has been the growth of the Internet, which allows us to research, retrieve, store, exchange, and communicate incredible volumes of bear information.

Related on these pages are current and historical observations, data, descriptions, anecdotes, comparisons, and beliefs of many people about the bears of the world. The information is presented in a format whereby the reader need not be concerned with continuity—beginnings and endings—but where one may read a paragraph, table, half page, chapter, or the entire almanac in a sitting and enjoy the overall world of bears.

There are two parts to the almanac, the first being a look at bears in their world—an examination of the natural history of a group of fascinating animals. The second discusses the influence bears have in the human world and our impact upon the bears. Obviously, there is considerable overlap and conflict between these two worlds, and I have often wondered in whose world we all truly live, that of the bears or of ours.

Bears are possibly the most dominant wild animals in our lives and have, through sharing the earth with humans, exerted distinct influences over our being. Mythical, exciting, revered, humanlike, and dangerous, they have altered our behavior and actions.

Bears are described in a variety of manner, generally colored by our own perceptions. We anthropomorphize, assuming their behavioral motivations to be the same as ours, applying our values, images, and perceptions. The behavior of bears is often termed "unpredictable," which actually means we do not understand the purpose for their actions and therefore judge them by our own.

The information available about some species of bears is extensive, collected and recorded by intensive research. However, there are unfortunate information gaps about specific species, populations, and countries. For example, there is minimal knowledge about Asiatic black, sun, and Andean bears compared to that of other species.

Bear descriptions, and reports of their behavior, are often conflicting, which creates confusion and uncertainty as to the "truth," but such variations may be in perfect keeping with each bear—an individual with its own personality, needs, traits, and character. (I would hate attempting to characterize the human race with a single or even a multitude of words.)

Paul Schullery, author of *The Bears of Yellowstone*, best describes this conflicting information: "No two bears live exactly the same life. They are nearly as different in physical appearance and in personality as are people. In attempting to summarize their lives, it is easy to speak of norms, averages, and probabilities, but one of the marvels of an animal as complex as the bear is its endless capacity to surprise us."

Hopefully, this almanac will pique your interest and encourage you to seek other informational sources about bears and, most important, cultivate understanding, appreciation, and respect for bears worldwide—in their world *and* in ours.

Gary Brown
January 2009

Part I
Bears in Their World

Always in season and accessible, ranged on the mountains like stores in a pantry. From one to another, from climate to climate, up and down he climbs, feasting on each in turn . . . almost every thing is food except granite . . . the sharp muzzle thrust inquiringly forward, the long shaggy hair on his broad chest, the stiff ears nearly buried in the hair, and the slow, heavy way in which he moved his head . . . how heavy and broad-footed bears are, it is wonderful how little harm they do in the wilderness. Even in the well-watered gardens of the middle region, where the flowers grow tallest, and where during warm weather the bears wallow and roll, no evidence of destruction is visible.

—John Muir, 1901
Our National Parks

CHAPTER 1

The Beginning
EVOLUTION

Bears have been evolving for about forty million years; today's bears descend from a family (Miacidae) of small tree-climbing carnivores. Fossils of the Hemicyon, or half-dog, found in the rocks of the Miocene Epoch, display the physical characteristics of both bears and dogs and indicate the related evolutionary descent of wolves, hyenas, weasels, other wild dogs, and bears.

Study of the evolution of any species is quite complex, as it requires reconstructing something that has long since disappeared, with the evidence primarily in fossils, living relics, and most recently genetic evidence. "Tracing the ancestry of the polar bear requires an intimate knowledge of every aspect of its present life," writes Thomas Koch in *The Year of the Polar Bear*, "and, possibly even more important, a wizard-like ability to guess the creature's past history." This is true of all bear species.

Fossil evidence is described by Lance Craighead in *Bears of the World* as ". . . a few scattered records; a fragment of bone, a jaw, a disjointed portion of a skeleton." Large skeletal parts are a rarity. The carbon-dating process originally was used to determine the age of these fossils. However, in recent years mitochondrial DNA and nuclear DNA have provided additional and more refined evidence of the ages of artifact material (see DNA, Chapter 9).

Fossil and genetic dating appears to be in general agreement, but I have used genetic (DNA) evidence where available. In many instances the DNA evidence indicates certain evolutionary times (the origin of a bear species) as "longer ago" than that of fossil evidence:

- *Panda bear (subfamily Ailuropodinae)*
  22 to 18 million years ago (DNA)
  15 million years ago (fossil evidence)
- *Short-faced bear*
  15 to 12 million years ago (DNA)
  6 million years ago (fossil evidence)

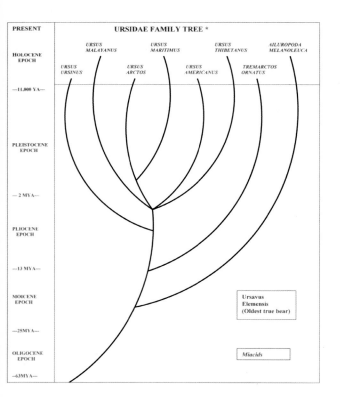

URSIDAE FAMILY TREE *

PRESENT

HOLOCENE EPOCH

URSUS MALAYANUS
URSUS MARITIMUS
URSUS THIBETANUS
AILUROPODA MELANOLEUCA

URSUS URSINUS
URSUS ARCTOS
URSUS AMERICANUS
TREMARCTOS ORNATUS

—11,000 YA—

PLEISTOCENE EPOCH

—2 MYA—

PLIOCENE EPOCH

—13 MYA—

MIOCENE EPOCH

Ursavus Elemensis (Oldest true bear)

—25MYA—

OLIGOCENE EPOCH

Miacids

—63MYA—

- *Polar bear*
  1 million years ago (DNA)
  300,000 years ago (fossil evidence)
- *American black bear*
  5 million years ago (DNA)
  3½ million years ago (fossil evidence)

- *Brown bear*
  1 million years ago (DNA)
  900,000 years ago (fossil evidence)
- *True bear (Ursidae family)*
  8 million to 4 million years ago (DNA)
  5 million years ago (fossil evidence)

EVOLUTION CHRONOLOGY OF BEARS			
Era	Period/Epoch	Duration (Years Ago)	Evolutionary Event
Cenozoic Era 63,000,000 to Present	**Tertiary Period**	63,000,000 to 2,000,000–500,00	
	–Early Oligocene Epoch	40,000,000– 30,000,000	**Bears** begin to evolve from small carniverous mammals (Miacid)
	–Late Oligocene Epoch	27,000,000	First **"true bear"** evolving from bearlike dogs
	–Mid-Miocene Epoch	22,000,000–18,000,000	** **Panda bear** (Ailuropodinae superfamily) originating in central Asia
		20,000,000	** Ursavus elemensis, oldest **true bear** (fox terrier size) in subtropical Europe; **modern bears** are from Ursavus
		15,000,000–12,000,000	** **Short-faced bear** (Tremarctinae subfamily) cross Bering land bridge, and spread in North America; **Old-World short-faced bear** going extinct
	–Pliocene Epoch	8,000,000–4,000,000	** **True bear** (Ursidae family) appearing in northern Asia
		8,000,000–7,000,000	** **Sloth bear** appearing in south-central Asia
		7,000,000	**Auvergne bear (Ursus minimus)** appearing
		6,000,000	Very large predacious **bear** developing; evidence of Protursus (Spain)
		5,000,000	** **Early American black bear** appearing in North America ** **Asiatic black bear** appearing in central Asia ** **Sun bear** appearing in southeast Asia

Era	Period/Epoch	Duration (Years Ago)*	Evolutionary Event
		3,500,000	** **True bears** into North America with the **black bears** (subgenus Euarctos) during the Pliocene epoch
		2,500,000	**Ursus etruscus, modern bear,** appearing Three lines of **bears** evolving in Europe: **black, brown,** and **cave bears**
		2,500,000–1,500,000	** **American black bear,** a separate species
	Quaternary Period	2,000,000–500,000 to present	
	–Early Pleistocene Epoch		**Giant panda-like bear** appearing; **black bear** and **brown bear** widespread
		2,000,000	Predecessors of **modern bears** are forest dwellers in Asia
			Ursus etruscus appearing
		1,500,000	*Ursus minimus* or *Ursus etruscus* crosses the Bering land bridge and moves south
		1,300,000	*Ursus etruscus* has disappeared
	–Middle Pleistocene Epoch		*Arctodus simus* (**giant short-faced bear**) widely spread throughout North and South America
		1,000,000	** **Polar bear** (*Ursus maritimus*) appearing in northern Siberia
			Ursus tremarctos floridanus (**Florida cave bear**) in area of present southeast United States
			Homo erectus moving out of Africa
			** **Brown bear** (*Ursus arctos*) appearing in northern Asia
		800,000	** **Brown bear** established in Europe; brown bear probably in central Asia
			Ursus arctos, Ursus deningeri, Ursus thibetans, and *Ursus spelaeus* appearing
			Ursus deningeri begins disappearing

Era	Period/Epoch	Duration (Years Ago)	Evolutionary Event
			Ice age; all **bears** extinct in North and South America except the **Andean bear**
			China: other lines from the Etruscan producing **black** and **brown bears**
	–Late Pleistocene Epoch	690,000–790,000	** Humans had fire
		500,000	** **Brown bear** widely distributed in Asia
			** Close human/**bear** associations
			Polar bear ancestors in the arctic evolving from the coastal **brown/grizzly bears**
		300,000	*Ursus spelaeus* (**cave bear**) widely distributed
			** **Early brown bear** "possibly" on North American continent
		250,000–100,000	Land bridge between Asia and North America
		200,000	** *Homo sapiens* appearing
			Brown bear crosses land bridge; also spreads in Europe and co-exists with cave bear
			Alaska, Kodiak, and **grizzly bears** in North America
		100,000–50,000	*Ursus maritimus* (**present-day polar bear**) evolving from the brown bear in northern Siberia
		80,000–30,000	Humans (*Homo sapien neanderthal*) and **bears** (**brown** and **cave bears**) living in Europe
		70,000	Beginning of last great glaciation
			Polar bear a distinct species
		40,000–35,000	** **Brown bears** on North American continent
		30,000	*Homo sapien sapiens*; **cave bear** and Neanderthal people begin declining
		20,000	**Modern-day polar bear** may exist

Era	Period/Epoch	Duration (Years Ago)	Evolutionary Event
	–Recent Epoch		**American black** and **Florida cave bears,** and species of the **short-faced bear** are widely distributed in North America, south of the continental ice sheet
			Andean bear in South America
		15,000–10,000	Humans to America
			Cave bear (*Ursus spelaeus*) extinct
		13,000	**Giant short-faced bear** in area of Texas
		11,000–10,000	End of last ice age
			** **Brown bear** in North America expands south
			** **American black bear** expands north, having been below the ice sheet for 3 million years
		8,000	*Tremarctos floridanus* extinct
		117–88	**Brown bear** extinct in Africa
		Present	*** **American black bear, brown bear,** and **polar bear** in North America
			*** **Andean bear** (short-faced) in South America
			*** **Asiatic black bear, brown bear, sun bear, giant panda, polar bear,** and **sloth bear** in Asia
			***Brown bear** and **polar bear** in Europe

* There are no definite beginnings or endings for some eras, periods, and epochs due to the enormous amount of time considered, as well as different dating methods utilized around the world.

** Genetic evidence (all other entries are from fossil records).

*** Bears living today

Evolutionary Bears

The fossil records, and now DNA, allow scientists to trace and track evolutionary development of the present-day species of bears. Some significant species are listed below:

Ursavus elemensis Appears to be the earliest "bear." The size of a fox terrier dog, the "Dawn Bear" was found in subtropical Europe.

Indarctos A rare, "bearlike" fossil mammal

Agriotherium A rare fossil mammal, found in Eurasia and North America. Larger and more massive than *Arctotherium*, it was short faced and had massive limbs. *Agriotherium* was extinct in most areas before the Pliocene Epoch.

Protursus A small bear of the Pliocene Epoch

Ursus minimus The Auvergne bear, a primitive species that lived in Europe during the Quaternary Period. Small (about one hundred pounds), approximately the same size as the present-day sun bear, *Ursus minimus* anatomically resembled the black bear and was the immediate ancestor of the Etruscan bear.

Ursus etruscus The Etruscan bear existed during the early Pleistocene Epoch. From European descendants, it populated much of Eurasia and North America and is apparently the ecological successor of *Agriotherium*. Living and fossil evidence exists that the polar, brown, and black bears evolved from *U. etruscus*.

Ursus sino-malayanus Consisting of small and large forms, *U. sino-malayanus* was the early sun bear.

Ursus savini Savin's bear, a transitional stage between the Etruscan bear and Deninger's bear. It was smaller, less heavily built, and not as advanced as *Ursus deningeri*.

Ursus deningeri Deninger's bear existed during the middle Pleistocene Epoch. It preceded, but was closely related to, *Ursus spelaeus* (cave bear), though without the size and heaviness of the cave bear. It was more rangy and slighter in build than the present-day grizzly and Kodiak bears.

Arctotherium The hyena bear was probably a forest dweller. Short faced and with massive limbs, it was a large bear. The species *Arctotherium californicum* was larger than the present-day Alaskan brown bear.

Ursus (Thalarctos) maritimus tyrannus The early polar bear. Very few fossil remains of polar bears have been found, but it is known that ancestors of the present-day polar bear moved into the arctic during the Pleistocene Epoch. Koch explains, ". . . it is accepted that during the age of the glaciers, perhaps during the mid-Pleistocene, a sizable group of brown bears was isolated from the main population. During this isolation, strong selection pressures forced them to change their style of life." *Tyrannus* was markedly larger and more *-arctos*-like than the present-day polar bear.

Arctodus pristinus	The lesser short-faced bear was found in a few locations of eastern North America, mostly in Florida. Its face was only slightly shortened, and the teeth were large and high crowned, with very large canines. The lesser short-faced bear was smaller than *Arctodus simus*.
Arctodus simus	The giant short-faced bear (bulldog bear) was not only the mid-Pleistocene Epoch giant but was the largest carnivorous land mammal ever. It inhabited North America (the north-central plains, Alaska, Canada to central Mexico, and California to Virginia). The most common of early North American bears, the bulldog bear was quite prevalent in California. It had a short, broad snout and a low forehead with eyes set far forward. The body was relatively short, with exceptionally long legs, and the fore and hind feet turned forward, with all surfaces of the feet touching the ground. It was gigantic, with powerful musculature, and measured more than 5 feet at the shoulders, over 11 feet tall when standing. It had a vertical reach of over 14 feet (a basketball rim is 10 feet high) and weighed 1,500 to 1,800 pounds in the spring, more than a ton in the fall. It was larger, but more rangy and slighter in build, than the Kodiak brown bear, and "comparing canine teeth," according to one scientist, *Arctodus simus* would make a mature Alaska brown bear look like a cub. Enormous specimens were found in Alaska and the Yukon. Large and swift, the giant short-faced bear was the most powerful predator of its time; it kept black bears in trees and probably humans off the North American continent. Possibly related to the lesser short-faced bear, it also appears to be related to the Andean bear.
Ursus spelaeus	The European cave bear is one of the best-known ice age mammals. It inhabited mountainous and hill regions in the area of present-day Germany, France, and Russia and lasted in Europe and Russia for two ice ages. Its head was very large, with a broad, domed skull and steep forehead; it had small eyes, upward-opening

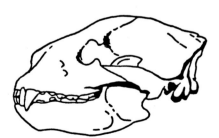

Skull of giant short-faced bear (*Arctodus simus*)
COURTESY INTERAGENCY GRIZZLY BEAR STUDY TEAM (IGBST)

Skull of cave bear (*Ursus spelaeus*)
COURTESY INTERAGENCY GRIZZLY BEAR STUDY TEAM (IGBST)

nostrils, and a grinding jaw. The body was stout, with long thighs; short, massive shins; and large in-turning feet; the large bones close in structure to those of the grizzly bear. Males weighed up to 400 kilograms (880 pounds). The cave bear was a specialist, a distinct herbivore, considerably more a browser than a predator. *Ursus spelaeus* was hunted and worshipped by Neanderthal man and has been found in burial positions.

The Florida cave bear was widely distributed south of the continental ice sheet, along the U.S. Gulf Coast, across Florida, and north to Tennessee, with some evidence in California, Idaho, New Mexico, Texas, Kansas, Georgia, and Mexico. Its forehead was domed, teeth relatively small, neck elongated, and body barrel-like. Its limbs were heavy, the humerus and femur long, the paws short. Large, with a heavier build than the short-faced bear, it was built more like the European cave bear, though not closely related to *Ursus spelaeus*. And though larger and heavier, it was possibly related to the Andean bear.

Ursus abstrusus   The primitive black bear was small, with a long, narrow skull, and was closely related to *Ursus minimus*, the ancestral black bear of the Old World.

Ursus americanus   The American black bear was found over most of North America. Similar to the European cave bear and evolving from the same line, it probably descended from *Ursus abstrusus*, as did the Asiatic black bear, to which it is closely related. The black bear split from the brown bear in the late Tertiary Period, but a black bear subgenus, *Euarctos*, came to North America during the Pliocene Epoch—before the brown bear. *Ursus americanus* and *Ursus thibetanus* have changed little since the early Quaternary Period. American black, Florida cave, and short-faced bears were distributed south of the continental ice sheet.

Ursus arctos   The brown bear derived from *Etruscus* and along the same line that produced cave bears. It evolved in open spaces, lived mostly in nonforest or woodland areas and, not being a forest animal, had to stand and fight for its territory, food, and cubs. Spread widely across the Pleistocene landscape, with the earliest bears living in China, the brown bear succeeded *Arctodus simus* over much of its range.

Ursus maritimus   The polar bear is a specialized descendant of the brown bear and the youngest of the living species of bears. The modern polar bear appeared 100,000 to 50,000 years ago, somewhere along the northern Siberian coast where the Asiatic brown bear population split.

Bears have evolved through an "orderly" development, generation after generation, with adaptation and new characteristics, both physical and behavioral. After forty million years their evolution continues, as does ours.

Cave Bears

Cave bears (*Ursus spelaeus*) were an important evolutionary bear and especially so beginning in the nineteenth century, when the study of their remains became more extensive. DNA science has now enhanced the investigations of the cave bear. According to *Science* magazine, June 2005, James Noonan and Edward Rubin (Lawrence Berkeley National Laboratory, Berkeley, California), ". . . were able to match the fossil DNA up against dog genes. And when they used the fossil DNA to build a bear family tree, the cave bear fit in right with black bears, grizzly bears, and polar bears."

Before becoming extinct as early as 15,000 years ago, cave bears had used predictable locations (such as caves) for shelter, hibernation, birthing, and safety. They appear to have lived and died in the caves. Bears and humans utilized some of the same caves (by humans as Paleolithic hunting stations) during different seasons and periods. These sites provided the hunters of the period opportunities to more easily locate and kill bears and have access to the species for cultural and survival purposes. In recent times their remains have told a broad evolutionary story.

Early discoveries of bear skeletal material, found in the caves of central Europe, were thought to be from unicorns and dragons, as well as bears. Considered of medicinal value, the material was pulverized and utilized in medieval pharmacies, and numerous central European caves were "commercially" exploited. However, the material was properly recognized by the mid-1600s, and because of the location of the discoveries, the bear teeth and bones were considered to be of the "cave bear." The exploitation of the caves continued, as phosphate fertilizer was produced from tons of cave-bear skulls and bones taken from the d'Aubert Cave in the Pyrenees between 1890 and 1894.

Scientific exploration and study also began, as caves provided excellent environments for fossilization and preservation of materials. Skulls, canine teeth, sometimes nearly complete skeletons, and other skeletal materials have been found not only in mountain caves but also in pits, tar pits, rifts, and "open-air sites" such as river deposits and other sediments on valley floors.

Theories of the causes or probable causes of the extinction of the cave bear have been put forth and thoroughly debated by numerous authorities:

- Changes in surroundings
- Changes in climate
- Changes in available foods
- Diseases
- Killings by the human populations
- Discrepancy between body size and chewing/grinding surface of the teeth
- Evolution into brown bears
- Smaller number of yearly births
- Degeneration (increasing number of dwarf forms; changing, high percentage of pathological cases; increasing number of males and resultant imbalance of sex ratio)
- Lack of adaptation to the cooling climate

Undoubtedly, there was a combination of causes, many of the above being interrelated, with some quite insignificant in themselves or only of local importance. According to some authorities, the most probable explanations may be the degeneration theory (which is internal) or the body size/tooth surface discrepancy theory (again, internal), both coupled with climatic changes (which are external).

"The cave bear was occasionally hunted by man, but the great accumulation of bones in the caves represents animals that died in hibernation . . ." explains Bjorn Kurten in *Pleistocene Mammals of Europe*. "Death in winter sleep was apparently the normal end for the cave bear and would mainly befall those individuals that had failed ecologically during the summer season—from inexperience, illness or old age. As a result the remains found are mostly of juvenile, old or diseased animals." Extinction was gradual, over thousands of years, and is not significantly attributed to Pleistocene *Homo sapiens* (humans).

There are numerous cave-bear grottos, caves, and "holes" considered significant and prominent in the modern-day discovery of the cave bear.

CAVE BEAR GROTTOS, CAVES, AND HOLES

Caves	Location/Comments
Abri-Sous-Roche	Hungary: near Pilisszanto
Altenstein	Germany: between Liebenstein and Altenstein
Arma de Faje	Italy: near summit of the Bricco di Peagna; near Calvisio, Finalese
Brillenhohle	Germany: bears used the cave seasonally and alternately with humans
Brixham	England: near Torquay
Cave a Margot	France: on the Erve river near Saulges
Contencher	France: in the valley of the Areuse near Rochefort
Cumberland	United States: Maryland
d'Aubert	France: near St-Girons in the Pyrenees Mountains
Drachenhohle	Austria: near Mixnitz
Drachenloch	Switzerland: near Vattis, in the eastern Alps; Saint Gallen canton; contained rectangular stone tombs (stone chests) filled with bear skulls
Dragons	Austria: more than 30,000 skeletons
Engihoul	Belgium: near Liege, on the Meuse River
"Erd" Cave	Hungary: near Erd; contained bones of 500 bears killed by Neanderthals 49,000 years ago
Furgelfirst	Switzerland: between Santis and Kamor
Gaylenreuth	Germany: Muggendorf
Grapevine	United States: West Virginia; lesser short-faced bear
Grotte des Dentaux	Switzerland: Rochers de Naye; Vaud canton
Hastiere	Belgium: near Hasitere-Lavaux
Hellmichhohle	Germany: contained cave-bear and brown-bear bones
Hohlenstein	Germany
Igric	Hungary: Gyula in the Transylvania region
Kents Cavern	England: Torquay
Labor-of-Love-Cave	United States: Nevada; *Arctodus simus, Ursus americanus*, and *Ursus arctos*

CAVE BEAR GROTTOS, CAVES, AND HOLES (CONTINUED)

Caves	Location/Comments
Lachaize	France: on the Tardoire River
Little Box Elder	United States: Wyoming, Converse County; *Ursus arctos* and *Arctodus simus*
Makapansgat	South Africa: near Potgietersrus, a limeworks excavation
Montespan	France
Podkala	Italy: Podklanec, near Nabresina (near Triest)
Port Kennedy	United States: Pennsylvania; *Arctodus pristinus*
Potter Creek	United States: California; *Arctotherium simus*
Rancholabrean	United States: Florida; *Tremarctos floridanus*, Florida cave bear
Regourdon	France; arm bone of a bear found as an offering in a human grave
Salzofen	Austria: in the Totes Gebirge
San Josecito	Mexico: state of Nuevo Leon; *Ursus americanus, Tremarctos floridanus*
Schnurenloch	Switzerland: Simmental canton, Bern
Schreiberwandhohle	Austria: Dachstein
Sibyllenhohle	Germany: near the Castle of Teck, southeast of Stuttgart
St. Brais (Cave I)	Switzerland: Bernese Jura; contains claw markings on cave walls
Steigelfadbalm	Switzerland: near Vitznau, Luzern canton
Sterkfontein	South Africa: near Pretoria
Sundwig (Sundwich)	Germany: near Iserlohn in Westphalia
Tamar Hat	Algeria (Africa)
Taza	Morocco (Africa)
Tischofer	Austria: near Kufstein, close to Austro-Bavarian border
Tornewton	England
Trou de Chaleux	Belgium
Tuc d'Audoubert	France: near St-Girons
Wildenmannistock	Switzerland
Wildkirchli	Switzerland: Appenzell canton; Santis Mountains
Wookey Hole	England: south of Bristol

CHAPTER 2

Bears of the World
NAMES AND TAXONOMY

Today's bears consist of eight species and numerous subspecies (the exact number of subspecies is debated) in more than sixty-five countries on four continents. They are identified under an assortment of names: scientific, common, historical, contemporary, descriptive, literary, romantic, emotional, and popular. Some have had their scientific names changed.

The sloth bear, originally considered a sloth (the "bear sloth"), was in 1810 discovered in fact to be a bear. In a more drastic adjustment, the giant panda was a bear, then was not, was once more, and now, with the use of DNA testing, is definitely known to be a bear. The term "grizzly bear" is synonymous with "brown bear," but I specifically use it where necessary to emphasize the individual significance of *Ursus arctos horribilis*. Although some Eurasian brown-bear populations are occasionally called grizzly bears, I maintain them in the brown-bear category. The use of the name "Andean bear," synonymous with spectacled bear, has become more common since the mid-1990s; therefore, I have adopted "Andean" as the name of the South American bear.

Classification

Bears are scientifically classified, as are all other animals and plants, in an orderly arrangement under a system of binomial nomenclature, developed in 1758 by Carolus Linnaeus, using the Greek or Latin languages of the early scholars. Original bear classifications:

- *Ursus americanus* (Palias, 1780), American black bear
- *Ursus arctos* (Carolus Linnaeus, 1758), brown bear
- *Ursus maritimus* (C. J. Phiipps, 1774), polar bear
- *Ursus thibetanus* (F. G. Cuvier, 1823), Asiatic black bear
- *Ailuropoda melanolueca* (Pere Armand David, 1869), giant panda
- *Melursus ursinus* (George Shaw, 1791), sloth bear
- *Helarctos malayanus* (Thomas Raffles, 1821), sun bear
- *Tremarctos ornatus* (F. G. Cuvier, 1825), Andean bear

Bears of the World
ORIGINAL ART BY AND COURTESY OF BARBARA PETTINGA MOORE

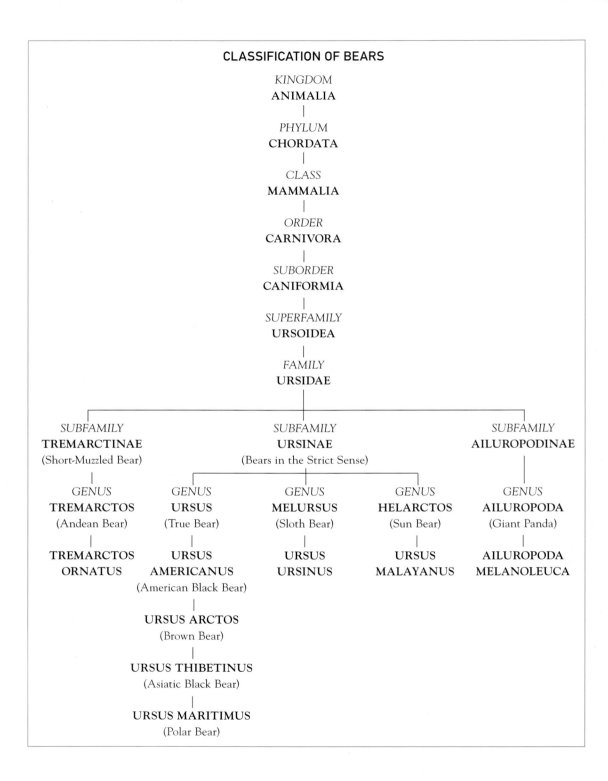

CLASSIFICATION OF BEARS

KINGDOM
ANIMALIA

PHYLUM
CHORDATA

CLASS
MAMMALIA

ORDER
CARNIVORA

SUBORDER
CANIFORMIA

SUPERFAMILY
URSOIDEA

FAMILY
URSIDAE

SUBFAMILY
TREMARCTINAE
(Short-Muzzled Bear)

SUBFAMILY
URSINAE
(Bears in the Strict Sense)

SUBFAMILY
AILUROPODINAE

GENUS
TREMARCTOS
(Andean Bear)

GENUS
URSUS
(True Bear)

GENUS
MELURSUS
(Sloth Bear)

GENUS
HELARCTOS
(Sun Bear)

GENUS
AILUROPODA
(Giant Panda)

**TREMARCTOS
ORNATUS**

**URSUS
AMERICANUS**
(American Black Bear)

**URSUS
URSINUS**

**URSUS
MALAYANUS**

**AILUROPODA
MELANOLEUCA**

URSUS ARCTOS
(Brown Bear)

URSUS THIBETINUS
(Asiatic Black Bear)

URSUS MARITIMUS
(Polar Bear)

American black bear in Yellowstone National Park
COURTESY YELLOWSTONE NATIONAL PARK

American Black Bear
Scientific name and origin
- *Ursus americanus*
- *Ursus:* Latin word meaning "bear"
- *Americanus:* Latin for "of America"; the first Europeans on the east coast of North America found "black-colored" bears

Common names and origins
- Black bear: black color
- Cinnamon bear: cinnamon brown color
- Glacier bear: bluish color, associated with glaciers
- Kermode bear: honors Francis Kermode for his scientific efforts with this subspecies

Continent
- North America

Brown Bear
Scientific name and origin
- *Ursus arctos*
- *Ursus:* Latin word meaning "bear"
- *Arctos:* Greek word meaning "bear"

Common names and origins
- Brown bear: brown color
- Grizzly bear: grizzled color
- European brown bear: resides in Europe
- Kamchatka bear: resides on Kamchatka Peninsula, Russia
- Kodiak bear: resides on Kodiak Island Archipelago, Alaska
- Red bear: reddish brown color; resides in Himalayas
- Silvertip: tips of hair silver color (grizzled)
- Several other common names based on general location

Continents
- North America
- Europe
- Asia

Adult male Kodiak brown bear in the Kodiak National Wildlife Refuge, Alaska
COURTESY U.S. FISH AND WILDLIFE SERVICE

The polar bear—symbol of wandering freedom
© SHUTTERSTOCK

Polar Bear

Scientific name and origin

- *Ursus maritimus*
- *Ursus:* Latin word meaning "bear"
- *Maritimus:* Latin word meaning "located on or near the sea"

Common names and origins

- *Nanook:* Eskimo word for the polar bear or white bear
- Polar bear: resides in polar regions
- Sea bear: resides near the sea
- Walking bear: travels great distances on the ice pack
- White bear: white color
- Water bear: excellent swimmer, lives at the water
- Ice bear: lives and hunts on the ice
- Snow bear: lives in the arctic snow

Continents

- North America
- Europe
- Asia
- Arctic Ocean

Asiatic Black Bear

Scientific name and origin

- *Ursus thibetanus (Selenarctos thibetanus)*
- *Ursus:* Latin word meaning "bear"
- *Selene:* Greek word meaning "moon"
- *Arctos:* Greek word meaning "bear"
- *Thibetanus:* Latin for "located in Tibet"

Common names and origins

- Asian black bear: black color; resides in Asia
- Asiatic black bear: black color; resides in Asia
- *Basindo nan tenggil:* Malayan for "he who sits high up in a tree"
- Collared bear: whitish collar; resides in Siberia and Manchuria
- Himalayan bear: resides in the Himalayas
- Moon bear: white crescent resembling moon on chest
- Russian black bear: black color; resides in Siberia and Manchuria
- Tibetan black bear: resides in Tibet

Continent

- Asia

Asiatic black bear with typical thick neck mane
© GARY BROWN

Giant panda in its shrinking China habitat
© SHUTTERSTOCK

Giant Panda

Scientific name and origin

- *Ailuropoda melanoleuca*
- *Ailuropoda:* black and white panda foot
- *Melano:* black, darkness of hair
- *Leuca:* white, colorless

Common names and origins

- *Daxiong mao:* large catbear (Chinese)
- Giant panda: large (giant) bamboo-eater
- *Panda:* Himalayan word for "bamboo-eater"; originally associated with the "small" red or lesser panda
- *Huaxiong:* banded bear (Chinese)
- *Maoxiong:* catlike bear (Chinese)
- *Pae-shioung:* white bear (Chinese)

Continent

- Asia

Sloth Bear

Scientific name and origin

- *Ursus ursinus (Melursus ursinus)*
- *Melursus:* dark (hair) honey bear
- *Ursinus:* Latin; characteristic of a bear

Common names and origins

- *Aswail (aswal):* Ceylon and India names
- *Bhalu:* India's favorite name (also used in Nepal)
- *Bhaluk:* Bangladesh name
- *Doni:* Bhutan name
- Indian sloth bear: resides in India
- Lip bear: has extendable lips
- Long-lipped bear: extends lips to suck up insects
- Sloth bear: originally considered a sloth ("bear sloth"); sloth: Old English for "slow"
- *Walaha:* Sri Lanka name
- Ursine sloth: bear sloth

Continent

- Asia

Sloth bear displaying its unkempt appearance
© SHUTTERSTOCK

Sun bear—the smallest species of bear
© SHUTTERSTOCK

Sun Bear

Scientific name and origin

- *Ursus malayanus (Helarctos malayanus)*
- *Ursus:* Latin word meaning "bear"
- *Helarctos:* Greek words for "sun" and "bear"
- *Helical:* pertaining to the sun (chest marking)
- *Malayanus:* Latin for "located in Malaysia"

Common names and origins

- Ape bear
- *Bruang (bruan):* in Sumatra
- Dog bear: resembles a dog
- Honey bear: Honey is a major food.
- Malayan bear: resides in Malaysia
- Sun bear: yellow crescent (rising sun) on chest

Continent

- Asia

Andean Bear (Spectacled Bear)

Scientific name and origin

- *Tremarctos ornatus (Ursus ornatus)*
- *Tremarctos:* tremendous bear
- *Andean:* resides primarily in Andes Mountains
- *Ornatus:* ornate design on face and around eyes (like spectacles)

Common names and origins

- *Achupalla:* Andean for "underbark eater"
- *Ocunari:* Andean for "cow-eating"
- *Pucca mate:* Andean for "red-fronted"
- Spectacled bear: light-colored rings around eyes, like eyeglasses
- *Ucumari:* Andean for "bear with eye in hole"
- *Yana puma:* Andean for "black puma"
- *Yura mateo:* Andean for "white-fronted"

Continent

- South America

Andean bear—the spectacled, South American bear
© SHUTTERSTOCK

SUBSPECIES

Several subspecies exist among the bears of the world. Distinctions have been made with DNA analysis and significant geographical, dietary, behavioral, and anatomical variations, as well as a consideration of relatively isolated populations. There are as many subspecies as there are disagreements as to what is a "valid" subspecies. Many bear authorities, though not all, recognize the subspecies below.

AMERICAN BLACK BEAR		
Scientific Name	**Common Name**	**Location**
Ursus americanus	American black bear	North America
Subspecies		
altifrontalis	Northwestern black bear (Olympic black bear)	Pacific Northwest
amblyceps	New Mexico black bear	Arizona (eastern); Colorado; New Mexico; Mexico (northern); Texas (western); Utah (southeastern)
americanus	American black bear	Pacific coast to Atlantic coast; Alaska
californiensis	California black bear	California (interior); Oregon (southern)
carlottae	Queen Charlotte black bear	British Columbia (Queen Charlotte Islands); Alaska
cinnamomum	Cinnamon bear	Colorado (eastern); Idaho; Montana (western); Oregon (eastern); Utah (northeast); Washington (eastern); Wyoming
emmonsii	Glacier bear (silver-black bear; blue bear)	Alaska (Glacier Bay to Prince William Sound)
eremicus	Desert black bear (East Mexico black bear)	Mexico (northeast); Texas (Big Bend area)
floridanus	Florida black bear	Florida; Georgia (southern); Alabama (southern); Texas (eastern)
hamiltoni	Newfoundland black bear	Newfoundland
kermodei	Kermode bear	British Columbia (northwest)
machetes	Mexican black bear	Mexico (northern)
perniger	Kenai black bear	Alaska (Kenai Peninsula)
pugnax	Dall black bear	Alaska (Alexander Archipelago; southeastern Alaska)
vancouveri	Vancouver black bear	British Columbia (Vancouver Island)

Old Ephraim, the grizzly bear, roamed most of western North America.
© GARY BROWN

BROWN BEAR

Scientific Name	Common Name	Location
Ursus arctos	Brown bear	Northern Hemisphere
Subspecies		
beringianus	Siberian brown bear	Kamchatka, Siberia
biensis	Gobi bear	Mongolia (Gobi Desert)
crowtheri	Atlas bear	Atlas Mountains, North Africa; (extinct)
formicarius	Carpathian bear	Carpathian Mountains
horribilis	Grizzly bear	North America (northwestern)
isabellinus	Himalayan brown bear	Himalayas (foothills; Tien Shan Mountains); Kyrgyzstan (reserve); Kazakhstan (reserve); Nepal; Pakistan; Northern India
lasiotus	Ussuri brown bear	Ussuri, Russia
manchuricus	Siberian brown bear	Siberia; coasts of Sea of Okhotsk; Amur Basin; Sakhalin Island
marsicanus	Marsican bear	Italy; Switzerland
middendorffi	Kodiak bear	Alaska (Kodiak Island Archipelago)
nelsoni	Mexican grizzly bear	Mexico (northern); (extinct)
piscator	Bergman's bear	Kamchatka; (extinct?)
pruinosus	Tibetan blue bear	Tibetan Plateau (eastern)
syriacus	Syrian brown bear	Armenia; Iran; Iraq; Israel; Lebanon; Syria; Turkey
yesoensis	Hokkaido brown bear (Yezo bear)	Japan (island of Hokkaido)

POLAR BEAR

Scientific Name	Common Name	Location
Ursus maritimus (Also known as ***Thalarctos maritimus***)	Polar bear	Arctic
Subspecies		
marinus	Polar bear	Arctic
maritimus	Polar bear	Arctic

ASIATIC BLACK BEAR

Scientific Name	Common Name	Location
Ursus thibetanus (Also known as ***Selenarctos thibetanus*** and ***Arctos thibetanus***)	Asiatic black bear	Asia
Subspecies		
formosanus	Formosan black bear (White-throated bear)	Taiwan
gedrosianus	Baluchistan bear (Pakistan black bear)	Iran; Pakistan
japonicus	Japan black bear	Islands of Kyushu, Shikoku, and Honshu
laniger	Himalayan black bear	Afghanistan; Iran (southeast); China (southern)
mupinensis	(No common name)	China (southwest)
thibetanus	Asiatic black bear	Asia
ussuricus	(No common name)	Siberia (southern); China (northeast); Korea

GIANT PANDA

Scientific Name	Common Name	Location
Ailuropoda melanoleuca	Giant panda	China
Subspecies		
melanoleuca	Sichuan panda	Sichuan province
qinlingensis	Qinling panda	Qinling Mountains

SLOTH BEAR

Scientific Name	Common Name	Location
Ursus ursinus (Also known as ***Melursus ursinus***)	Sloth bear	India; Sri Lanka
Subspecies		
inornatus	Sri Lanka sloth bear	Sri Lanka
ursinus	Indian sloth bear	India

SUN BEAR		
Scientific Name	**Common Name**	**Location**
Ursus malayanus (Also known as *Helarctos malayanus*)	Sun bear	Asia (southern)
Subspecies		
euryspilus	Borneo sun bear	Borneo
malayanus	Sun bear	Asia

ANDEAN BEAR		
Scientific Name	**Common Name**	**Location**
Tremarctos ornatus	Andean bear (Spectacled bear; Short-faced bear)	South America
(Also known as *Ursus ornatus*)		
Subspecies		
None recognized		

Kodiak, Kamchatka, Kermode, and Glacier Bears

There are four subspecies of bears, of which two are distinguished by location and size and two by "color" or the lack thereof.

Kodiak Brown Bear
(Ursus arctos middendorffi)

The largest bear in the world according to many bear aficionados, this unique subspecies is found on three islands in the Kodiak Archipelago (the northern section of the Gulf of Alaska); some sources also consider the bears in nearby areas to be Kodiaks. Kodiak Island (the second-largest U.S. island), Afognak, and Shuyak have concentrations of bears second only to that of the Kamchatka Peninsula. Approximately 3,500 bears—one bear per square mile—inhabit the islands. Concentrations are due to an abundance of streams (Kodiak alone has 117), most of them heavily laden with salmon, and the isolation offered by the island habitat.

Kodiak brown bear in Kodiak National Wildlife Refuge
COURTESY U.S. FISH AND WILDLIFE SERVICE

Kamchatka brown bear on the Kamchatka Peninsula, Russia
© SHUTTERSTOCK

Kamchatka (Siberian) Brown Bear
(Ursus arctos beringianus)

These huge bears inhabit the 750-mile-long Kamchatka Peninsula, of Russia's far-eastern coast (across the Bering Sea from Alaska). The Kamchatka bears are the largest bears in Eurasia (nearly as large as the Kodiak) and comprise the densest population of bears in the world: two bears per square mile. Kamchatka is a land of geysers, volcanoes, and abundant wildlife that includes one of the world's largest concentrations of salmon. Though the region is sparsely populated, protection of the bears has drastically declined since the collapse of the Soviet Union, with the bear population declining from 20,000 to 12,500. Lack of tight governmental control

has opened up the peninsula to poaching, tourism (supported by the United Nations), hunting, guided fishing, logging, mining, and petroleum extraction. Worldwide conservation groups are seeking improved protection.

Kermode Bear
(Ursus americanus kermodei)

The unique Kermode bear is "white" in color; that is, white to degrees of cream and tan. This rare subspecies has a recessive trait in its genes that provides approximately 10 percent white bears (DNA samplings of 220 Kermode bears) with the remainder black, brown, cinnamon, and other shades of these colors. A total Kermode bear population is unknown, considering all American black bears of a large region would require DNA sampling. It is not an albino; foot-pads are reddish and eyes brown. Larger than the "basic" black bear of North America, it averages 250 to 300 pounds, with some males reaching 500 pounds.

Found primarily in areas of the northwest British Columbia coast, including Prince Royal and Prince Rupert Islands, these bears are found inland as far as the Hazelton and Terrace, British Columbia, areas (Terrace is called the "Home of the Kermode Bear"). Surprisingly, a Kermode was observed in the Juneau, Alaska, area in 2002. The British Columbia "provincial" mammal is the Kermode bear.

Named after Dr. Francis Kermode in 1928, the Kermode bear has several names, including Spirit Bear, Ghost Bear, and Moksgm'ol (in the Tsimshian language) and is sometimes called the "white grizzly." Legend gives the Kermode "supernatural powers." Laws exist to protect the subspecies from hunting harvests, but those bears that

Kermode bear—the Spirit Bear/"white" American black bear
©2008 STEVEN KAZLOWSKI/ALASKASTOCK.COM

genetic manipulation of the black bear. According to the American Bear Association, "The undercoat of the glacier bears is a rich blue-black, the outer guard hairs are long and white (or light yellow) with silver tips." The glacier bear has ideal camouflage, as the coloration blends with the backdrop of glacial ice and snow and makes the bear highly difficult to observe if it is motionless. This color phase is becoming increasingly rare as the glacier bears mate with black bears of other colors, resulting in fewer offspring of this coloration.

are not white have minimal protection due to lack of recognition. Logging, mining, and other human pressures also threaten the Kermode bear. The Great Bear Rainforest Park (with sixteen million acres) was established in 2006 to protect the Spirit Bear.

Glacier Bear
(Ursus americanus emmonsii)

The very uncommon glacier bear is a blue-gray or silver-black American black bear found in southeastern Alaska (in the St. Elias range, coast of Yakutat Bay), northwestern British Columbia (in the Tatshensitini-Alsek Park, where they are protected), and possibly (this is unconfirmed) in the southwestern Yukon Territory. The color phase of this subspecies is a result of natural

Glacier bear—the blue-gray American black bear
© 2008 JOHN HYDE/ALASKASTOCK.COM

OTHER BEAR NAMES

There are many historical and contemporary names ascribed to the different bear species. They include emotional and reactive impressions of those people whose lives have been touched or otherwise influenced by bears—people who have met, feared, worshipped, hated, killed, respected, or observed bears. Many names come from individual human perceptions, and some are simply geographic. Individual bears were occasionally named because of their notoriety, and many became legendary. The origins of many names given to bears have been lost and forgotten with time.

The grizzly bear has elicited more names than any other species of bear and possibly any other animal. The list of names includes the descriptive "Old Ephraim," commonly used among the North American settlers of the 1800s and early 1900s. "The king of game beasts of temperate North America," wrote Theodore Roosevelt (Paul Schullery, in *American Bears*), "because the most dangerous to the hunter is the grizzly bear; known to the few remaining old-time trappers of the Rockies and the Great Plains . . . as 'Old Ephraim'. . . ." The biblical character of Ephraim is the leader of a "warlike" tribe.

Some Historical and Contemporary Names

Hopefully many of these names will trigger your imagination. Can you picture a *Gap Crosser*? A *Happy Hooligan*? A *Phantom*? A *Honey Paw*? A *Lord of the Woods*? A *Renegade*? A *Vagabond*? And, a *He without a Shadow*?

American Black Bears

- Black bear
- Black food (Cree Indians)
- Brownie
- Bruin
- Cinnamon bear
- Gap crosser (Appalachian Mountains)
- Happy hooligan
- Honey paw
- King of American wilderness
- Lava bear (central Oregon lava cone and flows)
- Owner of the earth
- Phantom of the woods
- Ridge runner (Appalachian Mountains)
- Smokey
- Spirit of the forest
- Teddy
- Variegated bear
- Yack-kay (Yankah)

Andean Bears

- Oso careto (ugly bear)
- Oso de anteojos (bear of eyeglasses)
- Short-faced bear
- Spectacled bear

Asiatic Black Bears

- Basindo nan tenggil (he who likes to sit high; day bedding)
- Black bear
- Black beast
- Dog bear
- Giant cat bear (Japan)
- Kala bhalom
- Kala reech
- Man bear
- Medved (Russian; honey bear)
- Moon bear (moon bear of Tibet)
- Pig bear

Brown Bears (including grizzly bears of Eurasia)

- Abruzzio brown bear (Italy)
- Alaskan brown bear
- Anijinabe (Ojibwa; Indian)
- Bad man (Sherpas)
- Bearcat
- Big brown bear
- Black grizzly (China, Mongolia)
- Blue tooth (Lapp)
- Brownie
- Caleb
- Cousin (Asiatic Eskimo hunters)
- Dog of God (Lapp)
- Dweller in the wilds (Ostyak)
- Fish-eating bear (Eurasian)
- Golden friend (Finn)
- Goliath
- Grandfather of the hill (Ural Mountains)
- Great grandfather
- Great grandmother
- Grizzly bear
- Hairy-eared bear (Eurasian)
- Himuga (Japan)

- Holy animal (Lapp)
- Honey paw (Tungus)
- Horse bear
- Kashmir bear (Isabelline bear)
- King of beasts
- King of the woods (ancient Greeks)
- Kodiak bear
- Light-foot (Finn)
- Little mother of honey (Finn)
- Lord of the mountains
- Lord of the taiga (Tungus)
- Ma hsiung (Chinese; horse bear)
- Man bear (Tibetans)
- Master of the forest (Lapp)
- Old man of the mountains (Lapp)
- Old man with the fur garment (Lapp)
- Owner of the earth
- Red bear
- Sacred man (Lapp)
- Sacred virgin (Lapp)
- Siberian bear (Kamchatka)
- Snowman (Kangme, Tibetans)
- Step-widener (Lapp)
- Thick fur (Lapp)
- Winter-sleeper (Lapp)
- Wise man (Lapp)
- Woolly one (Lapp)
- Worthy old man (Ural Mountains)

Giant Pandas

- Ailurus (early scientific; also common)
- Bai bao (white leopard)
- Bai hu (white bear; white tiger)
- Bamboo bear (German; bambushbar)
- Cat bear (hsiung-maou)
- Chitwa (Himalayan; 1800s)
- Fiery fox (Himalayan; 1800s)
- Harlequin bear
- Meng shi shou (Chinese; beast of prey)

- Metal-eating bear (entered villages and licked cooking pots)
- Mo (white leopard)
- Pi (ancient for panda; white fox)
- Pixiu (ancient for panda)
- Raccoon (Himalayan; 1800s)
- Shi tie shou (iron-eating beast; entered villages and licked food pots)
- Zhi yi (white bear; white tiger)

Grizzly Bears (North America)

- Aklak (Eskimo)
- Akshak (Eskimo)
- Baldface
- Bar (North American mountain men)
- Barren ground grizzly
- Beast that walks like man
- Big cinnamon
- Big hairy one (Blackfoot Indians)
- Bruin
- Buffalo grizzly
- Chief's son (Cree Indians)
- Cinnamon bear
- Colored bear (Iroquois Indians)
- Cousin (Northeast Native Americans)
- Elder brother (many Native Americans)
- Eldest brother (many Native Americans)
- Enemy of man
- Evil genius
- Fine young chief (Navajo)
- Food of the fire
- Four-legged human (Cree Indians)
- Glacier bear
- Grand old gladiator
- Grandfather (Northeast Native Americans)
- Gray bear
- Great bear
- Great grandfather (Northeast Indians)
- Hog back

- Hohhost (Native Americans of northern Rocky Mountains)
- Kenai giant bear
- King of beasts
- King of the plains
- Lord of the woods
- Matohota (Sioux Indians; gray bear)
- Moccasin Joe (early frontiersmen; hind paw print)
- Monarch of American beasts
- Monarch of the mountains
- Monarch of the plains
- Monster (Lewis & Clark Expedition)
- Monster, the
- Old Caleb
- Old Ephraim
- Old man (Sauks Indians)
- Old man of the mountains
- Oso grande (Mexico)
- Owner of the earth
- Pig bear
- Real bear (Blackfoot Indians)
- Red bear
- Renegade
- Roach bear (early frontiersmen; raised hackles)
- Silver bear
- Silvertip
- That hairy one (Blackfoot Indians)
- Thing, the
- Uncle
- Unmentionable one (Blackfoot Indians)
- Uzumate (Indians of the Yosemite region)
- Variegated bear
- White bear (Lewis & Clark Expedition)
- Yackah (Native Americans; Northern Rocky Mountains)
- Yellow bear
- Yosemite (Miwok Indians)

There are fewer, but perhaps more exotic, names for the other six species of bears:

Polar Bears

- Arctic bear
- Atertak (Eskimo; one who goes to sea)
- Eternal vagabond (Eskimo)
- Farmer (nineteenth-century whalers; "walked icy fields, his alone to tend")
- Great wanderer
- Hairy foot
- He who is without a shadow
- Ice bear
- King of the Arctic
- Lord of the ice and snow
- Maritime bear
- Monarch of the north
- Nanook (Eskimo; ever wandering one; also nahnook)
- Nanvark (Eskimo; polar bear cub)
- Nomad of the Arctic
- Pigoqahiaq (Eskimo)
- Sea bear (ancient Greeks)
- Snow bear
- Tiger of the north
- Traveler, the
- Wahb'esco (Cree Indians)
- Walking bear
- Wapusk (Cree Indians; white bear)
- Water bear
- White bear
- White giant

Sloth Bears

- Aswail
- Baloo (wise old man; Rudyard Kipling)
- Honey bear
- Lip bear

Sun Bears

- Ape man
- Beruang Madu (Malaysia; honey bear)
- Bruang
- Dog bear (Thailand)
- Honey bear
- Malay bear

Social Names of Bears

Boar: adult male bear (from the Old English "bar" and West Germanic "bairoz"; wild pig, male pig)

Cub: young bear (novice or learner, the young of certain carnivorous animals; an inexperienced or ill-mannered youth)

Dam: female parent (normally used for a quadruped, common with dogs; rarely used to refer to a bear; possibly originated in California during the mid-1800s)

Group: a pack or sloth (sleuth) of bears

He-bear: adult male bear

She-bear: adult female bear

Sleuth: a grouping of bears

Sloth: a grouping of bears (Middle English "slowthe")

Sow: adult female bear (adult female hog, Old English "sugu")

POPULATIONS

Determination of bear populations is extremely difficult, with exact numbers impossible. Scientific methods provide for reasonable estimates in most bear populations; however, many estimates in Asia (brown, sloth, sun and Asiatic black bears) are unreliable.

Difficulties in Determining Population Counts

There are many reasons that contribute to the difficulty of keeping track of numbers of bears, including the following:

- Bears are secretive and normally solitary, except for sows with cubs; not found in herds like deer, elk, wildebeests.
- Bears are transient, frequently moving in search of food (and often for reasons unknown to humans).
- Bears will alter state or country populations by moving across political boundaries.
- Polar bears, "the wanderers," are in a near-constant state of movement in vast ranges, frequently altering country and continental populations.
- Population information from many countries is often unavailable due to a lack of research funding or interest.
- Political conflicts, including war, place bear research and management low on the list of priorities.

Population counts have improved considerably in some areas and countries. The International Union for Conservation of Nature and Natural Resources (IUCN) Specialist Groups are now providing management and research guidance to many countries to help them determine bear populations.

Population Determination Methods

Numerous census methods exist, from roadside, boat, aircraft, and field sightings to incident trends (conflicts with humans), harvest reports, counts of sows with cubs, sex ratios, and trapping samples. However, all of these methods meet a single premise: The sample is "representative" of the population. The sample data, *though not of the total population,* is utilized over time to build a life table that depicts the sex and age structure (the number of observed bears of a sex in a specific age group) of the population. Knowing the proportion of each age and sex segment allows the biologist in subsequent counts to sample one segment and determine by ratio an approximate total number for the population. As the count of a specific segment of a population improves, the total number (or high-to-low range) for the population becomes more reliable. Most importantly, the information identifies the trend of the population, indicating whether it is increasing, decreasing, or stable. (The < symbol stands for *fewer than*, and the > symbol for *more than*.)

WORLDWIDE AND CONTINENTAL POPULATIONS

Worldwide Populations (Species)	Population
American black bear	900,000
Brown bear	> 200,000
Asiatic black bear	< 60,000
Polar bear	20,000–25,000
Andean bear	< 20,000
Sloth bear	10,000–20,000
Sun bear	6,000–10,000
Giant panda	1,000–2,000

Continental Populations	Species	Population
Africa	Brown bear	Extinct
Antarctica	Bears have never existed	—
Asia	Asiatic black bear	60,000
	Brown bear	< 70,000
	Giant panda	1,000–2,000
	Polar bear	*
	Sloth bear	10,000–20,000
	Sun bear	6,000–10,000
Australia	Bears have never existed	—
Europe	Brown bear	59,700
	Polar bear	*
North America	American black bear	900,000
	Brown bear	58,500
	Polar bear	*
South America	Andean bear	< 20,000

* Population groups of polar bears are listed on page 32.

There are approximately 187 countries in the world, with the number often changing due to political uprisings, wars, and so on. Populations of bears exist in at least 65 countries.

COUNTRY POPULATIONS

American Black Bear

Canada	396,000–476,000	United States	339,000–465,000
Mexico	Uncommon		

Brown Bear

Afghanistan	Low	Kazakhstan	900–1,000 (a)
Albania	250	Korea (North)	Unknown
Andorra	Few	Kyrgyzstan	300 (a)
Armenia	Unknown	Latvia	< 10
Austria	2–30	Macedonia	90
Azerbaijan	Unknown	Mexico	Extinct
Belarus	250	Mongolia	25–50
Bhutan	Unknown	Nepal	Few
Bosnia-Herzegovina	1,200	Norway	26–55
Bulgaria	700	Pakistan	150–200
Canada	25,000	Poland	60–100
China	7,000	Romania	5,500
Croatia	600	Russia	> 100,000
Czech Republic	2–3	Serbia-Montenegro	430
Estonia	250	Slovakia	600–800
Finland	800–1,000	Slovenia	350–450
France	4–10	Spain	100–130
Georgia	Common	Sweden	1,000
Greece	110–130	Tajikistan	700 (a)
India	500–1,000	Turkey	Common
Iran	Few	Turkmenistan	Low
Iraq	Few	Ukraine	300–400
Italy	< 100	United States	32,000
Japan (Hokkaido)	2,000	Uzbekistan	Low

(a) Data 10 to 12 years old

Polar Bear (Population Groups)

Polar bears exist in Canada (C), Greenland [Denmark] (G), Norway (N), Russia (R), and Alaska [United States] (A). The polar-bear population, both country and continental, is ever changing as the population groups span international boundaries.

Population Groups	Countries	Number of Bears
Arctic Basin	A, C, G, N, R	Common
Baffin Bay	G	2,074
Barents Sea	C, G, N, R	2,997
Chukchi Sea	A, R	2,000
Davis Strait	C, G	1,650
East Greenland	G, R	Common
Foxe Basin	C	2,197
Gulf of Boothia	C	1,523
Kane Basin	C, G	164
Kara Sea	R	Common
Lancaster Sound	C	2,541
Laptev Sea	R	800–1,200
M'Clintock Channel	C	284
Northern Beaufort Sea	C	1,200
Norwegian Bay	C	190
Southern Beaufort Sea	A, C	1,500
Southern Hudson Bay	C	1,000
Viscount Melville Sound	C	161
Western Hudson Bay	C	935

Asiatic Black Bear

Afghanistan	Rare	Korea (South)	< 60
Bangladesh	Few	Laos	Unknown
Bhutan	Unknown	Myanmar	Unknown
Cambodia	Unknown	Nepal	Unknown
China	28,000	Pakistan	1,000
India	7,000–9,000	Russia	5,000–6,000
Iran	20–30	Taiwan	Uncommon
Japan	8,400–12,600	Thailand	Common
Korea (North)	Unknown	Vietnam	Unknown

Giant Panda

China	1,000–2,000

Sloth Bear

Bangladesh	Extinct?	Nepal	Common
Bhutan	Unknown	Sri Lanka	Common
India	4,000		

Sun Bear*

Bangladesh	Extinct?	Laos	Common
Borneo (Indonesia)	Unknown	Malaysia	Uncommon
Brunei Darussalam	Unknown	Myanmar	Common
Cambodia	Unknown	Sumatra (Indonesia)	Unknown
China	Unknown	Thailand	Common
India	Few	Vietnam	Unknown

* Reliable population estimates do not exist.

Andean Bear

Argentina	400	Panama	Possible few
Bolivia	Unknown	Peru	Unknown
Columbia	3,000–7,000	Venezuela	300–2,000
Ecuador	2,000		

Definitions of Population Terminology

Common: considered common; population unknown

Extinct?: possibly extinct

Few: exists in very low numbers

Low: exists in low numbers

Uncommon: considered uncommon; population unknown

Unknown: known to exist; population unknown

North American Bear Populations

Bears were more than just "common" in North America as the early explorers and settlers approached, crossed, and settled the continent.

In September 1824 explorer and trapper James Ohio Pattie, while traveling in the eastern part of the present state of Colorado, encountered over 220 grizzly bears in a single day (twenty men stood guard around camp that night).

"In January, 1827," according to Tracy Storer and Lloyd Tevis in *California Grizzly*, "Duhaut-Cilly wrote that 'bears are very common in the environs; and without going farther than five or six leagues from San Francisco, they are often seen in herds. . . .'"

Alaska grizzly bear
©JOHNNY JOHNSON

Frank Dufresne, in *No Room for Bears*, describes an 1848 scene: ". . . grizzlies lined the shores of San Francisco Bay and the nearby river banks."

Author Ernest Thompson Seton noted that the Black Hills region of South Dakota (1800s) had grizzly bears "in bands like buffalo."

Storer and Tevis also relate the comments of George Yount, an early American pioneer in California during 1831. Yount wrote that bears ". . . were everywhere—upon the plains, in the valleys, and on the mountains . . . it was not unusual to see fifty or sixty within the twenty-four hours. . . ."

"School" Bears

Many schools were closed in California during 1852 as the trails were unsafe for children due to grizzly bears. In 2007 a few schools were temporarily closed in northern Montana due to grizzly-bear activity.

American Black Bear

When Europeans began to arrive in North America, 500,000 American black bears roamed the continent. Today there are 900,000 black bears displaying a remarkable adjustment to an ever-increasing human population. In the United States the American black bear is present in forty-two of forty-nine states (bears have never existed in Hawaii) and is considered transient in four other states. They exist in twelve of thirteen Canadian provinces or territories (they have been extirpated from the Prince Edward Island province) and in ten Mexican states.

Grizzly Bear

One hundred thousand brown (grizzly) bears originally inhabited the present forty-eight contiguous states. They were described simply as "abundant." However, only 1,200 to 1,400 exist today, belonging to six ecosystems in areas of four American states and a small portion of British Columbia.

United States	Population	United States	Population
Alabama	50–100	Montana	16,600
Alaska	100,000	Nebraska	Transients
Arizona	2,500	Nevada	200–300
Arkansas	3,500	New Hampshire	4,600
California	30,000	New Jersey	3,500
Colorado	10,000–14,000	New Mexico	5,500–6,000
Connecticut	200	New York	4,300–7,500
Delaware	None	North Carolina	11,000
Florida	2,500–3,000	North Dakota	100–300
Georgia	2,300–2,500	Ohio	50–100 (b)
Hawaii	Bears have never existed	Oklahoma	200+
Idaho	20,000–25,000	Oregon	25,000–30,000
Illinois	None	Pennsylvania	15,000
Indiana	None	Rhode Island	0–10 (d)
Iowa	Transients	South Carolina	1,200
Kansas	Transients (a)	South Dakota	Transients
Kentucky	< 500	Tennessee	2,000–2,500
Louisiana	200–400	Texas	Unknown
Maine	25,000	Utah	2,500
Maryland	550	Vermont	4,000–4,300
Massachusetts	2,900–3,000	Virginia	5,000–6,000 (c)
Michigan	15,000–19,000	Washington	25,000–30,000
Minnesota	20,000–30,000	West Virginia	10,000–12,000
Mississippi	70–80	Wisconsin	12,350
Missouri	Unknown (b)	Wyoming	5,000–7,000

Canada	Population	Canada	Population
Alberta	40,000	Nunavut	Unknown
British Columbia	140,000	Ontario	75,000–100,000
Manitoba	25,000–35,000	Prince Edward Island	None
New Brunswick	16,500	Quebec	70,000
Newfoundland/Labrador	8,000–11,000	Saskatchewan	40,000
Northwest Territories	10,000	Yukon	10,000
Nova Scotia	10,000–12,000		

Mexico	Population	Mexico	Population
Chihuahua	Unknown (e)	San Luis Potosi	Unknown (e)
Coahuila	(e)	Sinaloa	Unknown (e)
Durango	Unknown (e)	Sonora	Unknown (e)
Jalisco	Unknown (e)	Tamaulipas	Unknown (e)
Nayarit	Extinct	Zacatecas	Unknown (e)
Nuevo Leon	Unknown (e)		

(a) *Confirmed sighting approximately every 10 years*
(b) *Extinct by mid-1800s; now immigrating*
(c) *Density: 3.5 bears per square mile in some areas*
(d) *Immigration from CT and MA*
(e) *Exist; reliable population information unavailable*

STATES)	
Yellowstone (northwest Wyoming, eastern Idaho, southwest Montana)	> 580
Northern Continental Divide (north-central Montana)	> 400
Selkirk (northern Idaho, northeast Washington, southeast British Columbia)	40–50
Cabinet-Yaak (northwestern Montana, northern Idaho)	30–40
North Cascades (north-central Washington)	< 20
Bitterroot (east-central Idaho, western Montana; no established population)	0

POPULATIONS (CANADA AND ALASKA)	
Alberta	< 500
British Columbia	10,000–13,000
Northwest Territories	4,000–5,000
Nunavut	4,000–5,000
Yukon	6,000–7,000
Alaska	32,000–43,000*
Includes Kodiak and coastal brown bears	

POPULATIONS (MEXICO)	
Chihuahua	Extinct

Brown/Grizzly Bears in Alaska

The separation of brown-bear and grizzly-bear populations and distribution in Alaska is not perfectly definitive. The easiest system of division considers the bears inhabiting the coastal areas as brown bears; they have ready access to salmon and are larger than the inland grizzly bears.

The bears (*Ursus arctos middendorffi*) isolated on the islands of Kodiak, Afognak, and Shuyak are Kodiak brown bears (population estimated at 3,500 bears). Brown bears of Canada and the contiguous forty-eight states are grizzly bears.

Polar Bear

Polar bears are generally grouped into nineteen populations, found in Norway, Greenland, Canada, Alaska, and Russia; therefore, North American populations are shared with Canada and other countries and with another continent, Asia.

DISTRIBUTION

The family Ursidae and its members presently live on every continent except Africa, Australia, and Antarctica. Brown bears inhabited the Atlas Mountains of northern Africa until 1891, but there is no evidence of their previous existence in Australia and Antarctica. The present distribution of the world's bears is not only different from that of prehistoric periods and early times, but most species are today experiencing rapid and extreme distribution alterations (see Worldwide Status of Bears, Chapter 9).

COUNTRIES WITH MOST SPECIES OF BEARS

China	India	Canada	Russia	United States
Asiatic black bear	Asiatic black bear	American black bear	American black bear	American black bear
Brown bear	Brown bear	Brown bear (including grizzly)	Brown bear (including grizzly)	Brown bear (including grizzly)
Giant panda	Sloth bear	Polar bear	Polar bear	Polar bear
Sun bear	Sun bear			

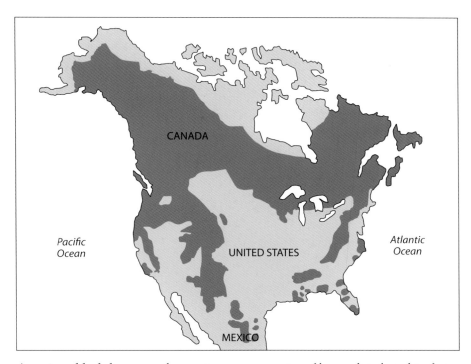

American black bear distribution— North America
C. SERVHEEN, U.S. FISH AND WILDLIFE SERVICE

American black bears are the most common species of bears, distributed in forty-two of the forty-nine mainland states and transient in four other states (bears have never existed in Hawaii). They are in twelve of the thirteen Canadian provinces and territories (extirpated on Prince Edward Island). Distribution in Mexico is currently uncertain, but they presently occur in ten states.

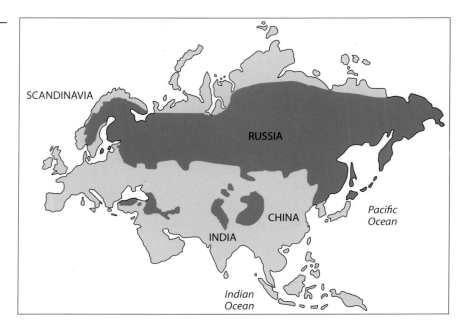

Brown bear distribution—
map of Eurasia
C. SERVHEEN, U.S. FISH AND
WILDLIFE SERVICE

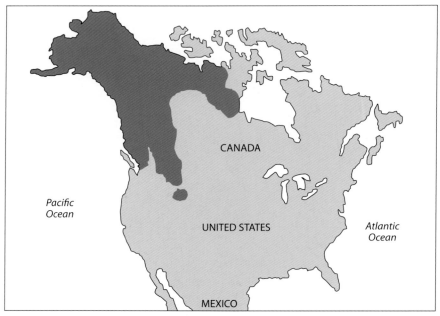

Brown bear distribution—
map of North America
C. SERVHEEN, U.S. FISH AND
WILDLIFE SERVICE

Brown bears have the widest world distribution, though the species has lost more than 50 percent of its range and population since the mid-1800s.

the gestation period is prolonged, with delayed implantation. More vegetarian and tree-dwelling (arboreal) than most species of bears, it is shy, solitary, and cautious.

Asiatic Black Bear
(Ursus thibetanus; also Selenarctos thibetanus)

The moon bear of Tibet, the Himalayan black bear, and the Tibetan black bear are names provided to the bear with the thick neck mane. A white, crescent-shaped, medallion-like mark on its chest accounts for the name "moon" bear.

The Asiatic black bear lives in a temperate climate, with a portion of its habitat shared with the giant panda. "It is a bear of eastern Asia, filling in the habitat that lies between that of the brown bear to the north and sloth bear and sun bear to the south," according to Paul Shepard and Barry Sanders in *The Sacred Paw*. Coloration is black, often with a white throat, and there is a highly pronounced, long, manelike mantle of hair around the neck, throat, and shoulders. The fur is soft, and the ears are thickly haired and relatively large. The head appears round, and the body is muscular and broad, with heavier front quarters and shorter legs than the American black bears and the worldwide brown bears. Hind legs and feet are slender. Claws are short.

The Asiatic black bear spends most of its day in trees, as protection from humans and other predators. It has a prolonged gestation period with delayed implantation and hibernates in northern regions of its range. Though basically shy and cautious, it has adapted to human pressures and is more aggressive than the brown bears of Eurasia. Despite its nasty disposition, it is often trained to perform in captivity.

Rudyard Kipling described the Asiatic black bears, with their strange appearance, many names, outstanding learning ability in captivity, and unpredictable temperament as "the most bizarre of the ursine species."

The subspecies *Selenarctos thibetanus geodrosianus* (Baluchistan bear) of Pakistan is considered one of the world's rarest mammals.

Brown Bear *(Ursus arctos)*

Brown bears, native to the Old and New Worlds, live in a temperate climate and are found from the Arctic tundra to the edge of the Gobi Desert.

The brown is the most diverse bear in size. Its color is variable, though generally brown, and an individual's is relatively uniform. It has a dished face (dished-in profile); short, round ears that are small compared to the skull; and long claws on the front paws. With its strong build, great strength, thick head, and large hump over the shoulder, it is the largest omnivore.

The remarkable and distinguishing "hump" is actually a mass of muscle that, coupled with long claws, provides the brown bear with great digging ability. Long guard hairs on the hump enhance this important feature of identification. Its gestation period is prolonged and with delayed implantation, and it hibernates.

The brown bear is dignified, majestic, and solitary. Europeans for thousands of years have treated brown bears with awe, fear, hatred, and respect. Erwin Bauer in *Bears in Their World* writes, "Magnificent is an adjective too freely used to describe too many creatures; but in my mind, the brown bear truly lives up to the words. It is impossible to spend much time in brown-bear country and not be almost overwhelmed by the environment as well as its inhabitants."

Giant Panda
(Ailuropoda melanoleuca)

As a national treasure of China (with cult status), the World Wildlife Fund's symbol of world conservation, one of the world's most esteemed animals, and creatures of mystery in the wild, these popular and appealing bears have long been the focus of a classification controversy. Though originally considered bears, their diet of bamboo, an uncertain ancestry, the inability to vocalize in the same manner as other bears, unbearlike foot pads, and remarkable eye patches all provided doubt as to whether they were true bears. Research—including genetic studies—however, indicates that giant pandas are "specialized"

THE PANDA CONTROVERSY

Disagreement dominated discussions for over 130 years as to whether giant pandas should be classified with bears or with the family that includes raccoons and lesser pandas. They were originally called giant pandas because of their bone and tooth similarities with the smaller red panda. Confusion reigned.

Giant pandas have traits that are similar to raccoons and bears, but they also have some unique characteristics of their own, including the following:

- Coloration: highly visible, distinct black-and-white markings
- Forelegs: larger and heavier than hind legs (a climbing asset)
- Dentition: heavy jaws and large teeth with multiple crowns for grinding
- Vocalizations: a bleating, unlike the growl or roar of other bears
- Shape of male genitalia: penis is very small

- (rodlike) and S-shaped.
- Forepaws: opposable (sixth) digit that is an extension of a wrist bone
- Scent gland: located in the anal region and used for marking
- Small intestine: shorter and less complex than that of other bears
- Hind-foot heel pad: none; no humanlike track

Giant pandas resemble bears with their shape; reproductive behavior, including delayed implantation; their walk or gait; and their number of teeth. During the early 1980s, serological studies were conducted in which the degree of rejection by various bears and raccoons to molecules of protein from an American black bear was measured. "When certain proteins (transferrins) from the black bear, *Ursus americanus*, are mixed with the blood of other animals, a measurable reaction occurs," relate Shepard and Sanders. "The degree of reactivity can be quantified and is interpreted as the degree of relatedness between animals descended from a common ancestor." The degree of genetic difference—with higher numbers indicating greater difference—between the study animals was found to be as follows:

- American black bears (own proteins): 0
- Brown bears: 6
- Sun bears: 8
- Spectacled bears: 8

- **Giant pandas: 18**
- Red pandas: 52
- Raccoons: 55

The study provided immunological evidence that giant pandas are more bear than raccoons and red (lesser) pandas, and they evolved from the bears, splitting off twenty million years ago. Solid proof has recently been established that giant pandas are justly part of the family Ursidae. Lance Craighead writes in *Bears of the World*, "There is now no doubt, based upon concordance of DNA and protein studies, that pandas are more closely related to bears than to any other group of species, and are close enough to be included in the family Ursidae."

white hair gives it the most distinctive coloration pattern of all bears. It is stocky, with a relatively short body that is squat and barrel shaped and a broad, massive, round head with a short muzzle. The legs are stout, powerful, and relatively short, and it possesses a specialized head and paws to handle bamboo stems. The forepaws are flexible, with a sixth toe that forms a modified opposable thumb. Its dentition is typical of carnivores, as is the digestive tract. The pupils of the eyes are vertical slits, as opposed to the horizontal orientation of other bears. The fur is coarse, extremely dense, and woolly and gives a cuddly appearance. A giant panda does not hibernate but has a prolonged gestation with delayed implantation. Retiring and elusive, it is a solitary and highly specialized and aberrant bear. "No other animal has so entranced the public . . . ," notes Schaller, ". . . an almost mythical creature in which legend and reality merge."

Grizzly Bear
(Ursus arctos horribilis)

North America's "unpredictable" bears have long been one of the most celebrated of all bears, having captured the attention and imagination of humans due to size, temperament, and conflicts with people. A feared species, not only from much western legend but also through considerable fact. "The term 'grizzly' is a colloquial name that refers to the animal's colorations," writes Domico. "It usually has a dark coat with shimmering silver-tipped hairs that give it a 'grizzled' appearance. . . ."

The grizzly bear is a North American subspecies of the brown bear, though a few brown-bear populations in Europe have at times been called

Giant panda—a disappearing mysterious symbol of wilderness
©2008 BRIAN JORG/CRITTERZONE.COM

bears, most closely related to the Andean bear. According to George Schaller et al. in *The Giant Pandas of Wolong*, ". . . pandas are related both to bears and to raccoons but more closely to the former. . . ."

The giant panda, rare in the wild (and in captivity), lives in a temperate climate, preferring forests of at least 66 percent cover. Its black-and-

"grizzlies." Diverse in color, which is brownish but varying from blond to black, it lacks uniformity in color on the body and head; the fur there often gives a grizzled appearance. Large—though smaller than other brown bears—the grizzly is strongly built. Dignified, the grizzly bear triggers the emotions of humans, at times being called the "bear of quotes."

"The story of the . . . grizzly bear," according to Harold McCracken in *The Beast That Walks Like Man*, "is an extraordinary heritage of legendary lore and historic melodrama, that goes back to the time when the saber-tooth tiger and the mastodon roamed where our farms and cities thrive today. "[The grizzly] . . . is invulnerable to all of life's hazards, except the artificial weapons of man, but he has a cast-iron constitution. As a species [sub-species], they are just about nature's healthiest children. Susceptible to practically no physical disease or lesser ailments, they have the natural ability of thriving on a remarkably wide variety of diets. Although carnivorous by physical evolution, they are widely omnivorous in adaptability."

Polar Bear (*Ursus maritimus*)

The "wandering bear" of monstrous size was called a polar bear (Nanook) long before the North Pole was discovered. ". . . there are Bears which are called Amphibia, because they live both on Land and in the Sea, hunting and catching fish like an Otter or Beaver, and these are white coloured," writes Edward Topsell in *The History of Four-footed Beasts*. Considered by many to be the most dangerous species of bear, and a formidable adversary, polar bears are one of North America's most magnificent animals. Arctic explorer Peter Freuchen said of the polar bears, "No more beau-

tiful animal walks on four feet," relates Ben East in *Bears*. This traveling "sea bear," according to East, "is the great white or cream-colored survivalist of arctic snow and ice."

Ian Sterling, a noted polar-bear biologist, has commented, "once polar bears reach maturity, they seem immortal."

The polar bear living in an arctic (polar) climate is the greatest wanderer of all bears and is considered by many as the largest. It is the most carnivorous of modern bears. Yellowish white in color, with a black nose, the polar bear has an elongated body with low, well-developed shoulders; a long, relatively thin but well-developed neck; highly developed hindquarters; and a small head. It has a straight profile, a Roman nose with a bulge at the bridge of the snout, large feet with membranes up to half the length of the toes, and long and thick claws. Four inches of blubber cover the rump and legs (except the inside of the back legs). The polar bear does not hibernate (with the exception of pregnant sows) and has a prolonged gestation period with delayed implantation. A shrewd hunter, it considers anything that moves on the ice as food.

As autumn passes through the arctic, ". . . the sun has already disappeared below the horizon," writes Charles Feazel in *White Bear*. "Its cheering rays won't be seen again for more than a hundred days. The huge Newfoundland dog lies curled beneath the building that is wrapped in a deepening blanket of snow. . . . And in the gathering gloom in the pack ice now frozen into solid sheets, there are bears. Hundreds of bears. Thousands of bears. Masters of darkness. White ghosts in the black night. No human, nothing in nature, challenges their supremacy; in the darkness of winter, the ice belongs to Nanook."

Sloth Bear
(Ursus ursinus; also Melursus ursinus)

These very active and elusive, long-lipped, and poorly groomed bears are highly specialized to allow them to seek and feed on termites. Sloth bears are sometimes referred to as the insectivores of the bear world. An unusual face, minus two upper front teeth and with a long lower lip, provides sloth bears with tubular vacuuming systems for the suction of insects. Originally classified as a "bear" sloth due to its sickle-shaped claws and the habit of hanging upside down from tree limbs, it was appropriately identified as a bear in 1791.

The sloth bear lives in a subtropical (monsoon) climate. Its fur is black, with a whitish Y, U, or V mark on the chest, and the coat is long, shaggy, and unkempt, with heavy fur on the back of the neck and between the shoulders, forming a mane. The belly and underlegs are nearly bare, and it lacks facial hair. The blunt, hooklike claws are highly developed, and a hairless web connects the pads of the toes. The sloth bear has a specialized, bulbous snout, with wide nostrils, pronounced lips, and a lower lip that can be stretched over the outer edge of its nose. The tongue is long and flat, and the palate is bony and hollowed out. There are no upper incisor teeth, which enhances the tubular space used to suck termites. It is a rangy bear, long in appearance (thirteen pairs of ribs in contrast to the twelve pairs of the other bears). The sloth bear does not hibernate, and there is prolonged gestation with delayed implantation.

"To get them the bear smashes a rotten log or tears open a termite mound with its long claws," write Shepard and Sanders when describing a sloth bear's specialized termite hunting. "At the same time it alternately blows away the dirt and wood chips and sucks up termites so noisily that it can be heard 100 meters away. It is called the 'lip bear' because its long lips form the end of a tube for this staccato in-huffing and out-puffing."

"The huffing sound that they make while feeding can often be heard through the forest even though the bear itself cannot be seen," writes Lance Craighead in *Bears of the World*. A sloth bear may consume 4,000 to 10,000 termites at a single sitting.

Sun Bear (Ursus malayanus; also Helarctos malayanus)

The world's smallest bear, the "Malay bear," occurs in a tropical climate, its population spanning the equator. One of the rarest tropical forest animals, it is also the most lightly built bear (one hundred pounds is considered big). Though small, a sun bear has a "chip on its shoulder," manifested in a very bad attitude, and it is known to attack humans.

Black to dark brown in color, it has a whitish to pale orange-yellow horseshoe-shaped chest marking that is thought to resemble the sun; hence the name. Its fur is short, the hair unusually thick for a tropical climate, and there is no hair on the soles of the paws. The head is short, wide, and flat, with small, beady eyes; a highly flexible snout; and an extremely long, slender tongue. The muscular body has short, bowed legs (the front legs are quite powerful); large inwardly set feet (making the bear bandy-legged); and long, sickle-shaped claws. The sun bear does not hibernate; its gestation period is not prolonged, and there is no delayed implantation.

Referred to in Malaysia as Beruang Madu (honey bear), this solitary, small, strange and fascinating animal is the least well known of all bears. Sun-bear research has long been a low priority on the Malay Peninsula and in other areas inhabited by the sun bear.

SIZE

The size of individual bears has long caused heated discussions and continual misjudgment. A bear's size is normally expressed in terms of weight, which is difficult to judge due to individual variations in height, thickness of fur, and physical stature, as well as the observer's proximity to the bear and particular level of stress. Under calm circumstances a bear's weight is often misjudged, but during a close encounter accurate weight determination is impossible by

nearly all except possibly a seasoned field scientist. To a general's question about how big the Alaska bears are, aviation pioneer Bob Ellis told him, ". . . the tracks weigh about 12 pounds. . ." (Ellis obituary, *Alaska* magazine, 1994).

To the untrained eye all bears are "big," as human perception of weight is most often much greater than an animal's true size. During a survey in Great Smoky Mountains National Park, responses to the weights of American black bears ranged from 400 to 4,000 pounds. The actual weights were 95 to 115 pounds.

"The boar was small," according to Ben East in *Bears*, "hardly more than 150 pounds, but still big enough to be a formidable antagonist . . . the men guessed him at four hundred pounds."

In nearly all species of bears, the male is rela-

Brown bears vie with polar bears as "the largest."
JOHN NICKLES/U.S. FISH AND WILDLIFE SERVICE

tively larger than the female, though differences vary. For example, the difference between the sun-bear females and males on Borneo is minimal, while on the Malaysian mainland the males may be more than one-third larger.

Weight

Weights of bears vary between species, with polar bears and Alaska brown bears more than ten times heavier than sun bears. Such differences between species, though due in part to genetics, are most often a result of variations in habitat, primarily diet (body mass is related to diet). For example, the Alaska brown bears of the coastal regions of North America, with a major source of fish and lush vegetation, are more than twice the weight of the inland brown (grizzly) bears.

- Average weight of coastal (Alaska) brown bears: 787.05 pounds
- Average weight of inland (Yukon) grizzly bears: 319.67 pounds

Causes of individual weight differences between bears of the same species, and sometimes the same habitat, may include:

- Individual health
- Individual ability to locate food
- Level of ability to withstand human impacts on the habitat
- Sex of the bear
- Individual ability to digest specific foods
- Age

Seasonal fluctuations in weights of individual bears are common. Fall (prehibernation) weights are normally much greater than spring (emergence) weights. Weights are affected by seasonally available foods. The state of Nevada

has identified an urban population of American black bears that spend all their time within city limits, in the Tahoe area, where the female bears average 19 percent heavier and the males 20 percent more than the nonurban bears, because of the availability of human foods and garbage. Some other urban-interface bears (living in or adjacent to urban areas) have 30 percent greater body mass than wildland bears.

Bear weights are obtained when bears are harvested during a hunt, illegally killed (poached), and when immobilized for management and research, though some management agencies do not maintain records of weight.

HEAVIEST RECORDED BEARS (SPECIES/WORLDWIDE)

American black bear	940
Andean bear	440
Asiatic black bear	440
Brown bear	2,500+
Giant panda	330+
Grizzly bear	1,496
Polar bear	2,210*
Sloth bear	385
Sun bear	145

* *Location undetermined*

BEAR WEIGHTS (MALES VS. FEMALES)

American black bear	Males 33% larger
Andean bear	Males 30% larger
Asiatic black bear	Males slightly larger
Brown bear (Kodiak)	Males 40–50% larger
Giant panda	Males 10–20% larger
Grizzly bear	Males 38% larger
Polar bear	Males 25–45% larger
Sloth bear	Males slightly larger
Sun bear	Males 10–45% larger

AMERICAN BLACK BEAR WEIGHTS

	Heaviest Recorded	Average Male	Average Female
United States			
Alabama	426	175	120
Alaska	800+	360	225
Arizona	350	275	150
Arkansas	600	200	150
California	630	275	190
Colorado	(b)		
Connecticut	200+		
Florida	635		
Georgia	581	250	150
Idaho	(b)		
Kentucky	435	225	130
Louisiana	(b)		
Maine	680	350	200
Maryland	615	400	200
Massachusetts	467 (a)	229	139
Michigan	615		
Minnesota	876	300	175
Mississippi	420	300	200
Missouri	400	200	130
Montana	(b)		
Nevada	660	253	143
New Hampshire	532 (a)	298	157
New Jersey	582		
New Mexico	(b)	200	300
New York	759	350	160
North Carolina	880 (f)	373	196
North Dakota	(b)		
Ohio	380	275	175
Oklahoma	525		
Oregon	456		
Pennsylvania	864	270	(b)
Rhode Island	(b)		

AMERICAN BLACK BEAR WEIGHTS (CONTINUED)

	Heaviest Recorded	Average Male	Average Female
South Carolina	594	235	209
Tennessee	586		
Texas	570		
Utah	500+	281	219
Vermont	514	200	135
Virginia	740	215	136
Washington	(b)		
West Virginia	485	220	150
Wisconsin	802½	300	150
Wyoming	(b)		
Canada			
Alberta	(b)		
British Columbia	(b)		
Manitoba	888 (c) (d)		
New Brunswick	690	236	147
Newfoundland/Labrador	496	220	121
Northwest Territories	(b)		
Nova Scotia	(b)	350	250
Nunavut	(b)		
Ontario	825	388	195
Quebec	690	192	126
Saskatchewan	(b)		
Yukon	940 (e)		
Mexico	350 (g)	263	200

(a) Dressed weight (add approximately 18% for live weight)
(b) Information unavailable/unknown
(c) Female; weighed without head/paws
(d) Three records of 800+ pounds
(e) Had been eating garbage
(f) Had been residing near a hog farm
(g) Heaviest sampled; ranchers claim "they get quite large"

Manitoba, Canada: In early May 2007 a 722-pound male American black bear was harvested in a spring bear hunt. While the bear was very large for the spring, if it had gained normal weight, considering its habitat and time of year, it would have weighed more than 1,050 pounds by early September. (Hank Hristienko, Manitoba Conservation, Wildlife and Ecosystem Protection Branch)

NORTH AMERICAN BROWN/GRIZZLY BEAR WEIGHTS (HEAVIEST)

Alaska	2,500+ (a)
Wyoming	1,120 (b)
Yukon	948
British Columbia	800+
Montana	790
Idaho	550
Northwest Territories	528
Alberta	(c)

(a) *Kodiak brown bear*
(b) *Yellowstone National Park*
(c) *Information unavailable*

NORTH AMERICAN POLAR BEAR WEIGHTS (HEAVIEST)

Undetermined location	2,210
Northwest Territories/Nunavut	1,780
Newfoundland/Labrador	1,768
Manitoba	1,549
Ontario	1,350

Bear Weights in Lore and Legend

Lore and legend have provided some very impressive weights of bears:

- Kamchatka (Russia) brown bear: 2,600 pounds
- California grizzly bear (early 1900s): 2,350 pounds
- American black bear (during the 1800s): 1,800 pounds

"Legendary" weights are not uncommon, even today. Ben East in *Bears* relates the comment of a zoo director about such weights: ". . . few grizzlies of record weight come from a part of the country where accurate scales are found." And Adolph Murie in *A Naturalist in Alaska* notes that ". . . a bear a long distance from a scale always weighs most."

polar-bear hair collects heat. The theory is each hair is a hollow, transparent tube that reflects and scatters the sun's rays to the black skin where the heat is absorbed; the hairs change 95 percent of the sun's rays to heat (see Body Temperature, this chapter).

- **Sloth bear:** long and straight; unusually coarse and shaggy; mane (ruff) behind head, on neck and shoulders; only bear with long hair on ears; underlegs and belly almost bare; lacks facial hair, minimal hair on snout; fur often matted and unkempt

- **Sun bear:** very short and dense; smooth and sleek; dark skin evident; fur cowlicks and whorls on forehead and behind ears

Polar bear in the Bering Sea
ELIZABETH LABUNSKI/NATIONAL PARKS SERVICE

COLOR

The coloration of bears is quite variable between species and within species. Color changes are not uncommon, due to maturation or seasonal fading and shedding in individual bears or with the angle and intensity of the natural light of the moment. Variations may include totally different color or different shades of a color. Color may change from shades of brown to black. The underfur color normally remains the same, while the guard hairs change.

American black bear cubs of the same litter may be different colors, and they may change as they mature from brown to black—or the opposite may occur: Light brown cubs often change to dark brown. Changes normally occur before the cubs reach one year old, but they have been known to change at two or three years.

A bear's underfur may be brown, while the outer, guard hairs are tipped in black, and some bears are entirely of a single color. Several species of bears have yellowish or whitish chest markings on many individuals, while the chest mark, or medallion, is found on nearly all members of the tropical bears—sloth, sun, and Andean. The markings vary in shape and size and may provide individual identification. In ancient eastern folklore, the yellow-whitish chest mark or medallion of a bear represented the "sun"; hence, the name sun bear.

Albinism

Albinism, though extremely rare, occurs in all bear species. In the early 1900s an albino American black bear was reported in New York State. There is record of a whitish American black bear with four cubs: one brown, two black, and one true albino. In Oregon an American black bear had a light chocolate brown head and feet, with the rest of the body a dirty white (this was not a true albino). An albino American black bear was killed near Kalispell, Montana, in 1983. And Ernest Thompson Seton made reference to two albino American black bears (late 1890s–early 1900s) in the eastern United States.

Color Descriptions and Variations

American Black Bear

- Black
- Blond
- Blue-gray (glacier bear)
- Brown
- Cinnamon
- Light brown
- Rich chocolate brown
- Silver
- White (Kermode bear)
- Yellow
- (Face *nearly* always brownish)

A white V-shaped patch (spot, blaze) sometimes occurs on the throat or chest. John Beecham and Jeff Rohlman in *A Shadow in the Forest* write, "We saw no differences in the number of black- or brown-phase bears who had white spots on their chests or in the number of males and females with white chest markings." The American Bear Association writes, "80% of all cubs are born with chest blazes, but many lose them as they age. If the mother has a blaze, the cub is more likely to retain [its] throughout its lifetime."

American black bear sow and its cub. Note the color variation that occurs within this species.
COURTESY YELLOWSTONE NATIONAL PARK

Color variations (phases) of American black bears are considerably geographical (that is, related to weather) and are greater in the western part of the continent. Even though 70 percent of American black bears are actually black, only 50 percent of those in the Rocky Mountains are black. Black coats are found more often in moist areas such as New England, New York, Tennessee, Michigan, and western Washington. Beecham and Rohlman stated they ". . . believe that brown-phase bears were better able to tolerate hot, dry, sunny habitat . . . than were black-phase bears. [B]lack-phase bears are more common in humid areas that receive lesser amounts of solar radiation." A study in Arizona found that 94 percent of the bears were brown-phase bears, and in Colorado a study reported 95 percent.

AMERICAN BLACK BEAR COLOR VARIATIONS IN THE UNITED STATES

State or Area	Color Breakdown
Arkansas	80% black; 20% brown, cinnamon, blond
Colorado	25% black; 75% shades of brown
Michigan	100% black
Minnesota	94% black; 6% brown
New England	100% black
New York	99% black; 1% brownish
Pennsylvania	99% black; 1% brownish
Tennessee	100% black; approximately 10% with white chest blaze
Washington (coastal)	99% black; 1% brown, blond
Washington (inland)	21% black; 79% brown, blond
Yosemite National Park	10% black; 90% brown, blond, cinnamon, tan

Andean bears with typical facial and chest markings
ERIC BACCEGA/NATUREPL.COM

Andean Bear

Andeans are jet black with a white or beige patch on the chest. They have a yellowish/beige line on the face, which often forms rings around the eyes. Markings are unique and allow identification of individual bears. The markings on the Andean bear are much less conspicuous in Bolivia than over the remainder of its range.

Asiatic Black Bear

Asiatic black bears are jet black and glossy; occasionally they are partly brown (brown color phase). Their muzzles are brownish and their upper lips usually white. They have a white or orange-yellow crescent (crest, horseshoe) on the chest.

Asiatic black bears of typical color—black with a white collar or crest
©GARY BROWN

Brown Bear

- Dark brown
- Ash brown
- Cream
- Rust (reddish)
- Yellowish
- Near black

Brown bears' coloration frequently shows white-tipped hairs, though it is less grizzled and more uniform in individual coloration than the grizzly bear. The lower part of the legs are a much lighter brown than those of the grizzly bear.

Eurasian Brown Bear

Eurasian brown bears show a wide variety of coloration: black, dark brown, reddish with a silver tip (the red bear of India), but mostly medium brown. Younger bears are lighter; some are bicolored with a yellow-brown or whitish cape across their shoulders (the "horse bear" of China).

Grizzly Bear

Grizzlies are dark brown (almost black) to cream (almost white) or yellowish brown; the black hairs usually have white tips. The intensity of color varies over the body; pale-tipped guard hairs extend beyond the mat of fur and provide a silver-tip or grizzled appearance. Black grizzly bears are seldom grizzled, but white collars on cubs are not uncommon. The grizzly bear is named for color, not disposition.

The grizzly bear with its "grizzled" coloration
©JOHNNY JOHNSON

Giant Panda

Pandas are white with black eye patches and ears; they have black forelegs, with black extending in a narrowing band over the shoulder, and black hind legs. The tip of the white tail is sometimes black, and there is some brownish black hair on the chest; some individuals are brownish. The giant panda's coloration makes it highly conspicuous in the forest. "The color pattern of the panda's pelage is unique among mammals . . . ," writes George Schaller et al. in *The Giant Pandas of Wolong*. "The giant panda requires no detailed description; its striking, black-and-white image is known throughout the world."

Japanese (Hokkaido) Brown Bear

These bears lack uniformity of coloration: They are mostly dark brown, with some nearly black or occasionally reddish/golden or silver-tipped (grizzled); yellow marking under neck.

Kermode and Glacier Bears

The unique colors of the white Kermode and Glacier bears are addressed in Chapter 2.

Polar Bear

Polar bears are white or cream, with orange-yellow coloring under the hairs (the hair is actually transparent but appears white or cream). Their color varies with the seasons, often pure white following the molt; during the summer they are a yellowish shade, due to oxidation by the sun.

"The natural color of a fully grown polar bear is a creamy, yellow white," writes Thomas Koch in *The Year of the Polar Bear*. "Depending on his surroundings and the type of light, he may seem to be more one shade than the other. If it is a brilliant day, he will seem to be more white than yellow. If it is a dark, dreary day, he will appear more yellow than white."

In some zoo situations, polar bears have developed a green hue caused by freshwater blue-green algae in the hollow hairs of their fur.

Sloth Bear

Sloth bears are dull black or sometimes rusty; white or grayish hairs mix with the black on some bears. They have a white or cream U or Y on the chest and a gray/white snout.

Sun Bear

The sun bear is glossy and coal black, sometimes brownish. It has a yellowish or whitish crescent mark on the chest, though the crescent sometimes is not present. Muzzle and ear tips are silver.

The coloration of bears of the world is simply described as ranging from "black to white." Coloration as a means of identification of species, except for the giant panda and the polar bear, is not as definitive as it may seem because of the enormous color variation within some of the species.

SKULLS

Generally, the skulls of bears are massive, typically long, wide across the forehead with prominent eyebrow ridges, a large jawbone hinge, heavy jaw muscles, and broad nostrils. When combined with their dentition, the structure of bears' skulls is very much oriented toward the carnivorous, though with omnivore modifications.

The skull may be the most important feature of an animal—housing the brain, providing a major protective and nutritional feature (a mouth with teeth), and containing sensory and communication features. "Bear skulls undergo a series of changes from early life to old age, and in most species do not attain their mature form until seven or more years of age," observed C. H. Merriam in a biological survey in *North America Fauna* in 1918.

Diet and other eating habits have influenced the individual development of the heads and skulls of each species. "Head shape and size . . . are influenced by dentition and jaw muscles," write Paul Shepard and Barry Sanders in *The Sacred Paw*. "[Skulls] are shaped to anchor the appropriate muscles. Because of the heavy jaw muscles it [Andean bear] uses for crushing palm nuts, its skull shape is unusual, rather resembling that of the giant panda, which has massive molars for grinding bamboo shoots."

Brown bears normally do not bite to kill but have grinding, crunching teeth with the massive muscles to accomplish the task. Polar bears are more carnivorous than other bears and do bite to kill; their skulls are specifically shaped for the appropriate teeth and muscles to hold, chop, and slash their prey. Each of the eight bear species has its own distinctive skull shape and size:

- **American black bear:** broad, narrow muzzle; large jaw hinge; female head may be more slender and pointed
- **Andean bear:** wide; short muzzle; lower jaw shorter than upper (overbite); unusual skull shape; resembles giant panda; young and female skulls narrow and long
- **Asiatic black bear:** large; sloping forehead
- **Brown bear:** massive; heavily constructed; large in proportion to body; high forehead (steeply rising); concave (dished face); domed head; long muzzle; flat nose tip; ears barely observed as bumps; eyes tiny
- **Giant panda:** massive; wide; dense; zygomatic arches widely spread; constructed for attachment of powerful jaw muscles; short muzzle
- **Polar bear:** large; small in proportion to body; long; snout long (warms air); Roman nose; large eyes
- **Sloth bear:** thick; long muzzle; small jaws; bulbous snout; wide nostrils
- **Sun bear:** wide and flat (unbearlike); short muzzle

Early animal classification was primarily based on skulls (". . . details of skull and leg bones are the usual criteria for the biologists," note Shepard and Sanders) and in part led to the "splitting" of the bear species. DNA has basically replaced skulls as the species-classification criterion. But skull size is still used as the criterion for the record-size bears in North America (see The Boone and Crockett Club, Chapter 6).

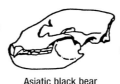

Brown bear
Polar bear
Asiatic black bear
American black bear
Giant panda

Skulls
COURTESY INTERAGENCY GRIZZLY BEAR STUDY TEAM (IGBST)

TEETH

A bear's teeth, combined with paws and claws, are its first-line tools for defense and obtaining food. Adventurer and author David Quammen writes in *Monster of God*, ". . . the crucial tools for most carnivorous creatures are teeth." The teeth are large and, though originally carnivorous, are adapted to an omnivorous diet of both meat and plant materials. The major difference between carnivore and omnivore dentition is the molars, which in bears are broad and flat. Dentition—the size, shape, and use of the teeth—and jaw muscles influence the size and shape of a bear's head.

Bears have forty-two teeth, except the sloth bear, which has only forty (less-toothsome humans have thirty-two, including wisdom teeth). Permanent teeth are normally in place by the time a bear is approximately two and a half years old.

DENTAL FORMULAE

Incisors	Canines	Premolars	Molars

	3-1-4-2 (upper each side)
Bears	———————— = 42
	3-1-4-3 (lower each side)

	2-1-4-2
Sloth bear	———————— = 40
	3-1-4-3

	2-1-2-3
Humans	———————— = 32
	2-1-2-3

Teeth Characteristics and Purpose

- **Incisors:** pointed, not specialized; for cutting and biting
- **Canines:** pointed, long, sturdy; for grasping, ripping, and tearing (catching, holding, and killing other animals)
- **Premolars:** not for shearing, as in carnivores; first three are unicuspids, with one root; last premolar has two roots—much larger; often missing in older bears; for holding and crushing
- **Molars:** heavy; "bunodont" crowns (flat, broad cusps); for crushing and grinding

Descriptions of Species Teeth

For each species the characteristics of the four kinds of teeth—incisors, canines, premolars, and molars—vary, depending on diet and habitat.

- **American black bear:** premolars and molars for grinding
- **Andean bear:** strong teeth; large molars for crushing palm nuts
- **Asiatic black bear:** heavy molars (causes round-headed appearance)
- **Brown bear:** flat and broad crowns on molars; premolars and molars for grinding; first lower molar and second upper molar wider and longer than in the American black bear (species comparison)
- **Giant panda:** massive (especially molars); highly modified for crushing and grinding (molars and premolars wide and flat topped),

including posterior premolars, a condition not found in other bears; first premolars sometimes missing

- **Polar bear:** canines larger, longer, and sharper than in other bears; molars smaller than those of land bears; molars more for shearing, premolars more for biting than grinding
- **Sloth bear:** missing two upper incisors; has forty teeth, cubs forty-two while nursing; two middle, upper incisors not replaced with permanent teeth; premolars and molars smaller than those of other bears (sloth bears chew less vegetation); have poor teeth due to sucking and grinding dirt as they eat insects
- **Sun bear:** flatter teeth than those of other bears; canines are long and protrude between lips

Cavities, Abscesses, and Worn-Out Teeth

Bears may have cavities, as they are one of the few wild animals susceptible to tooth decay, probably due in part to a sugary diet. Abscessed teeth are not uncommon and may contribute to the poor disposition of a bear. Any problem with a bear's teeth potentially affects its ability to eat and in some situations has led to starvation.

Teeth wear down with age, and broken teeth are not uncommon. "One old male grizzly showed excessive tooth wear: four of the molariform teeth were worn in two, only two root stubs remaining in each, and one molar was missing," describes Adolph Murie in *The Grizzlies of Mount McKinley*. "[T]he upper and lower incisors were worn to the gums; the two upper canines were worn but still retained their shape, but the two lower canines were worn until only blunt stubs remained." This bear was shot breaking into a building.

Determining a Bear's Age

A bear's age may be determined by the study of one of its teeth, in the same manner as growth rings are counted to age a tree. A small vestigial tooth (the premolar) is removed, softened with a nitric acid solution, and sliced into thin sections that are then stained. The staining highlights the tiny rings, or "cement deposits" (cementum annuli), that are formed each year. The rings are counted under a microscope to determine the bear's age.

Ring width may provide a general indication of a bear's health—thin rings indicate poor development and health. Rings close together in a female bear's teeth may indicate lactation. The cementum annuli are less well defined in polar bears, possibly due to the lack of winter denning—growth being more continual.

PAWS (FEET)

A bear's paws are important for a multitude of activities, including the following: sensing, feeding, digging, raking, locomotion, pulling, turning, lifting, killing, defense.

Bears walk plantigrade like humans, their paws with durable pads down flat on the ground, and pigeon-toed (forepaws turning inward). A bear's heat loss (thermoregulation) is primarily through its paws. "All the pads [paw soles] are surfaced with tough, cornified epidermis over a substantial mass of resistant connective tissue," describe Tracy Storer and Lloyd Tevis in *California Grizzly*. "This coverage of the foot is the sturdy, self-renewing 'shoe.'"

All bears have relatively flat feet (paws) with five toes, except the giant panda, which has six on its forepaws. The hind paws of bears are larger than their forepaws and resemble the feet of humans, except the "big toe" is located on the outside of the paw. Bears are predominately "right handed."

Bears are renowned for their forepaw dexterity and sensitive touch. Tiny objects are deftly manipulated with paws and claws, just as humans use their hands and fingers. Bears can pick pine nuts from cones and unscrew jar lids.

"I constantly marveled at . . . [the] bear's lightness of touch, or the deftness of movement of his fore paws," wrote Enos Mills in *The Spell of the Rockies*.

Specialized Paws

Giant pandas have a sixth digit on the forepaws, forming an opposable thumb (actually an enlarged wrist bone with independent movement and no claw), which allows them to handle bamboo stems and leaves with dexterity and precision.

Polar bears have swimming membranes that join more than half the length of their toes, and the paw pads are nonskid on ice due to a tread of tiny nipples on the soles.

Other bear species have paws with specializations geared toward their natural habitat.

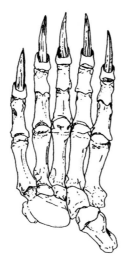 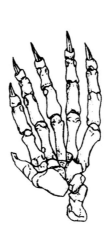 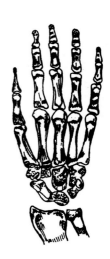

Skeletal paws and hand (left to right: brown bear paw, giant panda paw, human hand)
RENEE EVANOFF

Paws of the Species

- **American black bear:** sole black or brownish; naked, leathery, and deeply wrinkled
- **Andean bear:** no hair on soles, except band of hair between second and fourth toes
- **Asiatic black bear:** forepaws not deeply divided (leaves more solid track); heel pads of forefeet larger than those of most other bears; hind paw narrow and tapers toward rear; pads are bare
- **Brown bear:** sole black, brownish, sometimes whitish; wrinkled
- **Giant panda:** no heel pad on hind paws; forepaws flexible and adapted with a sixth toe (an opposable thumb) that has independent movement. Lance Craighead writes in *Bears of the World*, "The panda's 'thumb' is unique in the entire animal kingdom; a wrist bone, the radial sesamoid, has become so enlarged that it now functions like a thumb and enables the panda to grasp the stems of bamboo . . . to hold them while eating."

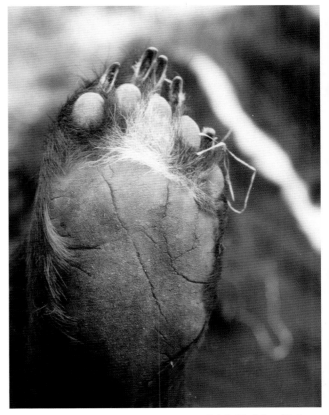

Asiatic black bear hind paw
©GARY BROWN

Grizzly bear hind paw
©GARY BROWN

- **Polar bear:** sole black; paws broad, paddle-like; flatter than those of other bears; pads concealed by hair; paws heavily matted with short, stiff hairs on soles; hair between pads for protection from cold; paws unique for swimming, shoveling snow, and traveling on and through snow; forepaws wider (up to 12 inches) than long
- **Sloth bear:** huge paws compared to body; minimal hair on soles; hairless skin web between toes; delicate finger (toe) control; paws extremely sensitive to touch
- **Sun bear:** paws similar to those of Asiatic black bear; no hair on soles

The tracks left behind by these paws that vary with the species and individuals are based on genetic characteristics. A bear may be identifiable by its paws or tracks.

CLAWS

Curved, nonretractable (unlike a cat's), fixed in an outstretched position, and longer on the forepaws than the hind paws, claws are a bear's more specialized tools, used for battle, digging (forepaws), climbing, and handling foods. Claw lengths of species and individuals within the species will vary with the time of year, amount of digging, and type of terrain where the bear travels and digs. Foreclaws are normally longer than hind claws.

Grizzlies have often been observed removing eggs from fish using a single claw. Robert Busch writes in *The Grizzly Almanac*, "At McNeil River, Alaskan writer Tom Walker once saw 'a bear try to shake the water out of its ears, then insert a single claw into its ear and gently scratch at the irritation.'"

Grizzly bear forepaw
©GARY BROWN

SMELL

An old, and much related, Native American saying may best describe the olfactory awareness of bears:

A pine needle fell in the forest.
The eagle saw it.
The deer heard it.
The bear smelled it.

The polar bear with its nose into the wind determines the direction of a food source along the Manitoba Arctic.
©JOHNNY JOHNSON

Whether low to the ground or held high in the wind, the nose of a bear is its key to its surroundings. "Smell," writes Herrero, "is the fundamental and most important sense a bear has. A bear's nose is its window into the world just as our eyes are."

The keen sense of smell—the olfactory awareness—of bears is excellent. No animal has a more acuteness of smell (seven times better than that of a bloodhound scent dog); it allows location of mates, avoidance of humans and other bears, identification of cubs, and the location of food sources. "[T]he nose provides the leading sense in the search for nourishment," notes Paul Schullery in *The Bears of Yellowstone*. The nose of the bear is somewhat "piglike," with a pad extending a short distance in front of the snout. The surface area of a bear's nasal mucous membrane, a hundred times larger than a human's, is the key to this incredible sense of smell.

A bear has been known to detect a human scent more than fourteen hours after the person passed along a trail. "The olfactory sense of the bears ranks among the keenest in the animal world," according to George Laycock in *The Wild Bears*. "A black bear in northern California was once seen to travel upwind three miles in a straight line to reach the carcass of a dead deer."

A grizzly bear's sense of smell is seventy-five times better than that of a human; therefore, it can detect a human 2 miles away. However, the sense of smell of polar bears may be the finest. They may smell a seal's breath emitted for only a few seconds from a small hole in the ice several miles away or detect a seal under 3 feet of snow a half mile distant.

PAIN

Bears have sensory end organs and experience pain stress from internal and external sources. Bear pain should not necessarily be compared with that of humans, which is possibly more complex. Generally, they do not appear to display obvious reactions, as humans do. Bears have numerous injuries due to the nature of their existence and have been compared to professional football players who "live in a world of constant pain."

American black bears appear to have a higher pain threshold than brown bears, as irritating and painful bear spray is found to be more effective on grizzly bears.

Persistent pain produces irritability and is possibly responsible for some "problem" bears, which display their discomfort by aggressive actions toward humans and other bears. These bears often are found to have abscessed teeth or other wounds.

A bear's wounds, or other problems, may be from natural or human sources:

- Abscessed teeth (bears appear to have more trouble with teeth than many other animals, probably due to sugary foods)
- External parasites (including bees that inflict obvious pain from stings as bears seek beehives)
- Fights with enemies or other bears

"ANOTHER SENSE"

Some bears in Alaska were observed moving to higher ground just prior to the 9.2-magnitude earthquake of 1964. Bears, geese, elephants, and other animals apparently are capable of sensing the initial earth movement preceding a major tremor.

- Gunshot wounds
- Internal parasites (tapeworms cause considerable misery for bears)
- Loss of teeth in old age resulting in inability to eat

STRENGTH

Bears possess enormous strength, regardless of species or size. The strength of a bear is difficult to measure, but observations alone (bears moving rocks, carrying animal carcasses, removing large logs from the side of a cabin, and digging cavernous holes) are indicative of incredible power.

A study team at Montana State University in Bozeman, Montana, found that a grizzly bear could treat a 700-pound garbage dumpster like a beach ball, while it took a minimum of two persons just to tip the dumpster. The team concluded the strength of a "calm" grizzly bear is two-and-a-half to five times that of a human.

No animal of equal size is as powerful. A bear may kill a moose, an elk, or a deer by a single blow to the neck with a powerful foreleg, then lift the carcass in its mouth and carry it for great distances. "The strength . . . is in keeping with his size," describes Ben East in *Bears*. "He is very powerfully built, a heavy skeleton overlaid with thick layers of muscle as strong as rawhide rope. He can hook his long, grizzly-like front claws under a slab of rock that three grown men could not lift, and flip it over almost effortlessly. . . . [A] brown [bear] . . . took a thousand-pound steer a half mile up an almost vertical mountain, much of the way through alder tangles with trunks three or four inches thick."

Strength and power are not only attributes of large bears but also of the young. The author observed a yearling American black bear searching for insects turn over a flat-shaped rock that was between 310 and 325 pounds "backhanded" with a single foreleg. The bear was captured the following day in a management action and was found to weigh only 120 pounds.

ODOR

Bears have a definite odor, as do other animals, including humans. However, the odor of a bear is quite pronounced, though not necessarily repugnant (depending on the individual nose), and is considered by many hunters as the easiest for a dog to track. The Eskimos often located polar bear dens by the scent emitting from the den vent hole.

The American black bear has a somewhat different odor from that of the grizzly bear, which, according to one bear biologist, smells musky and musty. Scientists, naturalists, hunters, and others who have experienced the odor of a bear agree that for them it is distinctive and could never again go unrecognized.

BAD BREATH

Yes! Bears have bad breath, too.

BODY TEMPERATURE

The normal body temperature of bears is approximately 98 to 101 degrees Fahrenheit. The temperatures vary, as do those of other mammals, based on individual differences and levels of activity. Temperatures are normally taken while the bears are immobilized (for obvious reasons) and under physical and psychological stress, resulting in elevated temperatures and the near impossibility of determining a "normal" temperature. However, two adult male grizzly bears in a captive situation had their temperatures taken under nearly normal circumstances. They each swallowed a tiny temperature-sensitive radio transmitter placed in their food. Their recorded body temperatures ranged between 98.5 and 99 degrees, with a mean temperature of 98.9. Interestingly, while the transmitters were still in their stomachs (before being passed with other feces), they were fed frozen fish, at which time the stomach temperatures dropped to the *low eighties*.

A bear's temperature may drop a few degrees when the animal is sleeping at night, resting on a snowbank, or in a cool day bed (see Hibernation, Chapter 4).

COMPARISON—AVERAGE BODY TEMPERATURES (DEGREES FAHRENHEIT)

Bears:	98–101
Blue whales	95.9
Cats	100.5–102.5
Dogs	101–103
Grasshoppers	101.5–108
Humans	98.6
Owls	104.4
Pigeons	106.6
Rabbits	101.3
Rainbow trout	53.6–64.4

Thermoregulation

Bears, like all mammals, must regulate their body heat. A bear's fur is an extremely effective insulation during the winter, maintaining body heat while absorbing heat from the sun. However, it does not allow adequate cooling during warm weather. As they don't have sweat glands, bears must cool themselves through several unique methods, shared by dogs:

- Balance energy expenditure and food intake
- Rest in shady day beds and cool summer dens
- Lie with bellies fully in touch with the cool ground
- Dissipate heat through slobbering tongues, panting like a dog; their paws (primary means of heat loss, as the pads are well supplied with blood vessels and are flat on the cool ground); and through areas with minimal hair, such as the face, ears, nose, and insides of hind legs
- Muscles behind shoulders contain a major supply of blood vessels and act as a radiator
- Submerge in water
- Shake off water as they emerge from a lake or stream
- Sprawl on snowfields or patches of snow
- Spread legs (thighs) wide
- Take mud and dust baths

Polar bears are faced with overheating like the other bears, but they also require additional heating during the subzero temperatures of the arctic winter. Their long snout warms the cool arctic air as they inhale. They avoid water, where heat loss is greater, when the weather is extremely cold. There are 3 to 4 inches of subcutaneous fat on their rumps and backs that provide additional insulation. An untested theory has existed for many years that they primarily bask in the sun because their outer fur functions as a unique system of heat transmission. "The theory," writes Ned Rozell in an Alaska Science Forum article, "goes like this: sunlight is captured by each hair, directed [like a fiber optic cable] to the bear's black skin, and converted there to heat, thereby providing warmth to the polar bear." However, in the late 1990s physics professor Daniel Koon of St. Lawrence University, New York, tested this theory and believes it is incorrect. According to Rozell ". . . less than .001 percent of red light and less than a trillionth of the violet light transmitted traveled the length of a typical, inch-long hair. Even less ultraviolet light made it from the tip to the base of the hair." The debate continues.

Giant pandas, according to George Schaller et al. in *The Giant Pandas of Wolong*, have a ". . . short, thick coat [that] provides excellent insulation; the animal readily sleeps on snow. The density and oily texture of the hairs probably prevent moisture from penetrating to the skin, an important adaptation in a damp, cool environment. And the hairs have a springy quality; they are resistant to compaction, which reduces heat loss when the panda lies on snow or cold ground."

A sloth bear, with its belly and underlegs nearly bare, is quite tolerant of heat.

HEART RATE

A normal (resting) heart rate for bears is forty to fifty beats per minutes (BPM) but during activity may increase considerably. The heart rates of some bears may slow to eight to twelve BPM when they are resting in a snowbank and during hibernation.

RESPIRATION

The lungs of bears are relatively large, and their breathing rate is six to ten breaths per minute while resting, forty to eighty when hot and panting, and sometimes over one hundred breaths per minute during extreme exertion. Hibernation reduces oxygen intake (resting) by approximately one-half.

DIGESTIVE TRACT

Bears have a simple intestinal tract, of which the colon is the primary site of fermentation. They have a long gut for digesting grass but do not digest starches well. Their small intestine is longer than that of the true carnivores but lacks other features of that group.

The barrel-shaped body of a bear is considered an indication of a long intestine, and according to Thomas McNamee in *The Grizzly Bear*, length means ". . . a highly developed ability to digest even low-quality foods." The brown bear's intestinal length is greater than that of the American black bear and giant panda. Polar bears have the longest intestine.

The short intestine of giant pandas results in poor digestion efficiency. Only 20 to 25 percent of what they consume is digested; thus they must eat enormous amounts—twenty-two to forty pounds of bamboo leaves and stems daily—to gain minimal energy. Because they eat fourteen hours a day, they produce considerable amounts of feces, mostly undigested bamboo, passing it in only five to eight hours. A giant panda's intestinal length is five to seven times its body length, similar to that of a house cat, whose intestinal length is five to six times its body length. By comparison, a horse's intestinal length is twenty times its body length.

The alimentary system of a sun bear cub must, for the first several weeks following birth, be externally stimulated for the urination and defecation processes to take place. The sow licks the cubs to provide this stimulation. The

American black bear must also at times perform this function.

SCAT (FECES)

Scat, or feces, is the excrement of animals. Scatology is the scientific study of scat; scientists collect and thoroughly analyze bear feces to determine many things about bears, including what they have been eating, how much of each type of food, and during what season of the year they were eating the specific food. The information provides more knowledge about the bears' requirements and activities and assists in the appropriate management of their habitat. Bear-research programs use hair found in scat for DNA analysis (see DNA, Chapter 9).

Bear scat is also beneficial to the land. It scatters and fertilizes seeds of the plants the bear has consumed and provides humus that enriches the soil.

For the traveler in bear country, the observation of bear scat triggers excitement and anxiety: It's exciting to find an indication of a bear, but at the same time, being unaware of its exact location provides anxious moments. However, bear scat may answer questions, too—how long has it been since the bear was here, how big is the bear, and what has it been eating?

Scat is a common sign of bear presence and activity. It may be distinguished by shape, size, and composition, though it is sometimes confused with horse and human excrement. "Bear scats are thick cords with blunt ends," describes James Halfpenny in *A Field Guide to Mammal Tracking in Western America*. "The quantity of scat is often great and you may see large piles. Bear scat often contains insects . . . plant remains are also common."

DISEASES AND PARASITES

Bears are susceptible to a variety of bacterial and viral diseases and parasites. Though these ailments may affect a bear's temperament, they are a minor factor in overall bear mortality.

Parasites

Bears are host to more than eighty types of known internal and external parasites, including more than fifty-five kinds of worms. Parasites weaken a bear, which may mean susceptibility to starvation, disease, injury, or death by other causes. External parasites are most common in the warmer climates, while quite scarce in the more northern areas of the world such as Scandinavia, Alaska, Canada, and Russia.

Typical grizzly bear scat
COURTESY YELLOWSTONE NATIONAL PARK

Internal Parasites

- *Ascaris schroederi* (intestinal worms)
- Cestodes (tapeworms)
- *Dirofilaria ursi* (blood parasite)
- Flukes (fluke fever)
- Hookworms
- Lungworms
- Nematodes (roundworms; very common—found in at least 50 percent of bears)
- Protozoa
- Toxoplasmosis
- Trematodes (intestinal and bile duct flukes)
- Trichinosis (trichinella worms)

The trichinella worm is most prevalent in northern bears, primarily those in the arctic—nearly all polar bears and three of four brown bears have the parasite. Charles Feazel writes in *White Bear*, ". . . the bears carry the *Trichinella* larvae, which form cysts in the muscle tissue. When the meat is eaten, the cysts dissolve in the small intestine, and the larvae invade their new host. They soon burrow into the human muscle, causing a wide variety of symptoms that mimic other diseases. If untreated, trichinosis may cause death within four to eight weeks." Humans may contract trichinosis by eating inadequately cooked bear meat.

External Parasites

- Black flies (pest to face and eyes)
- Fleas
- Lice
- Midges (tiny flylike insects; pest to face and eyes)
- Mites (chiggers; mange)
- Mosquitoes (pest to face and eyes)
- Ticks

Bears are susceptible to:

- Anthrax
- Blood poisoning
- Bronchopneumonia
- Brucellosis (approximately 20 percent of North American brown and grizzly bears test positive; no effects to the bears)
- Candidiasis (gastroenteric and encephalitic)
- Canine adenovirus type 1 (hepatitis; respiratory infection)
- Canine distemper
- Canine parvo
- Clostridium perfringens infection (gas gangrene)
- Encephalitis (several types)
- Feline infectious peritonitis (inflammation of the membrane that lines the walls of the abdominal cavity and surrounds the viscera)
- Leptospirosis (bacterial infection involving the kidneys)
- Metabolic bone disease (bears in captivity)
- Pseudorabies (viral infection of the central nervous system)
- Q-fever (a tick-borne fever)
- Rabies
- Staphylococcal septicemia (blood poisoning)
- Tuberculosis (especially polar bears)
- Tularemia
- West Nile virus (encephalitis)

Other Health Problems

- Actinomycosis (inflammation; tumors; "lumpy jaw")
- Arthritis
- Bites from other animals
- Broken teeth and lacerations while in research and management captivity
- Cataracts
- Cavities
- Chemical buildup in body
- Dermatitis
- Domoic acid poisoning (Red Tide; increasing accumulation in the ocean food chain; polar bears display evidence)
- Enterotoxemia (diarrhea)
- Flesh wounds (from rocks, trees, other objects, fights)
- Fractures from falls
- Gunshot wounds
- Hemorrhoids
- Hepatic and bile duct neoplasia (liver tumor)
- Hypothyroidism
- Indigestion (especially giant pandas)
- Joint injuries
- Mineral poisoning (mercury, etc)
- Pesticides
- Snow blindness
- Starvation (inadequate fat reserves before hibernation; inadequate diet due to poor teeth)
- Trauma (assorted)
- Tumors (on eyelids, liver, uterine horn, scrotum)
- Worn, broken, or lost teeth

Ernest Thompson Seton wrote about an Alberta guide's observation of a grizzly and an American black bear "wandering aimlessly" with snow blindness.

Bear Health Care

Nature provides excellent health-care benefits for bears:

- Acidic skin secretions act as insecticide.
- Acidic skin secretions prevent wound infections.
- Bears can survive amputations.
- Bears have natural resistances.
- Fractures readily mend.

Bears can contract tapeworms, especially bears that eat large amounts of fish, such as the Alaska and Kamchatka brown bears. Before hibernation, these bears instinctively seek and eat blue clay, if available in their habitat, which rids them of these internal parasites. American black bears do not appear to have this instinct.

Disease and Infirmities of the Cave Bears

Cave bears were also susceptible to various health problems. "When large predators are kept for many years in the confinement of cages, peculiar diseases of the spinal column develop," writes Terry Domico in *Bears of the World*. "These include inflammations, fusing, and atrophy. An extraordinarily large number of cave bear remains are from diseased or physically degenerate bears." Cave bears' remains indicate they suffered with:

- Anchylosis of vertebrae (fusion of spine)
- Cavities
- Exostoses (tumors) of bones (mandibles, vertebrae)
- Fractures of skull, humeri
- Hyperostosis of mandible (resorption of teeth)

- Necrosis in femur of young (tissue death)
- Nematodes (worms of the type found in recent mammal kidney problems)
- Osteomyelitis (inflammation of bone marrow in young bears)
- Periostitis (inflammation of bone membrane)
- Rachitis (rickets; spinal disease; as well as inflammation)
- Renal calculi (kidney stones)

LONGEVITY

Factors determining the lifespan of a bear vary between and within species (see Bear Mortality, Chapter 9).

The "aging" of bears has not always been a common practice of states, provinces, and countries; therefore, longevity records do not exist for some species of the world's bears and for other specific populations.

AMERICAN BLACK BEAR AGES (OLDEST RECORDED - WILD)

Alaska	30	Louisiana	34	New Hampshire	30.5	Tennessee	19
Arizona	29	Maine	34	New Mexico	25	Texas	8+ (d)
Arkansas	28	Maryland	20	New York	42 (b)	Utah	29
California	32	Massachusetts	28	North Carolina	26.75	Vermont	43.75
Colorado	23	Michigan	31	Ohio	4 (c)	Virginia	26 (e)
Florida	20 (a)	Minnesota	34	Oklahoma	10+	West Virginia	27
Georgia	21	Mississippi	27	Pennsylvania	30	Wisconsin	18.5
Kentucky	12	Nevada	23	South Carolina	15		

Canada		Nova Scotia	25	**Mexico**	15 (f)
Manitoba	34	Ontario	30		
New Brunswick	35.5	Quebec	33		
Newfoundland/Labrador	34	Yukon	27		

(a) Weighed 180 pounds
(b) 42 years and 9 months
(c) Immigrating population; young bears moving in
(d) Only recent records maintained
(e) Three 26-year-old female bears
(f) Oldest in recent research

RECORD AGE (OLDEST) BY SPECIES

	Wild	Captivity
	(in Years)	
American black bear	31	44
Andean bear	25	40
Asiatic black bear	(a)	33
Brown bear	40	55 (b)
Giant panda	30	30
Polar bear	34 (c)	41 (d)
Sloth bear	(a)	40
Sun bear	(a)	24 (e)

(a) Information unavailable
(b) Sunset Zoological Park, Manhattan, Kansas
(c) 34 years, 8 months
(d) Record polar bear is presently in the Assiniboine Park Zoo in Winnipeg, Manitoba, Canada. The female bear is considered the oldest polar bear in captivity in the world, and possibly the oldest ever recorded.
(e) 24 years, 9 months

BROWN BEARS AND POLAR BEARS IN THE WILD

Brown/Grizzly Bears (United States)

Alaska	40 (Kodiak brown)
Montana	37 (Grizzly)
(Wyoming, Idaho, Washington data unavailable)	

Grizzly Bears (Canada)

Newfoundland/Labrador	25
Yukon	37

Polar Bears (Canada)

Manitoba	30
Yukon	27
(Only data available)	

"The legs of this bear [grizzly] are somewhat longer than those of the black, as are its talons and tusks incomparably larger and longer," recorded Meriwether Lewis in his journal. ". . . Its colour is yellowish brown, the eyes small, black, and piercing; the front of the fore legs near the feet is usually black; the fur is finer thicker and deeper than that of the black bear. These are all the particulars in which this animal appeared to me to differ from the black bear; it is a much more furious and formidable animal, and will frequently pursue the hunter when wounded."

The American black and grizzly bears are often compared, as they are the two bear species most familiar to the majority of North Americans. A few features of comparison:

Feature	American Black Bear	Grizzly Bear
Size	Generally smaller at comparable age/sex	Relatively larger. Adult female grizzly bears weigh 1.7 to 2.3 times as much as an adult female black bear
Highest Body Part	Rump	Hump
Head/Skull	More pronounced forehead	
	Convex (Roman) face profile	Concave face profile
	Ears somewhat pointed	Ears rounded; appear smaller
	Nose doglike	Nose piglike
Teeth	Smaller relative to skull size	First lower molar and second upper molar wider and longer; teeth adapted to heavier chewing due to diet
Paws	More hair between toes and footpad	More skin webbing at the base of the toepad
Claws (shape)	Short and hooked; front and hind claws similar in length; claw marks seldom visible in tracks	Long and moderately curved; front claws much longer than hind claws; claw marks normally visible
Hump	No shoulder hump	Prominent shoulder hump
Fur	Hair overall shorter than that of grizzly bear; more uniform length	Hair long and thick; moderately long mane at back of head
Color	Black, varying shades of brown, blonde (Kermode white); light-colored muzzle; rarely shows grizzled appearance; white chest patch present on some bears	Black, brown, blond; often silver-tips provide the "grizzled" appearance; white chest patch on some cubs, rarely on adults
Speed	25 to 30 mph (short distance)	35 to 40 mph (short distance)

Travel	Wanders more than grizzly bear	Develops deeply worn trails
Habitat	Typically forests, though moves into open areas	Open areas close to forests; often found in forest meadows and other openings
Range	Smaller than that of grizzly bears	Adult female has range 2 to 5 times larger than that of adult female black bear
Food Habits	Eats more green vegetation and berries; bites grass and stems with incisor teeth	Food comes in windfalls (spawning fish, large carcasses), therefore may congregate; bites grass and stems with molars; eats more roots, corms, bulbs, and tubers
	Rarely buries a carcass	Often buries a carcass in dirt and debris
Digging	Uncommon	Common in seeking rodents and other subsurface foods; better digger due to hump (shoulder muscles) and longer claws
Climbing	Excellent climber	Does not generally climb
Reproduction	Age of sow at first litter: 3–5 years; 2 years between litters; average litter size 2	Age of sow at first litter: 5 years; 3 years between litters; average litter size 2
Hibernation	Hibernates earlier; dens at lower elevation, in less-steep areas, and close to roads; uses a natural hole or opening for its dens	Digs and develops a more elaborate den
Life Expectancy	14 to 20 years in the wild; up to 35 years in captivity	Same as black bear
Disposition	Less aggressive; adapts better to human presence; more apt to flee	More aggressive; defends food sources and its space
Nuisance	Commonly known as the "nuisance" bear	Considered more dangerous than a nuisance

CHAPTER 4

Bear Behavior and Activities

DISPOSITION AND PERSONALITY

Bears have a wide range of behavior but generally are curious, suspicious, self-reliant, clever, cautious, independent, and dangerous. The only certainty of a bear's behavior is unpredictability.

Behavior Characteristics

While there are behaviors common to most bears, there are more specific behaviors and characteristics documented within each species.

- **American black bear:** easily food conditioned; extremely clever; creature of habit; inquisitive; playful
- **Andean bear:** timid
- **Asiatic black bear:** easily annoyed; not necessarily fierce
- **Brown bear:** dignified; deliberate; fearless; bold; generally peaceful; solitary unless at a concentrated food source
- **Giant panda:** shy; restrained
- **Grizzly bear (subspecies):** generally shy and peaceful; secretive; ferocious when provoked
- **Polar bear:** silent; cunning; casual demeanor; fierce fighter; untrustworthy in captivity. "Although provided with a fighting equipment second to none on the continent [North America]," wrote Vilhjalmur Stefansson in *Arctic Manual*, "these [polar bears], like their Arctic land cousins, try to live peacefully and inoffensively."
- **Sloth bear:** bad temper; cranky; aggressive; playful; aberrant; teases other animals
- **Sun bear:** generally good natured; older bears bad tempered; extremely fierce in a fight

Age may be an important element in a bear's behavior. Charles Feazel notes in *White Bear*, "Old bears move slowly, their joints stiff with age. When angered, though, even the oldest whirls around with surprising fury, teeth and claws at the ready. . . . The oldest, largest bears are often the worst tempered, having survived a thousand challenges by lesser bruins."

CURIOSITY

A bear's curiosity may be attributed to many things, but most often a potential meal is the source. They will inspect odors, objects, and often noise to determine if the origin is edible or possibly a plaything. Actually, their intense curiosity should be considered "investigation."

"It was not unusual to find the tracks of a bear leading straight up to one of the large [steam] vents, where evidently he had stopped to peer into the mysterious hot hole," following the 1912 eruption of Alaska's Mount Katmai, Robert Griggs wrote in *The Valley of Ten Thousand Smokes*. "In one of the steaming areas Hagelbarger found a place where the hot ground had apparently excited the bear's curiosity, for he had dug into it until he started a small fumarole [vent with smoke and gases] of his own. The appearance of a cloud of steam under his claws as he broke into the hot crust must have given him a great surprise. It did not scare him away, however, for not satisfied with a single experiment, he tried again in several places, each time digging down till he started the steam before turning away."

Curiosity is often what brings a bear into the human world. "Young adult grizzly bears are particularly curious," according to Stephen Herrero in *Bear Attacks: Their Causes and Avoidance*, "and their curiosity is not yet tempered with a knowledge that humans can mean trouble."

INTELLIGENCE

Bear intelligence is difficult to assess and should not be compared or measured in human terms. Bears are considered by scientists and naturalists to be highly intelligent animals, based on their ability to learn rapidly and to reason.

Curiosity, combined with a high capacity for learning and an excellent memory, may be the key to a bear's "intelligence." It leads to learning and knowledge, which is the basis of survival—adaptability to environmental changes and unusual circumstances. Bears learn and remember from a single experience—a food source, a threat, a trap, or a rifle shot. "Bears . . . have the biggest brains relative to body size of any carnivore, giving them ample capacity to interpret and remember . . . ," according to Candace Savage in *Grizzly Bears*.

Studies at the University of Tennessee psychology department indicate that American black bears are highly intelligent, probably more so than many other mammals of the world. "Bears are highly intelligent and individualistic," relates Terry Domico, "and are capable of nearly as many responses in a given circumstance as a human.

Some biologists believe the highly adaptable brown bear is intelligent enough to be ranked with primates, like monkeys and baboons."

Bears display many "intelligent" actions that include:

- Hiding dark nose with a paw (polar bear) (considered a myth by some researchers)
- Hiding behind ice blocks (polar bear)
- Learning quickly in training situations
- The display of a cunning mind
- Navigation abilities
- Sneaking
- Bluffing
- Concealing self in ambush; hiding from humans
- Beginning hibernation during heavy snowfall to conceal tracks to den
- Choosing alternatives
- Adapting to other influences (including human, if allowed)
- Baiting other animals (polar bear)
- Resourcefulness
- Capacity to reason
- Avoiding problems
- Outwitting humans
- Memory (of food sources, threats, etc.)
- Calculating (think, plan, scheme)
- Retreating in the face of great odds (human impacts)
- Hiding tracks (jump to side, step on own tracks, wade in stream)
- Backtracking
- Using tools

"I would give the grizzly first place in the animal world for brainpower," noted Enos Mills in *The Grizzly*.

ASSOCIATIONS BETWEEN BEARS

With few species exceptions, adult bears are basically solitary. They are together during the courting and mating period and as a family group of a sow and her offspring. Streams with spawning fish, dumps, and other major food sources may attract a concentration of bears, resulting in a temporary proximity—a touchy truce.

"In a garbage dump in Yellowstone Park I have seen thirty grizzlies wallowing together with bodies practically touching," describes Adolph Murie in *A Naturalist in Alaska*. "Here, apparently, wild natural habits are being lost, and the dump is making of our lone philosopher bears a bunch of gregarious characters. They perhaps are gregarious, however, only at the dump."

Males normally do not recognize their offspring and have no interest in them, unless as a food source, and sows with cubs usually do not associate with other family groups. Bears of different species do not associate, though a large bear may prey upon the young of another species.

"Each unit, such as the lone bear, breeding pair, mother and cubs, sets of old cubs on their own, is independent and does not fraternize ordinarily with other units," explains Adolph Murie in *The Grizzlies of Mount McKinley*. "When bears do feed within two hundred to three hundred yards of each other, where they have been attracted by good rooting or grazing, a certain amount of uneasiness and watchfulness prevails, the degree of anxiety depending upon the types of bear units that are present and perhaps the extent of previous acquaintance."

Specific association behavior between bears of the same species includes:

- **American black bear:** suspicious of any intruder; nongregarious; sow short tempered with mate following courting and mating; sow short tempered with cubs when she forces them out on their own; large males dangerous to smaller bears; brief congregations at food supplies; basically harmless in fight with same species; minimal encounters with grizzly bears—being submissive, avoiding, and fleeing
- **Andean bear:** adult male occasionally with family
- **Asiatic black bear:** occasional family group or pair of adults and two successive litters of young; walk in a procession of largest to smallest; basically harmless in conflict with same species
- **Brown bear:** adult males kill young bears and occasionally a sow; occasional congregations of sows with cubs; brief congregations at concentrated food supplies; have been known to fight to the death
- **Giant panda:** closely share a small range; attempt to avoid each other; solitary and silent; rare face-to-face meetings
- **Polar bear:** solitary; often tolerate close associations; occasionally play together or feed together on large food supply, such as a whale carcass
- **Sloth bear:** get along better within the species; adult male occasionally with a family (gentle with cubs); occasionally travel in pairs; mostly ignore each other; will fight for food
- **Sun bear:** occasionally travel in pairs; pair of adults may be accompanied by infants

HIERARCHY

Bears are generally shy and attempt to avoid trouble. They are socially hierarchic, with a definite determination of which bear is dominant and controls a situation such as feeding, breeding, or occupying a location. Hierarchy's *most important* function is to prevent these large and powerful animals from entering into seriously violent battles that would adversely affect the species. There may be threat displays with vocalization and body or facial language until dominance is established, or hierarchy may be subtly expressed and understood.

There is a linear dominance/avoidance system: The subordinate retreats, based on psychological factors; physical condition, including health, size, and age; knowledge from experience; and confidence. There is extreme sensitivity to the roar of large males, as indicated by the doubling of a subordinate's heart rate. Females with cubs may tolerate other females without cubs or their own independent young, but they are the most cautious of all bears. Generally, size is power, and young bears are subordinate. The dominance order is as follows:

- Large, old males
- Females with new cubs (sometimes most dominant)
- Single subadult males
- Other adult males and females
- Other subadults

Unrestrained fighting may occur between males during mating season or between a sow protecting her young and another bear, but major confrontation is normally short and not fatal. Everything is based on the individuals. Their health varies; they grow older, larger, and

Grizzly bears in a short hierarchy-establishing fight
©2008 ROBERT BARBER/CRITTERZONE.COM

more confident; and the hierarchical arrangement is constantly being tested and occasionally readjusted.

COMMUNICATION

Bears communicate their mood between each other with expressive signals such as posturing, marking with odors and other sign, and vocalization. They communicate to humans with posturing and vocalizations (and, though not intentionally, leave a message of their presence with their markings and scat). Their ability to communicate with facial expressions is poor, as they rarely display teeth or curl a lip like dogs, and their small ears, though possibly expressive, are positioned in most species as to be unnoticeable. However, they strongly compensate with body language, vocalization, and attitude.

Vocalization

Bears are generally quite silent but have a repertoire of vocalizations, each with a specific significance, for important intraspecies social situations and encounters with other species.

Some bear species, and individuals, are more communicative than others. Giant pandas vocalize infrequently, except when courting and in a few other social interactions. The sloth bear is especially noisy when mating, and the roar of the polar bear is described as the bellow of Chewbacca the Wookiee in the movie *Star Wars*.

Vocalizations may be singular or multiple, and a particular sound may have more than a single meaning, depending on the situation. Various sounds may be expressed toward humans, bears, and other animals.

The cubs of most species vocalize in the same manner, whining, whimpering, and crying when upset; bawling and crying when hurt; humming when content (such as when nursing); and hissing when frightened.

A "vocalizing" grizzly bear
©2008 ROBERT VOLPE/CRITTERZONE.COM

A yawning expression on
a grizzly bear in Wyoming
COURTESY YELLOWSTONE
NATIONAL PARK

BEAR VOCALIZATIONS

Species	Emotion	Emitted Sound
American black bear	Annoyance (startled)	Chomp, cough, growl, huff, woof
	Contentment (eating)	Mumble, pant, squeak
	Disappointment	Howl, moan, sob, squall, wail
	Fighting	Roar
	Frightened	Moan (often in subordinate situation)
	Jealousy	Chomp, cough, growl, woof
	Nursing cub	Motorlike pleasure sound; hum
	Pain	Bawl
	Resting	Yawn (loud)
	Threat	Bellow, chomp, grunt, honk, huff, puff, snort
Andean bear	Alarm	Owl-like screech
	Contentment	Soft purr
Asiatic black bear	Courting	Cluck
Brown bear	Aggravation	Chomp, smack, woof
	Anger	Growl
	Anger (extreme)	Roar
	Contentment (sow with cubs)	Hum
	Express transient feelings	Cough
	Gastric problem	Belch
	Nervous	Grunt, woof
	Pain	Bawl
	Summon young (sow)	Bleat
Giant panda	Aggression	Growl, roar
	Anxiety	Chomp, honk, grunt
	Apprehension (aggressive threat)	Huff, snort
	Apprehension (defensive threat):	Chomp
	Birth (sow):	Cry (loud)
	Courting/mating	Bark, bleat, chirp, moan, roar, squeal
	Distress	Grunt, honk, squeal
	Friendly/social	Bleat
	Meeting	Chirp, yip
	Threat	Huff, snort
	Warning	Bark, moan, yip

Species	Emotion	Emitted Sound
Polar bear	Agitated	Chuff
	Anger	Hiss, rumbling growl
	Aroused (highly)	Roar
	Contented	Purr
	Display respect	Silent
	Hurt	Bellow, roar, rumbling snarls
	Uneasy	Hiss, rumbling growl
	Upset shriek (temper)	Shriek, squall, whimper
Sloth bear	Anger (deep)	Bark, scream, grunt, snarl, yelp
	Asleep	Snores loudly
	Attack	Bark, grunt, roar
	Danger	Snarl
	Digging (in company)	Drone
	Eating (sucking)	Huff, snuff (vacuum noise)
	Fighting	Roar, snarl
	Fright	Shriek
	Hurt	Howl, squeal, whimper
	Injured	Yowl, whimper
	Mad (temper)	Woof
	Mating	Buzzing, melodious humming
	Paw sucking	Babble, buzz, gurgle, hum
	Play	Grumble
	Resting	Buzz, hum
	Sow with cubs	Croon
	Teasing animals	Bellow
Sun bear	Attack	Bark, grunt, roar, growl, shrill screech
	Paw sucking	Hum

Posturing

Posturing—the display of the body—may be a bear's most significant and productive act of communicating. When combined with vocalizations, posturing expresses attitude, dominance, and subordination and questions intent. It is an element of hierarchy. During posturing, a bear may display its size and stride, stand tall, specifically orient its body or head, and utilize any of many visual signals. It demonstrates its position and "bearing," while assessing the other bear. Posturing may include:

- **Orientation (body):** frontal (head high); side; sitting; lying down; body at higher elevation (standing tall); lying down and waiting; sitting down facing; standing bipedal (sniffing)
- **Orientation (head):** down; facing away; neck stretched; neck and head oblique; head dropped; staring; looking for clues; touching noses; bobbing head; head high
- **Mouth:** shut; open; open with canines displayed; twisting muzzle; occasionally extends upper lip; moving jaw; clicking teeth; licking lips; snapping jaws loudly; yawning; spitting; panting; blowing wet bubbles; waving open mouth
- **Nose:** raised snout, sniffing
- **Ears:** back and up
- **Movement:** approaching (walking or running); retreating (walking, running, backing up); walking stiff legged; charging; circling; moving downwind; strutting; gesturing with paws

A stare or oblique neck is aggressive and a serious threat, while lowering of the head is submissive and a display of respect—a desire for peace. Extending the upper lip or blowing wet, smacking bubbles is definitely petulance. A bear may posture with humans in much the same manner as with other bears.

Grizzly bear charging other bears at McNeil River, Alaska
©2008 JOHNNY JOHNSON/
ALASKASTOCK.COM

Marking (Scenting)

Marking by bears is a highly ritualized chemical and visual communication function performed by resident *and* transient bears. Marking is accomplished by several methods, including scratching, biting, rubbing, leaving feces, and scenting with urine or secretions from the anal gland. Approximately 90 percent of all bear communications is scent, and overall, males scent more than females.

Often marking appears to be just the act of a bear scratching its back against a tree or other object, but whether or not that is the intent, an odor, hair, or a rubbed area remains for the next bears to find. Tree marking appears to be the most common form of marking and is most customary among males. Rubbing appears to be a separate marking ritual from biting or clawing an object.

The marking of trees by rubbing or clawing is the most visible sign normally observed by humans. Marked trees are found along well-traveled trails and other travel routes. Some trees are used once, others year after year until the trail up to the tree may be as worn and rutted as a well-used bear trail.

Tree marking may involve any of the following actions or signs:

- The bear stretching its body to scratch its back, leaving hair and odor
- Clawing and biting, leaving scratches and tooth marks in the bark
- Depositing urine, feces, and other secretions
- Worn areas at the tree base
- Strips of bark on the ground
- Limbs broken and chewed

A high frequency of marking occurs just prior to the breeding period and is also quite common during courting and mating.

The specific purpose of marking is not completely understood by naturalists and biologists, though there are numerous theories. ". . . [I]t is clear to the human observer that few other animals in the Northern Hemisphere other than themselves could make so striking a five-fingered print," notes Paul Shepard and Barry Sanders in *The Sacred Paw*. "Other than the bear, perhaps only the big cats give the impression of making a meaningful mark on a tree."

The many theories of marking include the following:

- Male bears warn other male bears.
- Marking signifies a dominance hierarchy between males.
- Male bears are indicating their dominance to avoid conflicts injurious to both bears.
- Marking provides evidence for other bears—a signal that it "was here."
- It is a sign of activity and presence (possibly indicates how long ago the "marking bear" was present).
- It is a display of dominance (that is, size).
- It marks a territory.
- It marks a territory, though quite possibly does not necessarily mean "keep out" but says, "I am here; just be careful and do not crowd me."
- Males are advising females (there may be an understanding that male markings allow a female to pass at any time).
- Females are warning other females to stay away (a territorial mark).

Marking may be any of the following:

- A means of identification
- A sign of belligerence
- An expression of well-being
- An expression of strength
- An expression of boredom
- An act of stretching
- An act of relaxing
- An act of manicuring (sharpening or blunting of claws)

Theories for marking trees that are associated with breeding include the following:

- It announces presence in the area to a potential mate.
- It is a means of promoting estrus in adult females of the area.
- It serves as a signal between males and females during the breeding season.

American black bear biologist and authority Lynn Rogers has long studied bear behavior. He believes tree marking by an aggressive male bear indicates its dominance and is to avoid conflicts injurious to both bears.

Marking by bears also occurred during prehistoric periods, as they appear to have "marked" the walls of caves. Extensive scratches found on cave walls and trees indicate seasonal occupancy by cave bears.

Specific marking methods observed by scientists and other observers include the following:

- **American black bear:** tree rubbing with shoulder, neck, head, rump; tree biting; tree clawing; pushing tree over and rubbing on downed tree; rolling on ground at base of tree; leaving scat

Brown bear leaving its hair and personal scent in Valley of the Geysers, Kamchatka, Russia
IGOR SHPILENOK/NATUREPL.COM

Giant Panda tree scratch marks, Changqing Reserve, China
GAVIN MAXWELL/NATUREPL.COM

- **Brown bear:** tree scratching; tree rubbing; may roll in urine before rubbing; tree biting; biting buildings, signs; rubbing on log in open area; pawing ground; leaving scat
- **Giant panda:** bark stripping; tree biting; tree clawing; ground pawing; rolling and rubbing on ground; tree scenting; spraying urine directly on trees. According to Lu Zhi in *Giant Pandas in the Wild*, one giant panda marked forty-five times in five-and-a-half days, and the marking substance "... smells sweetly acidic."

The giant panda primarily communicates by scent, having what appears to be the most involved method of marking. It has scent glands in the area of the anus that produce a secretion that smells acetic to humans. The tail acts as a brush to spread urine and the secretion at the scent areas, which are established along primary travel routes. The giant panda backs up to a surface, such as a tree, raises its tail and rubs. On some occasions, the bear will continue to "back up" a surface, by walking with its hind legs until it is standing on its forepaws in a handstand, brushing with its tail, scenting as high as it possibly can.

- **Sloth bear:** tree scraping with forepaws; tree rubbing with flanks; slashing tree with foreclaws
- **Sun bear:** tree scratching and rubbing; minimal scenting

ENEMIES

Bears' enemies are not necessarily other bears, animal species, or humans that precipitate direct mortality. Other causes result in indirect death, such as habitat degradation, chemicals, or food loss. "Although giant pandas have few natural enemies," notes George Schaller et al. in *The Giant Pandas of Wolong*, "the periodic die-off of bamboo, their main food, threatens their survival" (see Major Concerns, Chapter 9). Enemies in this segment are those other animals that prey upon bears or cause direct harm when the species otherwise come in contact.

Some "enemies," far inferior to the bear if they were in battle, only harass. Eagles will swoop down over bears, as do other birds such as ravens, magpies, and long-tailed jaegers. Ticks, fleas, mosquitos, flies, and other pests are also annoyances. Internal parasites weaken bears, and bears that kill porcupines may suffer serious infection and discomfort in their mouths and throats, be unable to eat, and possibly die of starvation.

Some enemies are a threat only to bear cubs, and there is an enemy common to all bear species—humans.

The Polar Bear versus the Walrus

Encounters between a walrus and a polar bear are violent battles, and there are several recorded observations of a walrus killing a polar bear, though walruses are also killed. Polar bear authorities of the Canadian Wildlife Service H. P. L. Kiliaan and Ian Stirling in an article in the *Journal of Mammalogy* entitled "Observations on Overwintering Walruses," describe ". . . a walrus that a polar bear killed with a blow in the head as it surfaced to breathe through a hole in the ice." They also noted another battle. "Tracks and blood in the snow around the walrus's breathing hole . . . indicated a fight had taken place very recently. The walrus was covered with blood and one tusk was broken. Despite a careful search, no bear tracks leading away from the site were found, suggesting that the bear may have been killed and sunk in the water."

"The polar bear and walrus, traditional rivals, occasionally come in contact while feeding on whale carcasses or while killing seals," writes Thomas Koch in *The Year of the Polar Bear*. "If a walrus is in the water, a polar bear will not enter. The walrus is the only polar animal that the bear really fears. If the two animals encounter each other on land, the polar bear will have an edge. When they meet in the water, the walrus has been known to grab the polar bear from below and, using his ivory tusks, which often grow more than thirty inches in length, to stab the bear in the back, driving the tusks to the hilt. The carcasses of polar bears and walruses have been found coupled in this manner."

". . . Nanook will usually leave a two-ton slumberer [old bull walrus] strictly alone," writes Frank Dufresne in *No Room for Bears*. "Rarely, when goaded by desperate hunger, the white bear will take a chance." However, he adds ". . . the ice was red with blood. The walrus was gone. The polar bear . . . in its gore, was punched full of holes and quite dead."

Enemies	American Black	Brown Bear	Polar Bear	Asiatic Black	Giant Panda	Sloth Bear	Sun Bear	Andean Bear
Alligator	X							
Bear (larger)	X	X	X	X				
Brown bear	X			X	X a			
Clouded leopard							X	
Coyote	X							
Dog (domestic)	X		X	X		X		X
Dog (wild, pack)					X	X	X	
Eagle	X (a)							X
Human	X	X	X	X	X	X	X	X
Jaguar								X
Killer whale (orca)			X					
Leopard				X	X	X	X	
Lynx	X (a)	X (a)						
Mountain lion	X							X
Musk ox		X	X					
Porcupine	X (b)	X (b)						
Snake (poisonous)	X	X					X	
Snake (reticulated python)							X	
Snow leopard				X				
Tiger (Bengal)						X	X	
Tiger (Siberian)		X		X				
Walrus (adult bull)			X					
Wild boar		X						
Wolf	X	X (a)	X (a)	X (a)		X		
Yellow-throated marten				X (a)				

(a) Primarily a threat to bear cubs
(b) Quills in throat; starvation
Patricia Brown

INTERACTIONS WITH SOME ENEMIES AND OTHER ANIMALS

Bears consider any other animals as food, if they are capable of catching and killing the specific individual. There are many interesting interactions between bears and large and small prey. Sometimes the prey is too elusive, or the bear may in some situations become the prey. A feeding bear often provides life for scavengers such as birds, martens, wolverines, coyotes, wild dogs, mountain lions, wolves, and foxes. Many interactions are not with what is typically considered prey or an enemy but are opportunistic contacts, and historically some were staged by humans. Some are simply curiosity and "social" contacts.

Axis Deer

Axis deer and sloth bears were observed feeding only 13 feet apart, and neither appeared disturbed by the other, according to Andrew Laurie and John Seidensticker in an article entitled "Behavioural Ecology of the Sloth Bear" in the *Journal of Zoology*.

A confrontation between distant relatives in Churchill, Manitoba
©JOHNNY JOHNSON

Bighorn and Dall Sheep

Bighorn and Dall sheep are too agile on terrain that is difficult for bears to negotiate. The author observed an American black bear stalk several bighorns that easily moved back and forth from one outcropping of rock to another.

Bison

The American buffalo (or bison) shares much of its range with grizzly bears, but there is minimal conflict between them. A grizzly bear normally does not attack an adult bison, for it may be the loser.

Coyote

Coyotes will dash in and steal food bits from a bear feeding on a carcass. However, with good reason, and relying on their quickness, they are at times willing to enter into a head-on confrontation, as witnessed by photographers and authors Erwin and Peggy Bauer. They write in Bears, ". . . two grizzly bears walking together downstream . . . two-and-a-half-year-old siblings. . . . Suddenly, a coyote appeared from nowhere and, unbelievably, attacked the grizzlies head-on. It snarled, snapped, lunged, and bit the bears in the face as if rabid, causing them to turn away and run up a steep bank. . . . The coyote followed, attacking their rear ends until the bears were out of sight." The Bauers later discovered the reason for the aggression—the coyote had a nearby den with pups.

Dog

Some dogs will stand up to bears. However, Charles Feazel in White Bear writes, "Bears . . . have been reported to walk slowly down a line of tethered dogs, killing each one in sequence." There can be exceptions: On five successive days in 2007, a polar bear came into the Churchill, Manitoba, area, where it "caressed" and "played" with a chained-up dog.

Eagle

"Any bear on the landscape is worthy of at least a brief inspection by an eagle . . . interested in carrion," writes Adolph Murie in The Grizzlies of Mount McKinley, "for the bear may be at a carcass."

Elk

Bears are a natural enemy of elk. Grizzly bears may under unusual circumstances kill an adult elk, but grizzlies and American black bears normally seek calves.

Fox

Adolph Murie observed a bear cub and a fox playing together. Arctic foxes rely on the scraps of seal that are left by polar bears for their winter survival.

Horses

Bears and horses or mules, in general, appear to have a healthy and mutual respect. They each prevent surprise encounters due to their acute hearing and smell and so normally avoid confrontation, and a horse's hooves pounding on the trail is an excellent warning to the bear. However, there are exceptions to this mutual avoidance. Bears, whether surprised and threatened or protecting a food source or cubs, have been aggressive, and horses and mules are defensive as well.

In *American Bears* (Paul Schullery, ed.), Theodore Roosevelt relates that the bear ". . . has much respect for the hoofs . . . of its should-be prey. Some horses do not seem to know how to fight at all; but others are both quick and vicious, and prove themselves very formidable foes, lashing out behind and striking with their fore-hoofs."

A park biologist in Yellowstone National Park in 1966, on horseback and leading a pack mule, encountered a grizzly bear at an elk carcass. As the bear charged, the biologist threw the mule's lead-rope upon the pack so the mule would have the freedom to run and escape. As the biologist rapidly retreated, he heard a "screaming-bray" from the mule, and turning, he expected to see the worst. However, the grizzly bear was departing as the mule with hackles raised, head down and outstretched toward the bear, was expressing its dominance of that moment.

House Cat

Interactions between bears and house cats are rare, and it is obvious what species would normally have the advantage. However, one situation found a 560-pound captive grizzly bear sharing its food and sleeping with a stray house-cat kitten.

Killer Whale (Orca)

Polar bears have one natural enemy—killer whales. They are vulnerable while swimming and are occasionally killed by these large, fast predators.

Leopard

Though the leopard is a major enemy (some leopard scat was found to contain 0.6 percent giant panda), the sloth bear is known to drive away a leopard from its prey.

Magpie, Raven, and Other Birds

There is no true conflict between these birds and bears, as they bide their time to take advantage of the scraps left by the feeding bear.

Moose

A grizzly bear preying on a moose calf finds the protective mother a formidable foe. Adolf Murie ". . . watched a mother, followed by her very young calf, determinedly chasing a grizzly and doing her best to overtake it."

An account is related of a Russian brown bear imitating the call of an elk (moose are called elk in Asia) during the rutting season, luring the unsuspecting moose to where it would be easier prey.

Mountain Goat

A goat was observed feeding near a grizzly, with neither indicating any aggression or fear; however, naturalist William Hornaday observed a goat use its horns to mortally wound a grizzly bear.

Mountain Lion

Grizzly bears steal from mountain lions, but each has a healthy respect for the other. Enos Mills wrote in *The Grizzly*, "Bears and lions are not neighborly, and at best each ignores the other; but one bear I knew followed a lion for weeks . . . profiting by the food-supply—the excessive killing of the lion."

Musk Ox

These shaggy animals of the arctic tundra, with their sharp, hooked horns, are formidable opponents when circled as a group. A grizzly bear will kill an individual musk ox by attacking from behind, grasping its neck, placing a foreleg over its shoulder, and pulling it to the ground. However, bears are sometimes killed or seriously injured during an encounter.

Porcupine

". . . I have sat and watched a grizzly bear and a little porcupine feeding side by side on the grass near the snow banks," wrote William Wright in *The Grizzly Bear*, "neither one paying the slightest attention to the other."

Bears are occasionally found with face and paws filled with porcupine quills, which may lead to infections and the inability to eat, with subsequent starvation. Author Ernest Thompson Seton described an emaciated dead bear with lips and mouth terribly swollen and "bristling with quills."

Pronghorn Antelope

Three pronghorns approached an American black bear sow with two cubs that were grazing on a hillside. Drawn by what appeared to be curiosity, the pronghorns approached to within 50 feet, while the bears only occasionally glanced at them. Curiosity satisfied, they departed, and the bears continued eating grass.

Rhinoceros

"Sloth bears avoid rhinos," according to Laurie and Seidensticker. However, "in one instance, a sloth bear roared when it encountered a rhino at close range, then ran away and was chased by the rhino 200 meters [656 feet] across an open river bed and into forest."

Seal

Seals harass swimming polar bears and according to Koch can ". . . literally swim circles around" them.

Skunk

A grizzly bear was observed moving aside to avoid a skunk. And when a family of skunks and an American black bear encountered each other at less than 20 feet, the bear stopped, but the mother skunk did not hesitate and with a raised tail moved toward the bear, which retreated.

Tiger

Tigers prey on bears in their respective habitat. The diet of some Siberian tigers is 5 to 8 percent Asiatic black bear, though the bears have been observed displacing tigers from their kills.

Bengal tigers kill sun bears, though they will often avoid them, and they must ambush or

An Alaska grizzly bear in Katmai National Park confronts a wolf that it perceives as a threat to its food source.
©JOHNNY JOHNSON

sneak up on a sloth bear. Brown bears are a more formidable challenge for a Siberian tiger, and most of those bears killed are young, orphaned, or bears too old or weak to defend against a tiger.

Wolf

Wolf-bear relationships have been considered neutral, with only occasional conflicts that are based on defense of home site, food, or young by each species. A wolf and a grizzly bear have fed side by side on a caribou carcass, while at other times a grizzly has fought off a pack of wolves to defend its food, and they each have killed the other.

Wolverine

Adolph Murie observed a wolverine chase a grizzly bear off a carcass, and a Russian brown bear was driven away from a carcass by a wolverine.

BEAR AGGRESSION (ATTACKS)

Bears attack other animals and humans for two basic purposes—for food (predation) and as a defensive reaction. Generally, bears display an avoidance behavior, which promotes species survival. However, aggression is often based on fright (defensiveness) when a bear is startled and reacts to protect a food source or protect its "space" when crowded or when a sow protects its cubs from a real or perceived threat. If there is an abundant food source, there is less aggression. Attacks are then rare, other than when preying on other wild animals. A bear would rather bluff, chase, or scare away an intruder, or flee, than enter into actual combat. However, if it attacks, the situation is serious.

Several reasons prompt a nonprey attack, and they are most often due to a short-distance contact with a person or other enemy:

- Defensive action
- Protection of food source
- Protection of cubs
- Their "space" is invaded
- Confusion
- Mating rivalry (males)
- Travel route is blocked
- Fear

In an attack, bears charge on all four legs, some in great, leaping bounds. They do not stand bipedal in an attack, unless in a final, close-quarters "reaching" action. They do not "bear hug" but strike, claw, and bite. The most effective method of attack is with a crushing blow of a forepaw; they have incredible forepaw speed; a single strike is so powerful that it can kill an adult elk, caribou, or moose. The bear ". . . strikes around with its paws," according to Frederick Drimmer in *The Animal Kingdom*. "The terrific strength of its weighty arms drives the claws deep into the body of its victims."

"When hunting large game, bears may stalk catlike, then run the prey down with a sudden spurt and kill it with blows of the forepaws and bites through the neck," describe Paul Shepard and Barry Sanders in *The Sacred Paw*.

Scientists, victims, and other observers describe various actions of the species:

- **American black bear:** not an efficient predator (has strength but not necessary speed); hunts with ambush and surprise; approaches

An aggravated grizzly bear, Brooks River, Katmai National Park, Alaska
©2008 MARK STADSKLEV/ALASKASTOCK.COM

low on four legs; swings powerful forelegs, with body strength behind them; bites and claws

- **Andean bear:** timid; attacks only in defense; raises up and bites; strikes head and shoulders
- **Asiatic black bear:** sits or stands up and knocks prey over with blows of forepaws; claws and bites; bites limbs, shoulders, and head if attacking a person; mostly attacks only to protect food; normally does not prey on other animals; climbing is principal means of defense
- **Brown bear:** uses speed to run down prey; charges in great, leaping bounds (while uttering a deep roar); rears up in fight to grasp head or neck with teeth; swings powerful forepaws, with enormous body strength behind them
- **Giant panda:** pushes with body; swats with forepaws; lunges; grapples with tremendous shoulder strength, heavy forepaws, and powerful jaws; bites neck
- **Polar bear:** uses stealth and sudden bursts of speed to approach prey; tucks forelegs under chest and pushes with hind legs or pulls itself along on ice; stops when prey, such as a seal, moves or looks; moves directly into wind; uses shadows or shields such as ice blocks and ridges; approaches within 30 feet; makes 12- to 15-foot bounds; pounces with teeth and claws; uses its long neck to place its huge canines out in front of the body to grasp the seal on the ice or through its breathing hole in the ice; often synchronizes its feeding on seals with the seals' patterns of sleeping alongside their breathing holes; will occasionally enter the water to stalk seals on an ice floe, but this is mostly in vain; has been known to prepare a seal's hole so it is large

An angry giant panda with powerful jaws
KITCH BAIN/ISTOCKPHOTO.COM

enough for its paw, then waits in ambush for the seal; successful in less than one-fourth of its attacks on seals

- **Sloth bear:** very aggressive, it attacks savagely when surprised; spectacular charge and bipedal display; may attack unaware person at night; approaches low, head first, and rears up to strike claws into head and upper body; bites and tears with teeth; stands and drives claws into humans' shoulders and temples while biting (major aggression, probably due to a life of conflict with Bengal tigers)
- **Sun bear:** normally attacks only in defense but is extremely aggressive and savage when cornered or threatened; barks loudly when attacking

"In hunting seals on icefloes," write Shepard and Sanders, "polar bears slither on their stomachs, pause when the seal looks up and cover their black noses with their paws, then rush the seal from fifteen or twenty feet. When ringed seal pups are in chambers three feet down in ice, the bear digs and smashes his way to them. . . ."

". . . [A] large Grizzly Bear [apparently fleeing] . . . sprang upon the Canadian," wrote Osborne Russell in *Journal of a Trapper*, ". . . and placing one forepaw upon his head and the other on his left shoulder pushed him [to] one side about 12 ft. with as little ceremony as if he had been a cat [while] still keeping a direct course as tho. nothing had happened."

Predation

Predation is considered the action of attacking, capturing, and feeding on another species. Bears, with the exception of the basically carnivorous polar bear and "insectivorous" sloth bear, eat predominately vegetation. However, they do prey on rodents, birds, small mammals, the young and the weak of larger animals, occasionally a healthy adult animal, and rarely a bear of another species. "Predators," according to George Laycock in *Wild Hunters*, "often kill the animals that are easiest to take: the young, the old, and the weak." Their success rate is low and accounts for a small percentage of their diet. One study of bears preying upon caribou found they were successful only 28 percent of the time, and the animals killed were primarily calves. Studies have found that a sow with cubs is the most successful in preying on elk and caribou. Though bears would prefer the easier prey, for success and to prevent injury, a grizzly bear sow, with two cubs, in Yellowstone National Park was observed attacking and killing an adult bison (see Interactions with Some Enemies and Other Animals—Bison, this chapter).

Some Prey Animals

- Antelope (Tibetan, American pronghorn)
- Birds, pikas, rabbits
- Bison
- Caribou
- Coyote
- Deer (musk, mule, tufted)
- Domestic pets
- Elk
- Livestock
- Llamas
- Marmots, squirrels
- Monkeys
- Musk ox
- Other bears
- Reindeer
- Seals
- Whales (stranded)
- Yaks

Natural food shortages have resulted in bears killing dogs at urban and rural homes. The Associated Press (North Carolina) related, "The killing or injuring of dogs happens each year when hungry bears head into developed areas looking for food then are provoked when dogs start barking at them, said Mike Carraway, a state Wildlife Resources Commission officer."

Bears preying on livestock and on other domestic animals (pets) are addressed in Sources and Causes of Interactions and Conflicts—Dogs; Livestock (see Chapter 8). Bears preying upon their own species is addressed in Cannibalism (this chapter).

BEAR TRAVEL

Moving from one location to another is the most common activity of bears. It is closely associated with seeking food and resting. "Bears," notes David Brown in *The Grizzly in the Southwest*, "make well-defined pathways to and from characteristic bedding sites in heavy cover where they avoid midday heat. These bedding sites are interconnected to favorite foraging areas and escape retreats by a system of well-worn paths that facilitate rapid movement with a minimum of noise."

Walk, run, wander, meander, climb, swim, and slide are all modes of travel that have a specific purpose for bears. Ben East notes in *Bears* that "if scent or an unnatural noise alerts him [the bear] at close range, he is likely to . . . go crashing off through the brush like a runaway truck. But if he picks up danger signals at a distance, he will probably melt away with hardly more commotion than a shadow. For an animal of his size, he can move through thick cover with astonishingly little noise. . . ."

Purposes of Travel

- Avoid people
- Escape
- Move to and from day bed
- Move to and from den
- Play
- Purposes not understood by humans
- Return to previous habitat following translocation
- Seek a mate
- Seek food

Travel Routes

The routes traveled by bears are varied in topography and purpose. Some serve a specific need, leading to a known destination, while others are the result of exploration. Cover and safety are important criteria in bears' travels; therefore, 95 percent of their travel is away from roads and other developments. Most commonly bears travel the routes of least resistance, while avoiding open areas, though if necessary they are capable of negotiating most any terrain, including the densest vegetation or extremely steep ridges and cliffs, areas humans would consider impenetrable.

"The more rugged and inaccessible the general character of the topography of any particular region, the more surely will the trails of white men, Indians, bears, wild sheep, etc., be found converging into the best passes," wrote John Muir in *The Mountains of California*. "Bears frequently accept the pathways laid down by glaciers as the easiest to travel; but they often leave them and cross over from canon to canon."

Frank Dufresne comments in *No Room for Bears*, "No other four-footed animal in all the world travels so far in its lifetime."

Common Travel Routes
- Base of cliffs
- Bear trails
- Forest edges
- Game trails
- Glaciers
- Hillsides (rock ledges to walk on)
- Human-constructed trails
- Ice floes
- Open forests
- Open ridges

Brown bear on a difficult route in the Cantabrian Mountains, Spain
JOSE B. RUIZ/NATUREPL.COM

- Open seas
- Ridge tops
- Roads
- Shorelines (streams, ponds, lakes)
- Small passes between hills
- Snowfields
- Stream bottoms

Trails

Bears have routes with specific purposes, and because they are creatures of habit, repeated use transforms a route into a well-defined trail. Many years of use by generations of bears result in a trail of deep indentations in the ground, in a zigzag pattern, due to the hindpaw stepping into the same location as the forepaw. Two well-defined ruts are formed with time. Where such a trail climbs over an embankment or up a steep ridge, the trail may become a stairway.

"We . . . came into the deepest bear trail I had ever seen," writes Harold McCracken in *The Beast That Walks Like Man*. "It was cut to an average of at least six inches into the solid ground . . . we marveled at how many thousands of footsteps by the padded feet of bears, through the untold expanse of years, it had taken to cut that primeval trail."

TRAVEL GAITS

The common gait of all species of bears is the walk. They amble, or pace, with both legs on one side moving together—alternate paws on alternate sides—the paws striking the ground in the sequence of:

	1
	(right forepaw)
2	
(left hindpaw)	
3	
(left forepaw)	4
	(right hindpaw)
	1
	(right forepaw)
2	
(left hindpaw)	
3	
(left forepaw)	4
	(right hindpaw)

Bears do not always start walking with their right forepaw, of course, but they *always* follow the above sequence. (Note the photograph of the sow and cub running at the camera.)

Their general gait and appearance is the following:

- A shuffling, lumbering walk
- Plantigrade (feet flat on ground)
- Feet turned in (pigeon-toed)
- At normal walking pace, the hind foot is often placed *slightly forward* of the forefoot track.
- At a faster walking pace, the hind foot is often placed *well in front* of the forefoot track.
- A slow pace is a walk.
- A hurried pace is a trot.
- A frightened or angry pace is a gallop.

An Alaska grizzly bear sow and its cub rapidly approach the photographer in Denali National Park.
©JOHNNY JOHNSON

Walking

- **American black bear:** graceful; rhythmic; surefooted
- **Andean bear:** wobbly
- **Asiatic black bear:** dignified; deliberate motion
- **Brown bear:** dignified; ponderous; travels a straight line if possible; head low, scenting; "swims" breaststroke through deep snow

- **Giant panda:** moves with ease and silence; rolling gait; extremely long stride; body somewhat diagonal; head low; clumsy appearance; wiggling pigeon-toed (all paws); trots when startled; not built for traveling great distances but adapted to move on difficult terrain
- **Grizzly bear:** fast moving, though with a slow-motion shuffling appearance; truly rapid; somewhat graceful; silent; moves with indication of power; flees danger at a waddling gait
- **Polar bear:** dignified; nimble; easy motion; fast moving; weighty shuffle; front paws move in rhythm like paddles; requires twice the energy to walk as other mammals of equal size; uses energy-conserving pace; slides downhill on rump and forepaws; will crawl spread-eagle (nondignified) when the ice is thin
- **Sloth bear:** slow; shambling; feet set down in a kind of flapping motion; noisy; crashes through vegetation
- **Sun bear:** extremely pigeon-toed; front paws often cross

Travel along the Beaufort Sea coastline, Alaska
SUSAN MILLER/COURTESY NATIONAL PARK SERVICE

The walk of the giant panda is different enough from other bears to be noteworthy. "Once seen, the giant panda's wiggling, pigeon-toed walk is never forgotten," write Desmond Morris and Ramona Morris in *Men and Pandas*. "Dwight Davis describes it, 'The head is carried well below the shoulder line, and the tail is closely appressed against the body. The stride is considerably longer . . . and as a result the gait is more rolling, with much more lateral rotation of the shoulders and hips than in *Ursus*. This gives a pronounced waddling character to the locomotion. The heavy head is swayed from side to side.'"

Bipedal Standing and Walking

Bears are plantigrade and capable of standing upright on their hind legs. They stand unaided to observe or increase sight distance, to fight, and to reach to feed, prey, or mark.

Some species of bears are capable of walking bipedally, though this is not a normal means of locomotion. They do not attack in this position, though they may raise their upper body to better reach and grasp their prey or enemy.

The American black, brown, grizzly, polar, sloth, and sun bears walk bipedally but only a few steps. The giant panda and the Andean bear do not walk bipedally. The Asiatic black bear walks bipedally extremely well. Circus, street, menagerie, and other performing bears walk bipedally, being trained to perform stunts and walk distances in this manner.

Running

Bears, with the exception of the giant panda, run quite well. They are fast and agile, though their speed is maintained only for short distances.

An Alaska grizzly bear in Katmai National Park stands to walk bipedally, though for only a few steps.
©JOHNNY JOHNSON

"The Bear," according to Ernest Thompson Seton in *Monarch the Big Bear*, ". . . came racing down the bank before he [not Seton] was fairly on the horse, and for a hundred yards the pony bounded in terror while the old Grizzly ran almost alongside, striking at him and missing by a scant hair's-breadth each time. But the Grizzly rarely keeps up its great speed for many yards. The horse got under full headway, and the shaggy mother, falling behind, gave up the chase and returned to her cubs."

Many bears run with power and are 50 percent faster than humans. ". . . [T]he grizzly can barrel, tanklike, through thick brush that would bring a man to a complete halt . . ." relates George Laycock in *The Wild Bears*. The stride of one galloping bear was recorded at 17 feet between tracks.

Bears run to catch prey, to inspect an unknown situation or movement, to escape from a threat, to play, and for no apparent purpose. Their endurance is exceptional, as they have been known to run without a break for 10 miles, though not with their short-distance speed. A sow with two cubs is reported to have traveled more than 20 miles through mountainous terrain in one hour.

SWIFTNESS OF THE SPECIES

Species	Speed
American black bear	25–30 mph
Andean bear	Fast, agile
Asiatic black bear	Quick, fast
Brown bear	35–40 mph
Giant panda	Quite slow; clumsy trot; seldom moves faster than a walk; does not gallop, though capable of running away rapidly when startled
Polar bear	25 mph; 35 mph over a short distance; easily overheats when running
Sloth bear	Gallops faster than a running human; gallops with leaps; gallops when it is frightened
Sun bear	Fast

A display of endurance as an Alaska grizzly bear easily runs through deep snow in Katmai National Park
©JOHNNY JOHNSON

Bears run uphill and downhill with speed and agility. "The rumor [bears cannot run downhill without stumbling] is untrue," relates Stephen Herrero in *Bear Attacks: Their Causes and Avoidance*. "I have watched grizzly bears chase one another, and . . . elk and bighorn sheep—downhill, uphill, sidehill—wherever the pursuit leads. I have never seen a . . . bear stumble. . . ."

"He was going so fast," relates W. P. Hubbard in *Notorious Grizzly Bears*, describing an American black bear, "his hind feet were up by his ears when his front feet were under and behind him. He was all action, a big black bottom, with four stems churning for all they were worth."

COMPARATIVE RUNNING SPEEDS OF OTHER SPECIES

Species	Speed
African lion	50 mph
American bison	30–35 mph
Cheetah	70 mph
Elephant	30 mph
Elk	40–50 mph
Horse (with rider)	48 mph
Humans (100 yards)	23 mph
Moose	35 mph
Pronghorn antelope	61 mph
Sloth	⅓ mph
Sprinter (Olympic)	Runs 100 meters (328 feet) in 10 seconds at 33 feet per second; grizzly and American black bears at 30 mph run 44 feet per second

NAVIGATION

Bears appear to have no difficulty navigating throughout their range. Obviously the size of the range might be significant, as one would not expect a giant panda to experience much difficulty when its home area is approximately 1 to 3 square miles. However, the ranges of other species of bears are hundreds of square miles (and those of polar bears are thousands of square miles), and the ability to navigate is remarkable—they appear to have a "mental compass." Bears also are unbelievably capable of finding their way home following a translocation to a totally new and unfamiliar area. Homing appears more developed in adults, and grizzly bears are more proficient than American black bears in returning to their home range.

"Their [bears'] sense of topographical orientation transcends simple familiarity with specific features," writes Paul Schullery in *The Bears of Yellowstone*. "They can find their way home from country they have never before visited."

Some biologists believe bears may navigate by possessing a level of sensory contact with their goal, and most believe that familiarity with the area of release is *not* a factor.

Bear biologist Lynn Rogers, in *The Translocation of Wild Animals* (Leon Nielsen and Robert Brown, eds.), describes the levels of the navigation ability of bears as:

- Orientation to familiar landmarks (visual or otherwise)
- Movement in a particular compass direction without reference to landmarks
- The ability of an animal in an unfamiliar area to orient toward home or some other goal beyond the range of sensory contact

Polar bears may be the most amazing of bear navigators. Scientists are baffled by the white bear's ability to travel in straight routes across an ever-changing, ever-moving, and constantly drifting icepack or how they remain in the same location when the ice beneath them is moving with the circumpolar drift.

SWIMMING

All bears seem to enjoy water, whether they wade, sit and splash, lie, soak, float, scratch, drink, or actually swim (sometimes long distances). Their buoyancy is excellent, and they swim "dog paddle" fashion and shake water off like dogs.

In general, bears will utilize bodies of water (streams, lakes, ponds, and the seas) for pleasure and purpose:

- Cool off
- Escape from insects
- Feed (fish, frogs, bugs)

Brown bear swimming in a display of a bear's enjoyment of water
©2008 NEIL BRAMELY/CRITTER ZONE.COM

- Hide their tracks
- Hunt (polar bear)
- Hydrate
- Locate a mate*
- Play
- Relax
- Relieve itching
- Travel
- When wounded, to heal or die
- Purposes unknown to humans

Male American black bears of the Pacific Northwest swim between the mainland and offshore islands seeking females during the mating season.

Swimming Ability

- **American black bear:** excellent, strong swimmer; swims for pleasure and to feed
- **Andean bear:** good swimmer
- **Asiatic black bear:** good swimmer
- **Brown bear:** strong and skillful swimmer; swims to feed (fishing, frogging) and for pleasure
- **Giant panda:** skeptical of water; will swim to cross streams or escape an enemy; does not appear to voluntarily swim
- **Polar bear:** "the swimmer" of all bears; swims to travel, move to other feeding sites, and for pleasure; moves through the water with efficiency and relative ease due to shape and strong, powerful strokes; displays enormous endurance (may swim 300 miles between ice floes); excellent buoyancy due to thick, oily fur and blubber; normally swims (paddles) only with front legs and paws, with hind legs and paws used as stabilizers and rudders to steer (used otherwise as paddles); shape cuts through the water, leaving a wake like a ship's bow; muzzle submerged in rough water but is

"The Swimmer" in the Beaufort Sea, Arctic National Wildlife Refuge, Alaska
©2008 STEVEN KAZLOWSKI/ALASKASTOCK.COM

regularly raised to breathe; swims 6 miles per hour; male swims 100 yards in 30 to 33 seconds (female in 40 seconds); swims 60 miles without rest; avoids water if possible during severe cold weather
- **Sloth bear:** good swimmer; primarily plays in water; sits and splashes self
- **Sun bear:** good swimmer

Polar bears are capable of leaping out of the water 7 to 8 feet in the air from a swimming start. They close their ears and nostrils when diving and may remain underwater up to two minutes, cruising 10 to 15 feet deep. Thomas Koch notes in *The Year of the Polar Bear*, "this bear's peculiar habit of diving every few minutes or so while swimming, as if the diving were part of its escape mechanism."

Bears that dive have been observed shaking their heads to remove the water from their ears. One bear placed a claw into its ear to "scratch the irritation." Grizzly bears and American black bears have been observed swimming underwater for more than a minute, apparently pursuing fish.

Bears not only enjoy wallowing in natural pools but also have on occasion bathed in developed pools. Tracy Storer and Lloyd Tevis in *California Grizzly* relate an account of a bear visiting Paso Robles Hot Springs in California. "A huge grizzly was in the habit of making nocturnal visits to the spring; plunge into the pool, and, with his forepaws grasping the limb [a cottonwood tree that extended low over the water], swing himself up and down in the water, evidently enjoying his bath. . . ." Not infrequently, American black bears visit residential swimming pools in urban and suburban areas.

The author observed a large grizzly bear in the Savonoski River of Katmai National Park, Alaska, swim from a gravel bar directly across a 30-foot channel to the riverbank. Upon reaching the 6-foot-high vertical bank, the bear turned upstream and swam, seemingly effortlessly, 60 feet against a swift (7-mile-per-hour) current, until it reached a more easily ascended embankment.

CLIMBING

Bears climb trees to feed, rest, hibernate, and play or for safety. Young brown bears, American black bears, and Asiatic black bears climb naturally (they do not need to learn), which allows the mother to defend only the base of the tree. When threatened while aloft, cubs climb out on thin branches and sit where a larger and heavier enemy is unable to access.

All species of bears except the polar bear are capable of climbing trees, though the adults of the larger species lose their climbing ability as

Adult American black bear effortlessly seeking safety
BILLLEA.COM

they become heavier. "Young grizzles are good climbers: They can go up a tree like a black bear," describes Frederick Drimmer in *The Animal Kingdom*. "However, they lose this ability as they get older, and most full-grown grizzlies are too big and heavy to climb." There are exceptions to the rule, as large grizzly bears have attained heights of at least 18 feet.

The best climbers are those whose paws have naked soles that provide rough skin, short and sharply hooked claws, and a more-pronounced inward turn of the paws. The brown bears are poor climbers due to fixed wrist joints, poor claw structure (long and relatively straight), and their weight. Grizzly bears have been observed "shinnying" up at least 10 feet.

American black bear cub seeking safety
BILLLEA.COM

Climbing Ability

American Black Bear

- Outstanding climber
- Climbs regularly and easily to feed, to escape enemies (principal means of defense), or in some situations to hibernate
- Climbing ability declines with age, with large adults climbing infrequently for food

Andean Bear

- Excellent climber
- Climbs to feed, rest, sleep, and to escape enemies
- Spends more time in trees than other bears
- Climbs quite high
- Able to climb vines and small trees (less than 4 inches in diameter)
- Known to have climbed a 23-foot-tall cactus for the fruit at the top

Andean bear in Peru, climbing to feed, rest, and sleep
FRANCOIS SAVIGNY/NATUREPL.COM

The most common method of ascent among bears is to use the front legs to grasp the tree trunk and pull while pushing with the hind legs. The motion appears somewhat like an inchworm. Claws are hooked into available cracks for a better hold. A bear may on occasion grasp, pull, and push, moving its legs in a sequence, as if it were walking. Bears may also "ladder" up trees by using the tree branches as rungs. This method allows the larger bears, such as grizzly bears, sometimes to climb trees. If a tree is bent over or leaning, a bear may walk in a normal manner up the sloping surface.

The descent from a tree is made in reverse fashion: head up, walking down backward, though sliding down or jumping down from low limbs may sometimes accomplish it.

Asiatic Black Bear

- Good climber
- Frequently climbs trees
- Climbs to feed (important in feeding habits), rest, sun, escape from enemies, and hibernate
- Excellent climber on rocks and cliffs
- Some older bears become too heavy to climb

Brown Bear

- Poor climber due to claw structure and body weight
- Climbs to feed (pursue prey, seek human foods)
- Climbs to travel, including steep rock ridges
- Capable of laddering up only trees with low branches
- Cubs climb trees

Giant Panda

- Poor climber
- Climbing is uncommon and less efficient than that of other bears
- Climbs slowly and clumsily, appearing inept; embraces tree, ascending with caterpillar movements
- Climbs for defense (escape dogs, humans, other enemies, and other giant pandas), and to rest and sun
- Females climb to escape courting males

Polar Bear

- Does not climb trees (none available)
- Agile climber of ice ridges
- Climbs to travel and pursue prey
- Capable of scaling 35-foot-high ice barriers
- Capable of jumping down 10 feet

Sloth Bear

- Excellent climber despite appearing slow and clumsy; can climb a smooth-bole tree or pole
- Climbs to feed and rest
- Hangs upside down like a sloth
- Does not climb to escape enemies; runs or fights, probably because its major predator, the leopard, is an excellent climber
- Can jump down 10 feet

Sun Bear

- Expert climber (nimble, skillful)
- Most agile species of the bears
- Hangs nearly upside down with its long claws
- Climbs to feed and rest
- Climbs trees like South Sea Islanders climb palm trees
- Hooks its long claws on a tree, extends its legs and keeps its body away from tree trunk
- Cubs climb better than they run

PLAYING

Humans appear to be most attracted to bears by their play, especially the humorous activities of cubs. A cub's active and amusing playfulness with its siblings and mother is not only sport, recreation, or idle activity, as we would interpret, but a natural necessity for survival. Play is actually "play fighting" and is extremely important to cubs as part of their education. The large variety of play fighting of the cubs, which they may engage in until five years of age, contributes to their preparation for survival in the "real" world. Play may occur anytime and wherever they may be—in the den, in trees, or on the ground, in water, or on ice and snow. This playful education helps develop social attitudes and physical coordination.

Alaska grizzly bear in a play-fight in Katmai National Park
©JOHNNY JOHNSON

"One of the most humorous play sessions I've observed," relates Stephen Herrero in *Bear Attacks: Their Causes and Avoidance,* "occurred . . . when two black bear cubs of the year came upon a young sapling pine tree. One bear climbed to near the top. Then the other bear followed, and their combined weight bent the tree to near the ground where one cub hopped off and the other was catapulted up as the tree straightened. Soon both cubs were up the tree again to repeat the sequence."

Adults also play very much like cubs, but it is a solitary activity except for females with their cubs. ". . . A big bear sat down like a dog at the top of the slide [long snowdrift]," relates Andy Russell in *Grizzly Country.* "[A] huge hind foot was elevated to scratch the back of an ear . . . with the paw still held up to its head, the grizzly took off in a plummet down to the bottom."

The play activities of some species in the wild are poorly documented, but there is evidence that cave bears, like today's bears, enjoyed play. D. P. Erdbrink, in his paper "A Review of Fossil and Recent Bears of the Old World," relates an explorer's description of a play area, the "toboggan of the bears." He noted the explorers found that "a gentle slope, covered with cave loam, ending in a shallow subterranean pond, has been the playground of local Cave bears, as indicated by numerous prints and even by imprints of separate hairs. . . ."

Play Activities

The list primarily includes recorded observations of play fighting of cubs. However, any activity in which a cub may engage is probably enjoyed by an adult, and a few adult activities are included.

- Acrobatic leaps
- Bite and wrestle with sow or sibling

Grizzly bear cubs play fighting
©2008 LAURA ROMIN & LARRY DALTON/CRITTERZONE.COM

- Box with sibling
- Chase and tease monkeys
- Chase own tail
- Chase sibling
- Climb on sibling
- Climb on sow
- Climb rocks, trees, stumps, ice floes, logs
- Crawl through hollow logs
- Crowd against sow
- Embrace sow or sibling
- Flip fish
- Flip stick or driftwood
- Frolic, roll, and tumble
- Grab hind paws and roll in water like a barrel
- Hang upside down
- Hide
- High dive onto ground or into water
- High-stepping run
- Jump out of hiding
- Jump up and flip
- Knock sibling off rocks and logs
- Leap
- Lie on back and grasp paws
- Lie on back and play with object
- Lie on back and wave legs
- Lie on back in mud and kick
- Make and play with snowballs
- Mouth sibling
- Nibble/nip sow or sibling
- Paw
- Play hide and seek
- Play tag
- Pounce
- Push sibling under water
- Rock ice floes back and forth
- Roll down hill
- Roll in water
- Roll logs
- Romp
- Run
- Run at sow or sibling
- Run up and down tree
- Shadow box
- Shove sibling
- Slap
- Slide down ice fields

- Slide down ice into water
- Slide down riverbanks
- Slide down snowbanks
- Slide off mother
- Slide off sow
- Splash water
- Squeeze between sow's legs
- Stand on head
- Stand up
- Swim through hollow logs
- Toss rocks or other loose items
- Toss stick, catch in mouth
- Tug of war with sibling

"I was rewarded by seeing a small light-colored grizzly," describes noted explorer Charles Sheldon in *The Wilderness of Denali*. "It was indulging in the most grotesque play imaginable, while not a hundred yards above it were more than thirty [Dall sheep] ewes quietly feeding, all completely indifferent to its near presence. The bear was repeatedly turning somersaults, rolling a few feet down the slope, and running short distances upward. Often it would lie on its back, throw up all four feet and attempt to strike them together. These antics continued for ten minutes or more, while only one of the sheep—a yearling lamb—looked directly at it. The others maintained their usual watch, apparently taking no interest in the bear."

"Suddenly, it jumped off [an ice wall] onto the almost perpendicular slope and came zooming out on the slick, wet ice of the glacier at a dizzy rate of speed," describes Frank Dufresne in *No Room For Bears*. "Then, to my amazement, it came sailing over the lip of the glacier to plunge fifty feet into a lake." The bear then started climbing back up the slope to possibly try again.

"Next to the apes and monkeys," wrote naturalist William Hornaday, in *Camp-Fires in the Canadian Rockies*, "I regard bears as the most demonstrative of all wild animals."

GROOMING

Bears are generally quite well groomed, utilizing a variety of methods to clean, smooth, and otherwise maintain their fur and skin. Their grooming activities include the following:

- Bathing
- Combing fur with claws
- Licking fur dry
- Licking to remove dirt
- Nibbling off dirt with teeth
- Rubbing against brush (vegetation)
- Rubbing against rocks
- Rubbing against trees
- Rubbing in grass

Scratching, this Alaska grizzly bear displays one of many grooming habits.
©JOHNNY JOHNSON

- Rubbing in gravel
- Scratching with fore- or hind paw
- Shaking off water like a dog
- Stretching in a catlike manner
- Swimming
- Wallowing in mud (removes insects and other debris but is followed with other grooming measures)

The natural activities (walking through brush and high grass) of bears and their lack of pores also contribute to cleanliness. The sloth bear is the major exception and is poorly groomed, while the polar bear licks and washes fastidiously after eating, even using snow if water is unavailable. "Like a cat, the [polar] bear washes his face with his newly cleaned paws," notes Charles Feazel in *White Bear*.

PAW SUCKING

Paw sucking occurs with all ages of bears in most species, and captive bears appear to suck their paws more frequently than those in the wild. Though its purpose remains something of a mystery, research and speculation attribute this activity to various reasons, which include the following:

- A means of displacement
- A pastime
- An indication of contentment
- Boredom
- Enhancing footpad sensitivity
- Obtaining footpad secretions
- Obtaining remnant food particles
- Paw cleaning
- Psychological reasons
- Softening or removing calluses

An ancient theory, over 10,000 years old, speculates that paw sucking provides bears subsistence

during hibernation. And as early as 1607, Edward Topsell in *The History of Four-footed Beasts* wrote, "Immediately after they have conceived, they betake themselves to their dens, where they (without meat) grow very fat (especially males) only by sucking their fore-feet." Such theories have been proven untrue. However, hibernating bears often sleep with their paws located directly against their face, and to add an element of confusion, studies have shown that American black bears shed their paw pads during hibernation and sometimes consume them upon awakening.

Little is understood about paw sloughing, though it is considered physiological. "In the den the skin of its paws is slowly sloughed off and replaced by new skin," according to Shepard and Sanders in *The Sacred Paw*. "The factors that cause shedding of old pads are unknown at present," relates Lynn Rogers in "Shedding of Foot Pads by Black Bears during Denning" (*Journal of Mammalogy*).

Sloth and sun bears suck their paws more than other bear species, babbling and gurgling as they carry out this activity for fifteen to twenty minutes each time. Asiatic black bears lie on their backs, placing their front paws together, and alternately suck each paw. Sun bears also lie on their backs, humming as they alternately suck their hind paws.

REPRODUCTION

Reproduction is similar among bear species, though some variations exist in the timing of reproductive and denning activities, reproductive rates, and litter size. Reproduction depends upon the nutritional condition of the female; therefore, reproductive rates of bears are highest in areas of abundant food. Generally, the species of larger bears have less reproductive potential, though the North American brown bear appears to have some decreasing potential with decreasing body size (due to declining habitat quality).

The number of litters a sow produces during her lifetime depends on her longevity, age of first litter, survival of litters (how soon she is able to breed again), and her individual health.

"The grizzly has one of the lowest reproductive rates of the terrestrial mammals," notes David Brown in *The Grizzly in the Southwest*. The rate for the sloth bear is also one of the lowest for mammals, and giant panda reproductive potential is lower than that of American and Asiatic black bears of the same size.

Young sexually mature males are often unable to participate in the breeding process, as they become sexually active earlier than their boldness allows them to compete. The polar bear is sexually mature at five to six years, though some authorities believe they are not bold enough until eight to ten years of age.

Bears have a mechanism, termed "delayed implantation," whereby the development of the embryo is temporarily suspended (see Gestation Period, this chapter).

AGE OF SOW AT FIRST LITTER

American black bear	3–5 years Some 7 years 2, if exceptional food supply
Andean bear	4–7 years
Asiatic black bear	4–5 years
Brown bear	4½–9 years (4–7 years in Europe)
Giant panda	4½–7 years
Polar bear	4–7 years
Sloth bear	Undetermined
Sun bear	3 years

BREEDING PERIODS

American black bear	Late May, June, July As late as August in the north 2- to 3-week period
Asiatic black bear	April–October Early as March; late as December 1- to 2-day period
Andean bear	March–October 1- to 5-day period
Brown bear	May, June (North America) April–August (Europe)
Giant panda	March, April, May Occasional fall estrus Estrus 1 to 3 weeks Receptive 2 to 7 days
Grizzly bear	May, June, July 2- to 3-week period
Polar bear	March, April, May 3-week period
Sloth bear	May, June, July (India, Nepal) Most of year (Ceylon) All year (Sri Lanka)
Sun bear	All year (undefined) 2- to 7-day period

Courtship/Mating Period

"The ultimate social interaction is finding a mate. Mating itself is a brief act," notes Feazel. Courtship and mating periods vary between and within each species, depending on habitat and climate. The giant panda and polar bear appear to have the earliest spring estrus periods, and the sloth and sun bears may breed nearly anytime of year.

In captivity bears may mate at any time, possibly due to boredom and good health, but the sow usually does not conceive except during the normal breeding season.

Courtship/Mating Activities

The male "comes to pay court with the delicate finesse of an animated locomotive running on a one-way track," notes Andy Russell in *Grizzly Country*, describing the arrival of the male when the female has come into estrus.

"He kept herding her from below, as though his objective was to keep her up the slope," describes Adolph Murie in *A Naturalist in Alaska*. "When she traveled, he traveled on a contour below her. Once, when a sharp ridge hid her from him, he galloped forward and upward to intercept her . . . when he saw her again she was two or three hundred yards away. He galloped after her, his hoarse panting plainly audible half a mile away. But she made no real effort to escape, and he was soon herding her from below again. The chase continued all day."

The courting and mating activities of the bear species are quite noisy and diverse. Sloth bears may be the most vociferous while mating. They are very boisterous and emit a long, melodious call.

Bears are polygamous, and a single male may mate with several females, with copulation occurring "dog fashion"; however, a female giant panda crouches while the male squats.

Courting and mating actions among the species include the following:

- Barking
- Clucking
- Male holding female's neck
- Squatting
- Biting
- Head bobbing
- Squealing
- Bleating

Grizzly bears in courtship behavior, Admiralty Island, Alaska
©2008 JOHN HYDE/ALASKASTOCK.COM

Grizzly bears—male approaching female during mating activities
CHRIS SERVHEEN, U.S. FISH AND WILDLIFE SERVICE

- Hugging
- Mock Fighting
- Wrestling
- Caressing
- Kissing
- Roaring
- Chirping
- Moaning
- Rubbing

"The male [grizzly bear] covered her for about an hour," relates Murie. "Much of the time the female wriggled about, apparently trying to escape while he held her with his paws in front of her hips and his head lying along her neck."

Gestation Period

Embryonic growth in all bears takes approximately two months, but due to embryonic delay (delayed implantation), the overall gestation period is considerably longer and varies between bears. Mating generally occurs during the summer, but implantation of the blastocyst (the fertilized ovum) is delayed until a more appropriate time for the female. When the ovum implants, the true gestation period begins.

The female is able to breed and give birth only when in her best condition and with the weight of fat reserves that is the "food" for her and her cubs during the winter. If the female is in poor condition, she aborts, and her body absorbs the blastocyst. Bear biologist Lynn Rogers has determined a correlation between an American black bear sow's body weight and implantation and is able to predict the "likelihood of her giving birth." All species of bears except the sun bear have this wonderful physiological mechanism.

GESTATION, BIRTH PERIOD, LOCATION

Species	Gestation Period (Days)*	Birth Period	Location
American black bear	180–240	January/February	Dens
Andean bear	240–255	November–February**	Nests on the ground most common
			Nests under large rocks or tree roots
Asiatic black bear	200–240	November–March	Caves
			Hollow trees
Brown bear	180–220	January/February	Dens
Giant panda	110–170	August–September	Nests on the ground
			Nests in caves or rock clefts
			Nests in hollow trees or stumps
Grizzly bear	235	January/February	Dens
Polar bear	200–270	Late November–early January	Dens in snowdrifts
Sloth bear	180–200	Late November-January	Caves
			Shelters under boulders
		All year in southern habitats	
Sun bear	90–170	All year	On ground (in vegetation)
			Hollow logs

* Period includes time of "delayed implantation."
** Andean bears' birth period is timed to the ripening of fruit.

Birth Location

The locations of births among the different species of bears are influenced by habitat and topography and whether the bears hibernate. The hibernating species most often have a true den.

LITTER SIZE		
Species	Average	Range
American black bear	2 (western USA)	1–5
		3 (eastern USA)
		3 not uncommon
		4 rare
		5 exceptional
		6 few recorded in Pennsylvania
		First litter usually 1
Andean bear	1	1 (2 uncommon)
Asiatic black bear	2	1–4
Brown bear	2	1–5
		Seldom 4 or 5
Giant panda	1.7	1–2 (normally only 1 survives)
		3 extremely rare
		3 in captivity in 1973
Grizzly bear	1.7–2.5	1–4
Polar bear	1.6–1.9	1–3 (2 normal)
		3 in 10% of litters
Sloth bear	2	1–3

Giant pandas normally have two cubs, but only occasionally in the wild does the mother care for both; normally she abandons one of the two, and it dies. "To hold, suckle, and carry two helpless young for four or five months until they are mobile is probably too difficult," notes George Schaller et al. in *The Giant Pandas of Wolong*. He also explains that the second cub is insurance, in case the other cub is not viable.

Don DeHart, a hunting guide, observed a brown bear on the Alaska Peninsula with six cubs, two of which were runts.

Interval of Litters

The interval (years between litters) may vary if the sow, following the period when she and her cubs separate, is unable to rebuild her weight and condition. Variations in food sources and forage seasons may determine the sow's preparedness, and density of bears, amount of human disturbance, and the sow's health and age are also factors. These elements also affect litter size. In captivity, cubs are removed from the sow earlier than in the wild, so litters may be at a shorter interval.

SPECIES	YEARS BETWEEN LITTERS
American black bear	2
Andean bear	Information unavailable
Asiatic black bear	2–3
Brown bear	3 (Europe: 2)
Giant panda	2.2
Grizzly bear	3–4
Polar bear	3–4
Sloth bear	2–3
Sun bear	3

Interbreeding

Interbreeding between the species is *genetically* possible between six of the eight species of bears: American black bear, Asiatic black bear, brown bear, polar bear, sloth bear, and sun bear. The early ancestors of the giant panda and Andean bear split from the *Ursus* ancestral line during the early evolution of bears. Interbreeding primarily occurs in captivity.

In Captivity

Captive interbreeding between bear species other than polar and brown bears is quite uncommon and occurs primarily in Eurasian facilities. Interbreeding has included the following pairings:

- American black bear/grizzly bear
- Grizzly bear/brown bear (same species, different subspecies)
- Asiatic black bear/brown bear
- Asiatic black bear/sloth bear
- Sloth bear/sun bear
- Polar bear/brown bear

"One of the most revealing facets of the relation between the brown bear and the polar bear has occurred in some of the zoos around the world," explained Koch. "When given the opportunity to mate, these two different bears will produce fertile hybrids. This conclusively proves their close relationship in the not-too-far-distant past." DNA testing has further proven the close genetic relationship.

"Successful breeding between polar bears and Alaska browns is not uncommon in captivity, and the polar bear has also been successfully crossed with the brown bear of northern Europe," explains Ben East in *Bears*. "In both cases the hybrid offspring are capable of producing young, too." The color of the offspring might be what you would expect. "Some are pure white, some silver-blue, some roan, and others grizzly brown," describes Frank Dufresne in *No Room for Bears*. "Some have the big head and hump of the grizzly [brown]; others the snake-like neck and narrower head of the polar bear."

When polar bears breed with other *Ursus* bears, the "hybrid cubs show many characteristics of their polar bear parent, including body and head shape, a white coat at birth, and good swimming abilities," describes Charles Feazel. "Some hybrids' coats darken as they mature."

In the Wild

Brown/grizzly bear and polar bear hybrids have been shot and reported in the past, even as early as 1864 in the Canadian north, but positive identification was not possible, as DNA testing was unavailable. However, in April 2006 a hunter legally hunting with a guide on Banks Island in the Northwest Territories killed what was thought to be a polar bear. Further examination displayed various brown bear characteristics. Wildlife Genetics International (Canada) conducted DNA tests and confirmed the bear was a hybrid of a grizzly bear father and a polar bear mother. Another bear of the same appearance has been observed in that region. Grizzly bears are roaming farther north into the arctic region, with recent sightings on Banks and Melville Islands (northern Canada), increasing the hybrid potential.

The convention in naming a hybrid usually is to use the male name first and the female name second; therefore, in the case of a grizzly/polar bear mix, "grolar." However, the Banks Island hybrid has been unconventionally, but maybe appropriately, given the name "pizzly."

BEAR CUBS

The human interest and fondness for bears is often centered on the cubs of the species. Cuddly in appearance and playful and amusing when most people first observe them, these youngsters are quite unattractive when they arrive in the bear world. They are born:

- With mother "half asleep"
- Toothless
- Almost helpless
- Unable to hear
- Blind
- Unable to smell
- Nearly naked (fine hair)
- Weak
- Poorly insulated
- Able to move to warm objects
- Uncoordinated
- Able to find sow's nipples
- Noisy
- Demanding
- Able to detect temperature changes

Motherhood
SCOTT SCHLIEBE, U.S. FISH AND WILDLIFE SERVICE

CONDITION OF CUBS AT BIRTH

Species	Weight (ounces)	Length (Inches)	Condition
American black bear	8–16	8	Fine, gray, downlike hair; hindquarters underdeveloped; drags self around den; 1/280 of sow's weight*
Andean bear	10–18	7	**
Asiatic black bear	13	**	**
Brown bear	16	9	Lightly furred; 1/720 of sow's weight
Giant panda	3–5	6	Yellowish pink skin; sparse white hair; black fuzz around eyes, on ears and shoulders at one week (fully furred at one month); squeaky voice; 1/900 of sow's weight
Grizzly bear	14	8	Lightly furred; 1/625 of sow's weight
Polar bear	16–24	8–9	Pink skin; short, thin hair; no blubber; size of a house cat; 1/700 of sow's weight
Sloth bear	**	**	Unattractive; very strong (toes and forelegs like a sloth)
Sun bear	12	7	Skin near transparent; more hairless than other species

Human infant is 1/25 of its mother's weight
*** Information unavailable*

Rapidly growing cubs along the Beaufort Sea Coast, Alaska
SUZANNE MILLER, COURTESY OF NATIONAL PARKS SERVICE

Characteristics of American Black Bear Cubs at Birth

A study of American black bear cubs' characteristics at birth was conducted in Pennsylvania by research biologist Gary Alt.

Characteristic	Average	Smallest	Largest
Weight	12.8 ounces	10.3	16.0
Total length	9.4 inches	8.2	11.2
Head length	2.8 inches	2.4	3.1
Ear length	0.4 inches	0.3	0.5
Nose width	0.4 inches	0.4	0.4
Tail length	0.4 inches	0.3	0.6
Hair length	0.1 inches	0.1	0.1
Neck girth	4.3 inches	3.9	4.7
Chest girth	6.5 inches	5.9	7.2
Foot length (front)	0.7 inches	0.7	0.8
Foot length (hind)	1.1 inches	0.9	1.3
Foot width (front)	0.7 inches	0.6	0.8
Foot width (hind)	0.6 inches	0.6	0.7
Claw length (front foot)	0.3 inches	0.2	0.3
Claw length (hind foot)	0.2 inches	0.2	0.2
Umbilical cord length	1.5 feet	0.6	5.7

Cubs' Eyes Open

Born unable to see, cubs generally open their eyes in a few to several days, depending on species and individuals:

Species	Days
American black bear	28–40
Andean bear	25–42
Asiatic black bear	7
Brown bear	28
Giant panda	40–48
Grizzly bear	21
Polar bear	28
Sloth bear	21
Sun bear	14

Both of a cub's eyes do not necessarily open at the same time. Paul Schullery in *Yellowstone Bear Tales* relates a story by E. E. Ogston of a young American black bear cub being transported through Yellowstone National Park. "One of his eyes had opened at Yellowstone Lake and the other at the Canyon," described Ogston.

American black bear cubs' eyes are bluish at birth, subsequently becoming brown in color.

Cub's First Walk

Unable to walk at birth (though a few are able to crawl), cubs first "walk" at varying stages, depending on species and individuals.

Species	Weeks
American black bear	5
Andean bear	4
Asiatic black bear	4
Brown bear	6
Giant panda	12
Polar bear	8
Sloth bear	4
Sun bear	2

Kodiak brown bears may have a weight increase of a thousand times from a newborn cub to a mature adult. Humans would weigh over 6,000 pounds if they shared this characteristic.

Growth and Development (Cubs and Adults)

The development of cubs varies between species, and geographically and individually within a species. Some cubs are born larger and stronger than others, while litter mates develop at different rates. Weight gain may be as much as several pounds a day during the first year.

American black bear

Six weeks: 2 pounds
Eight weeks: 5 pounds
Six months: 40–60 pounds
Three years: sexually mature
Five years: fully grown

Andean Bear

Information unavailable

Asiatic black bear

Three to four years: sexually mature

Brown bear

Six months: 55–80 pounds
During first year: Kodiak cubs double weight every two months
Eighteen months: 150–200 pounds
Three years: 8 feet long
Four to five years: sexually mature
Seven to eight years: mature
Eight to ten years: fully grown

Giant panda

Thirty-six days: 3½ pounds
Three months: 11 pounds
Twelve months: 77 pounds
Thirty months: 114–121 pounds
Forty months (female): 134 pounds
Forty months (male): 153 pounds
Five to seven years: sexually mature

Grizzly bear

Eight to ten weeks: 10–20 pounds
Seven months: 50–80 pounds
Twelve months: 125–175 pounds
Twenty months: 200–400 pounds
Three years: 350–425 pounds
Four to five years: sexually mature
Seven to eight years: mature
Eight to ten years: fully grown

Polar bear

Forty days: 2 pounds

Three months: 28 pounds

Six months: 130 pounds

Four years: sexually mature

Eight to nine years: Fully grown

Earliest maturing bear

Females grow minimally after fourth year

Sloth bear

Rapid growth

Early growth is in legs

Begin to travel sooner than other cubs

Third year: sexually mature

Sun bear

Information unavailable

Cub Mortality

The first few months of a bear's life are the most perilous. There are many enemies in a cub's world, all considerably larger than this youngster, who must depend upon its mother for protection.

American black bear cubs

| First year: | 75 percent survive |
| Second and third years: | 50 percent alive at end of three years |

Brown bear cubs

| First one-and-a-half years: | 60–90 percent survive |

Grizzly bear cubs (Yellowstone National Park)

First year:	83 percent survive
Three years:	50 percent survive
Five years:	40 percent survive

Grizzly bear cubs (Yukon Territory, Canada)

| Three years: | 79 percent survive |

Polar bear cubs

| First year: | 60–80 percent survive |

The primary causes of cub mortality are larger bears (adult males—no strange bear is a safe bear) and other large predatory animals including humans.

Not stranded or abandoned, but curious, these Alaskan grizzly bear cubs in Katmai National Park have their mother nearby.
©JOHNNY JOHNSON

Cub Activities

Possibly the main attraction to bear cubs is their playful and comical antics. Many activities begin in the den and increase as a new world is opened to their imagination. Deceptively cuddly, cubs emerge from the den with apprehension and require considerable encouragement by the sow. Some walk and run on unsure legs—American black bears initially climb better than they walk—and giant panda mothers carry their cubs from the den.

Their play is a near-constant variety of stomping, vocalizing, exploring, and climbing, with a full display of curiosity and mischievousness. All cubs fight as the learning process begins and will play-fight up to five years of age. They share all of their mother's activities—travel, caution, and feeding—as she prepares them for their life alone.

"Getting them into a sack was one of the liveliest experiences I ever had," Enos Mills in *The Spell of the Rockies* writes of two orphaned cubs. "Though small and almost starved, these little orphans proceeded to 'chew me up' after the manner of big grizzlies, as is told of them in books."

Juvenile giant pandas playing
LYNN M. STONE/NATUREPL.COM

MOTHERHOOD

The drowsy "hibernating" mother, from the moment of giving birth, begins her long effort to ensure her offspring's survival. From initial nourishment through constant protection to teaching them how to survive alone, she is fully and solely responsible. Her maternal behavior is paramount—she is "cubbing," without fatherly assistance.

There is a deep family bond. The mother is affectionate, devoted, protective (aggressive toward threats), sensitive, strict, and attentive to the training of her cubs. Her primary concern is for their safety and education. Considerable knowledge is necessary for the cubs to survive; therefore they remain with their mother for long periods of time, learning from her during this lengthy infancy. The female cubs are the fastest learners.

True motherhood is demonstrated by this grizzly bear sow in Katmai National Park, Alaska.
©JOHNNY JOHNSON

A SOW'S MOST CRITICAL LESSONS FOR HER CUBS

Food

- How to find and eat specific food
- How to catch prey, large and small (a brown bear sow brings a fish to the cubs and opens its side for them to eat)
- What to eat by letting cubs smell her breath
- How to dig
- How to fish

Safety

- How to recognize specific threats (enemies, hazards)
- Sow spanks her cubs to make them obey (very important to their survival)
- Sow cuffs her cubs, sending them up a tree (cubs are natural-born climbers) or scurrying away to safety
- Sow will lure an enemy away from the cubs

"Behind her were two cubs. I caught her impatient expression when she beheld me," wrote Enos Mills. "She stopped, and then, with a growl of anger, she wheeled and boxed cubs right and left like an angry mother. The bears disappeared in the direction from which they had come, the cubs urged on with spanks from behind as all vanished in the falling snow."

A sow with cubs is typically the most dangerous bear. She defends her cubs to whatever degree she believes necessary, bluffing or attacking until she has lessened the threat. She is occasionally persistent, killing and even eating the threat. The sloth bear mother is considered the most fierce defender of her cubs, though the most sensitive and patient teacher. The American black bear sow is less apt to charge than some other species of bears, as she sends her cubs up a tree.

However, if she does charge, she may be quite persistent in the attack. The grizzly bear is more apt to charge to lessen the threat.

Motherhood is not always perfect—cub mortality is high. Sows habituated to human activities and conditioned to human foods teach their offspring these bad and often deadly habits.

Sows will occasionally abandon their young. "Picnickers disturbed a family group," explains James Cardoza in *The Black Bear in Massachusetts*. "The sow treed her three cubs and left the area, not responding even when one cub was captured and carried to a car."

Nursing

"Mammary glands are of course unique in mammals and together with hair distinguish them from all other classes," writes Jean Craighead-George in *Beasty Inventions*. "Because of the position of these glands on the warm chest and bellies, and because the infant needs the mother and the mother the infant, the most intimate relationship of all life is between the mammalian mother and child."

Nursing activities vary with the species and individual cubs. The cubs locate the nipples by sensing the sow's warmth, and individual cubs are known to dominate a specific nipple, appearing to have a favorite side on which to nurse. They are demanding, and nursing is often noisy, with humming, trilling, and purring sounds accompanying feeding. The sow initially nurses on her side, with two nipples normally used during the den period, then sitting up, using four nipples, following emergence from the den. Nursing (lactation) is the greatest energy demand on a sow's body. Sows do not come into estrus while nursing.

American black bear nursing two cubs
BILLLEA.COM

NURSING CHARACTERISTICS

American black bear	Sow has three pairs of functional nipples.
Andean bear	Sow must assist extremely undeveloped cubs for first eight weeks.
Asiatic black bear	Sow has three pairs of functional nipples.
Brown bear	Sow has three pairs of functional nipples.
	Cubs nurse five minutes at a time, four times a day.
Giant panda	Sow has two pairs of functional nipples.
	Cubs nurse six to fourteen times a day (first one to two days); three to four times a day (next sixty days); one to two times a day (next 150 days).
Polar bear	Sow has two pairs of functional nipples.
	Cubs nurse fifteen minutes at a time, six to seven times a day.
Sloth bear	Information unavailable.
Sun bear	Information unavailable.

Alaska bear biologist Larry Aumiller relates an observation of two Alaskan brown bear sows with eight cubs between them. The sows would alternate caring for the cubs, and on one occasion a sow was observed nursing six of them, describes Tom Walker in *The Way of the Grizzly*.

Bear Milk

Bear, and marine mammal, milk is richer in fat and protein, providing three times the energy of the milk of humans and cattle. Bear's milk contains an average of 30 to 33 percent (high of 48 percent) fat, 11 to 15 percent protein, and 0.3 to 0.6 percent carbohydrates. In comparison, human milk contains 3½ to 4 percent fat.

Polar bear milk is the richest, followed by that of brown bears, then black bears. The milk of the tropical bears (sun, giant panda, sloth) is less rich, as they do not face the cold temperatures of the Northern Hemisphere.

"Polar bear milk has the appearance and consistency of condensed milk, with a fish odor," according to Thomas Koch in *The Year of the Polar Bear*. "The composition of polar bear milk reflects the animal's high-fat dietary requirements. Thirty per cent of the milk is fat, whereas the milk we drink contains only 4 per cent fat. The cubs receive almost the same amounts of protein and lactose from their milk as do their young cousins, the seal, the porpoise, and the whale." Barry Lopez comments in *Arctic Dreams* that "those who have tasted of it say it tastes like cod liver oil and smells of seals or fish."

Weaning of Cubs

Weaning is a gradual, sometimes slow, process and will vary with species of bear and the individual family group. Lactation generally peaks in 150 days and ends in approximately 245 days, and by then the cubs will be well established on other foods. However, they may continue to nurse occasionally, some doing so until they separate from their mother.

- **American black bear:** typically nurses for 30 weeks but can eliminate complete nutritional dependence in 22 weeks
- **Andean bear:** typically nurses for 8 weeks
- **Asiatic black bear:** nurses for between 104 and 130 weeks
- **Brown bear:** can nurse for up to 82 weeks but eliminates complete nutritional dependence in 24 weeks
- **Giant panda:** nurses for between 30 and 46 weeks but usually eliminates complete nutritional dependence in 7 to 9 months
- **Polar bear:** nurses for between 74 and 104 weeks
- **Sloth bear:** nurses for between 104 and 156 weeks
- **Sun bear:** usually nurses for 17 weeks

Adoption of Cubs

Sows occasionally adopt cubs. "Adoption and interchange of cubs, thought not common, has been observed in some circumstances," writes Paul Schullery in *The Bears of Yellowstone.*

"Sometimes the cubs of two sows will have the opportunity to play together . . . and actually mix, leaving with the wrong mother. One case of this sort . . . resulted in one of the two sows assuming responsibility for all cubs."

The congregation of bears at major food sources provides the opportunity for cub swapping or adoption as cubs mingle while the sows are fishing. As one sow travels on, her cubs follow, and their newfound friends may follow as well. Tom Walker in *The Way of the Grizzly,* in describing an adoption situation at Alaska's McNeil River, comments, ". . . the females were either quite tolerant of strange cubs or that they had difficulty in identifying their own."

Sows Transporting Cubs

Sows carry their cubs when necessary, normally with their mouths. "Cats grip the back of the neck and dogs take the scruffs, but grizzly and black bears take the entire head of the cub in their mouths to carry them," notes Craighead-George. In some species, the cubs routinely ride on their mother's back to facilitate transportation and to further cement the close sow/cub relationship.

Sloth bear sow transporting cubs, Bandhavgarh National Park, India
E. A. KUTTAPAN/NATUREPL.COM

TRANSPORTATION METHODS

American black bear	Cubs rarely ride on the sow's back
Andean bear	Cubs ride on sow's back if she is frightened and attempting to escape; sow may carry a cub, held against her body with a paw, as she runs on three legs
Asiatic black bear	Information unavailable
Brown bear	A few observations in Alaska of cubs riding on the sow's back
Giant panda	Cub carried in sow's mouth when young; larger young held to chest while sow travels
Polar bear	Cub rides on sow's back on land or in the water; may hang onto sow's tail or rump hairs while walking or swimming
Sloth bear	Cubs ride on sow's back while she walks, runs, and climbs trees; cubs grasp thick tufts of fur between the sow's shoulders, and maintain individual riding positions that do not change (fights occur to maintain the proper positions); sow may carry cubs until they are nine months old; some have been carried until they are a third their mother's size
Sun bear	Information unavailable

"One of the cubs . . . scrambled up to a point of vantage on some rocks and then hopped onto her [sow's] back," describes Frederick Drimmer in *The Animal Kingdom*. "The little fellow rode off in style, hanging on with his paws embedded in his mother's fur. The others in the family trailed along behind."

"We observed female Sloth bears transporting small young on their backs . . . one or two young up to one-third the size of the mother were carried either crosswise or with heads forward," Andrew Laurie and John Seidensticker, "Behavioural Ecology of the Sloth Bear" (*Journal of Zoology*), noted during their studies at Royal Chitawan National Park, Nepal. "A young Sloth bear (age 3 to 5 months) rode on the back, hip and shoulder of the female. Usually the cub was situated on the lower back, grasping the fur if it began to slip or if the female stood up. Fre-quently, if the cub seemed off center, the female would shake vigorously, occasionally flipping the cub all the way over her back; if the cub was too far forward, she would elbow it back."

Social Independence of Cubs

Considerable knowledge is necessary for cubs to survive; thus they remain with their mothers for lengthy periods that vary with species. They may remain with their mother longer in undernourished populations that require more time to learn critically important feeding strategies. Upon sep-

Orphaned cubs, depending on age and climate, are capable of surviving on their own. American black and grizzly bear cubs less than a year old have been known to survive their first winter alone.

Cannibalism in Motherhood

A sow may kill and eat her cubs if she is extremely malnourished. However, a mortally wounded cub may be consumed whether the sow is malnourished or not. The author observed an American black bear sow eat one of her cubs that had just five minutes earlier been struck and killed by a vehicle. The remaining sibling joined its mother at the meal.

HIBERNATION

Hibernation is a state of dormancy and inactivity that is utilized by bears and various other animals to adapt to short winter food supplies. Their body temperature, breathing, and metabolic rate decline during this state. "Hibernation is not so much a response to extreme cold as to a seasonal shortage of food," notes Schullery. "The bear's warm coat is as necessary to it in the den as it would be outside."

arating from the sow, siblings most often remain together for more than a year. "Siblings may remain together for up to four years even without their mother," notes David Brown in *The Grizzly in the Southwest*.

Hibernation of bears is different from some other "hibernators" such as bats, marmots, squirrels, woodchucks, and rodents that are in a deep sleep or state of torpidity, with a very low metabolic rate and temperatures many degrees below normal. Several weeks are required to reach this state of dormancy.

During a bear's hibernation its body temperature drops only about ten to twelve degrees, and its metabolic rate is reduced only by about half. A bear may awaken during a warm period in the winter and move about outside the den, though it remains nearby.

Specific lengths of hibernation depend on climate, location, and the sex, age group, and reproductive status of the individual bear. Some bear species do not hibernate, and populations of hiber-

PERIOD OF TIME WITH SOW

American black bear	16 to 18 months
Andean bear	6 to 8 months
Asiatic black bear	24 to 36 months
	Sow observed with two sets of different-age cubs
Brown bear	In general 17 to 36 months
	Usually den with sow for two additional winters (Arctic: with sow 2 to 4 years; Montana 1 to 3 years)
	Males move out of mother's range
	Females may remain in mother's range
Giant panda	18 to 30 months
Polar bear	16 to 17 months
	Often into third year
Sloth bear	24 to 36 months
Sun bear	Until nearly fully grown

nating species in areas of available foods and warm winter weather may also remain active. Some American black bears in California do not hibernate, as they have an available supply of human foods and garbage. Bears in poor condition, with an inadequate fat reserve, may not hibernate or for only a short period. Early Native Americans considered nonhibernating bears "winter bears."

GENERAL CHARACTERISTICS OF HIBERNATING BEARS

- Do not eat
- Give birth to young
- Do not defecate
- Curl up to conserve heat
- Change position in den
- Are sensitive to their surroundings
- Awaken and move about
- May be aroused and attack an intruder

- Do not urinate
- Temporarily leave den
- Lactate (nurse their young)
- Provide warmth for cubs
- Lick and groom cubs
- Lick self
- Slough paw pads
- Lose weight

"A bear is wiser than man," an old Abnaki Indian sage once philosophized, "because a man does not know how to live all winter without eating anything," related George Bird Grinnell in *When the Buffalo Ran* (as cited by Harold McCracken in *The Beast That Walks Like Man*).

HIBERNATION CHARACTERISTICS OF THE SPECIES

American black bear	Hibernates; some southern populations do not during mild winters; bears of Louisiana, Florida, and Arizona sleep only a few days at a time in a den (nest in hollow tree, cave, shelter under rocks or a fallen tree or in just a shallow excavation in a wooded area); pregnant females hibernate in southern populations; this is the most active bear during the winter
Andean bear	Does not hibernate
Asiatic black bear	Does not hibernate over most of range; may hibernate in colder (northern) regions of habitat; some bears descend to lower elevations; nearly all pregnant females hibernate
Brown bear	Hibernates; considerable variation depending on severity of weather (some male Kodiaks do not hibernate); may den early (September) in far northern regions and hibernate for eight months
Giant panda	Does not hibernate, primarily due to inability to put on fat; descends to lower elevations during harsh winters
Polar bear	Males and nonpregnant females do not hibernate; pregnant females will enter a dormant stage referred to as "denning"
Sloth bear	Does not hibernate
Sun bear	Does not hibernate

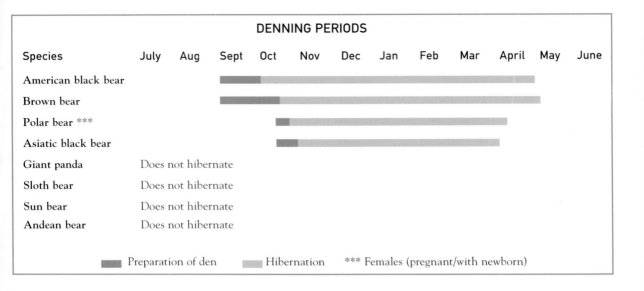

Species	July	Aug	Sept	Oct	Nov	Dec	Jan	Feb	Mar	April	May	June

DENNING PERIODS

American black bear — Preparation of den / Hibernation (Sept–May)
Brown bear (Sept–May)
Polar bear *** (Oct–April)
Asiatic black bear (Oct–April)
Giant panda — Does not hibernate
Sloth bear — Does not hibernate
Sun bear — Does not hibernate
Andean bear — Does not hibernate

■ Preparation of den   ■ Hibernation   *** Females (pregnant/with newborn)

Hibernation Periods

The periods of hibernation typically begin earlier and last longer in the north than in the south, and coastal bears begin hibernation later than inland bears. In North America black bears hibernate earlier than brown bears. Generally, the hibernation periods are longer at the higher latitudes (the polar bear is the exception). Brown/grizzly bears in the Yukon Territory hibernate for approximately seven months, while those in the Yellowstone area only do so for five months. Pregnant females enter their dens early and, with cubs, emerge later. Probably the shortest hibernation period is the sixty to seventy days of the brown bears in Iran.

Preparing to Hibernate

Preparation to hibernate—to den up—begins during late summer and early fall when bears enter hyperphagia (eating enormous quantities of food) to build up fat. According to Robert H. Busch in *The Grizzly Almanac*, "By late fall, a grizzly's weight may be 85 percent higher than it was in the previous spring. One big male on Alaska's Kodiak Island put on 205 pounds (93kg) in 70 days during one fall season."

To accumulate fat, bears:
• Eat high-caloric foods
• Eat nuts
• Drink great quantities of water
• Eat acorns
• May eat 20,000 to 40,000 calories per day
• Eat natural sugars (fruits, berries)

Fat serves as:
• Insulation
• As a food and water reserve

Prior to hibernation (hyperphagia):
• American black bears add 4 inches of fat, gaining two to three pounds a day
• Brown bears add 6 to 8 inches of fat
• Some female bears more than double their weight

- Polar bears do not put on heavy fat for hibernation
- Giant pandas do not hibernate due to their minimal ability to accumulate fat, resulting from the poor nutritional value of bamboo

The Trigger

Bears stop eating shortly before denning. The conditions that trigger their entering the den—the beginning of hibernation—are a combination of the first inclement winter-type weather, a reduction in the supply of high-quality food, decreased mobility due to snow, and increased energy costs of keeping warm. Grizzly bear researchers John and Frank Craighead in *Track of the Grizzly*, noted that a "trigger" was a snowstorm (following an earlier cold snap) with drift-

ing snow that would not thaw and would cover the bear's tracks to the den.

Bear Dens

Bear dens vary in location, aspect, elevation, size, and general construction. Dens are excavated or natural openings and holes or, in some cases, simply a ground nest. They typically have an entrance, tunnel, and chamber, and a vent hole in the case of polar bears. Chamber size depends on the individual bear, but it invariably has good drainage. Though a bear may move up to a ton of material when digging a den, it will relocate if it is disturbed.

Dens are prepared in a secretive manner. Hidden and secure, they provide a quick escape for a bear in danger. Some are even located high up

European brown bear in den entrance, Switzerland
©2008 THOMAS SBAMPATO/ALASKASTOCK.COM

in trees or often protected by surrounding water. A black bear den with three cubs, in Glacier National Park, was found 70 feet up in an opening of a tall tree.

Bedding in a den may consist of grasses, moss, leaves, conifer needles, and tree branches, 7 to 9 inches deep. A den is partially closed with vegetation, which also serves as camouflage. A pregnant sow uses a larger den. Some bears use the same den for several years, while others prepare a new den each year, and some dens are used for decades by *different* bears.

American Black Bear Dens
Location

- Under large boulders
- Scraped-out depression under brush
- Under logs
- Tree cavity, well above ground
- Base of tree or in cavity of tree roots
- A tree den in Louisiana was 96 feet above ground.
- Culverts

- Under buildings
- Small opening (prevent intrusion)
- Half of Louisiana bears use brush piles (fallen treetops), ground nests, and trees.
- Southern slope exposure
- Steep slopes, 20 to 40 percent

Description

- 2 to 3 feet high
- 2½ to 5 feet in diameter
- 6 feet deep
- Good drainage

Brown Bear Dens
Location

- Slope aspect (exposure) varies in different areas.
- 30 percent slope
- Located above valley floor
- Southern slope (North America and Asia)
- Dug under large boulders
- Dug in dry earth

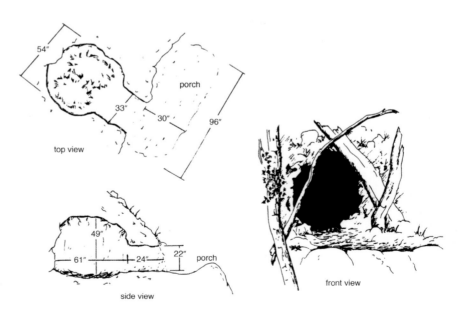

Grizzly bear den
COURTESY INTERAGENCY GRIZZLY BEAR STUDY TEAM (IGBST)

54"
33"
30"
96"
porch
top view

49"
61"
24"
22"
porch
side view

front view

- Eastern slope (Alaska Peninsula)
- Under fallen trees in wet areas (Alaska)
- Northern slope (Kodiak, Alaska)

Description

- 59 inches long
- 39 inches wide
- 25 inches high

Grizzly Bear Dens
Location

- 61 percent on northern slopes (Rocky Mountains)

Description

- 9 to 27 feet into ground
- 1½ feet high
- Tunnel leads to chamber
- up to 9-foot diameter

Polar Bear Dens
Location

- Most on ice within 5 miles of coast
- South facing, 20 to 40 percent slope
- Bear determines correct snow.
- Dug in ice, snow, frozen ground
- Uses deep, drifted snow
- Snow is an excellent insulator.
- May be in a sheltered snowdrift in lee of an ice ridge
- Dug through snow into earth in some areas

Description

- 10- to 15-foot long tunnel, 2-foot diameter, sloping upward into den (cold-air trap like igloo)
- Den temperature may reach 40 degrees Fahrenheit, while below zero outside; den seldom below 32 degrees

Normally only a female digs a den, which is then used by all bears. The den is used for temporary winter shelter, cooling during the summer, and birthing. Pregnant females remain in the den for months.

- Typical den 71 inches in diameter, 36 inches high
- May enlarge den after cubs are born
- Just enough room to turn around

Asiatic Black Bear Dens
Location

- Steep, mountainous, sunny slope
- Hollow log
- Caves, under rocks
- "Old" brown bear dens
- Burrows excavated in hillsides
- Dug out in hollow tree (possibly 60 feet above ground)
- Ground nest (hole in ground)

Description

- Cave (hole), 1½-foot diameter, 6 feet deep
- Thick bed of branches, leaves, grass, and other vegetation

Noticing a steamy vapor rising from a hole in the snow by protruding roots of an overturned tree," describes Enos Mills in *Wild Life on the Rockies*, "I walked to the hole to learn the cause of it. One whiff of the vapor stiffened my hair and limbered my legs. I shot down a steep slope, dodging trees and rocks. The vapor was rank with the odor from a bear." Eskimos have long hunted polar bears using the odor and steam to locate dens.

A Bear's Physiology during Hibernation

Medical research continues to better identify the remarkable physiology that occurs in bears during hibernation. Recycling calcium appears to be the key to the months of inactivity without disastrous physiological effects. According to Seth Donahue, professor of biomedical engineering at Michigan Technological University, in *Good Nappers*, by Lee Dye, 2004 (ABC News), "Bone loss is related to keeping blood calcium at certain levels. . . ." Bears are able to maintain calcium near the correct level because of some "unique features." Bones of mammals, including humans, become thin and brittle with age and inactivity; however, according to Dye, "Donahue and his fellow researchers have found that the bones of a black bear get stronger as it gets older, while ours get weaker."

Lynn L. Rogers of the North American Bear Center writes, ". . . bears living off their accumulated body fat have hibernating cholesterol levels more than twice summer levels and more than twice as high as the normal cholesterol levels of most humans. Yet bears exhibit no hardening of the arteries or formation of cholesterol gallstones.

"Medical studies reveal hibernating bears produce a bile juice, "ursodeoxycholic acid," that may help them avoid problems with gallstones. When this acid is given to people it dissolves gallstones and eliminates the need for surgery. Hibernating black bears also exhibit reduced kidney function. They do not urinate for months but still do not poison their bodies with waste products such as urea. Urea is somehow broken down and its nitrogen is reused to build protein. The ability to build protein while fasting allows black bears to maintain their muscle and organ tissue throughout the winter. They only use up fat. Evidence is accumulating that hormone-like substances control physiological changes in hibernating black bears. These substances also produce hibernation-like effects when injected into other species—both hibernators and non-hibernators, suggesting potential human medical applications."

Physiological Changes in Hibernating Bears

- Bears do not eat, drink, defecate, or urinate during hibernation (approximately four-and-one-half to five months).
- Metabolism slows to approximately 50 to 73 percent of normal (metabolism varies considerably between individuals).
- They use 4,000 calories a day from their fat reserve during hibernation (cholesterol does not develop).
- They lose 15 to 30 percent of their body weight as fat breaks down, providing food and water (polar bear sows may lose 40 percent with hibernation and birthing).
- One gram of fat produces more than a gram of water.
- Digestive organs and kidneys shut down almost completely.
- They exist on foods and fluids stored in body.
- Blood contains high levels of circulating fat, including cholesterol.
- Blood is more concentrated to head and upper body.
- Poisonous wastes and byproducts are broken down and reabsorbed.
- Paw pads are sloughed and replaced with new pads.

- They do not dehydrate.
- Their temperature declines.
- Females begin lactation.
- The heart rate declines.

Respiration
- Only one-half of the normal oxygen intake is required; breathing declines to half that of an active bear.

Heart rate
- Declines to 8 to 12 BPM (resting: 40 to 50 BPM)
- Returns to normal over a few weeks if it is disturbed

Temperature
- Declines into a basic range of 87 to 95 degrees Fahrenheit
- Polar bear's temperature drops one degree below normal; needs body temperature due to pregnancy and arctic conditions
- Declines in relation to the outside temperatures but does not drop below 59 degrees in the den

Anal plug
A tough, fibrous plug often found in and about a den has long been identified as an anal plug, with an uncertain purpose. Two opposing theories attempt to explain the development of this block in a bear's lower digestive tract:

- Formed by food remnants and dead cells that occur during hibernation
- Formed by indigestible materials (animal hair, own hair, nut hulls, wood, dirt, moss, grass, and other plant materials) eaten during the final few days before hibernation, for the specific purpose of blocking the anus

Emergence from the Den

Early civilizations of the world, especially Native Americans, considered a bear's emergence from the den a return from the dead—a rebirth. The emergence process is typically slow with sniffing, limping, stretching, limbering stiff muscles, grooming, yawning, and scratching. The bear appears groggy but is healthy.

- Males and poorly conditioned bears emerge first; sows with cubs, last.
- Sows emerge ready to protect their young, remaining close to the den, probably acclimating cubs to the outside.
- Cubs may begin climbing the first day.
- Bears are drowsy and lethargic for several days.
- They display some weakness.
- Some bears are extremely emaciated.
- Some bears emerge at one-half their prehibernation weight.
- A few bears weigh near their pre-den weight.
- Most often, they are in good shape.
- Some bears continue to lose weight for approximately two months.
- They are not immediately interested in food.
- They seek large quantities of water and will eat snow if water is unavailable.
- They feed lightly at first, but before long they will seek:
  - High-protein foods
  - Roots and herbs to clear kidneys and digestive system
  - Chaff (nondigestible) to clear system
  - Old berries and rose hips left from the fall
  - New grasses, small roses
  - Winterkill carcasses

Robert Busch, in *The Grizzly Almanac*, relates a comment by Beth Day (*Grizzlies in Their Backyard*, 1994). "Some grizzlies are remarkably constant in their dates of emergence; one old male in the Knight Inlet area of British Columbia emerged on the same day (April 15) for eight years. . . ."

DAY BEDS

Located near food sources and often with a commanding view, day beds are utilized by all bears for short- or long-period resting. A bear may have several day beds throughout its range. Nonhibernating bears may use day beds as birthing beds.

"There is a dense grove of Englemann spruce and lodgepole pine nearby, in a particularly dense part of which the mother bear scoops out a cozy bowl just big enough for her and the cubs," describes Thomas McNamee in *The Grizzly Bear*. "She rips down green spruce boughs and lines the depression to form a springy, heat trapping mattress. Curled up here, concealed to perfection within defensive-charging distance of their meat cache, the bear and her young may sleep their breakfast off in watchful security."

American black bear	In trees, stretched out on limbs; on ground (bare areas, grass, conifer needles)
Andean bear	Platform of broken branches in a tree or at junction of tree trunk and first major limb; nest of small branches, leaves, sticks, twigs, and other plant material; rests sitting with forelegs in front of its chest; often used as a feeding platform
Asiatic black bear	In trees, 15 feet or higher, nest of branches; may use treetop nest to feed; nests on ground; spends much of winter in day bed; sleeps in sitting position
Brown bear	On ground (grassy areas, conifer needles); in shallow depressions dug in soil or snow (lined or unlined)
Giant panda	Base of trees; under stumps or overhanging rocks; crevices of ledges; hollow trees; rock caves; bed of bamboo sticks, wood dust, twigs, and other vegetation; enough room to sit upright; prefers 6 to 9 percent slope
Polar bear	Digs "dens" in snow, ice, or dirt for summer cooling; digs pits at the shoreline and anywhere in the snow (some as simple as a shallow scraping); sow and cubs have day beds as high as possible to detect danger; lines resting sites with moss and lichens
Sloth bear	Anywhere; nests of broken branches in a tree or at junction of trunk and first major branch; cave during rainy season
Sun bear	Platform (nest) of broken branches, 6½ feet to 23 feet high in a tree; rests lying on belly

The Asiatic black bears in Japan, "Have a queer habit not found among bears elsewhere," writes Phyllis Osteen in *Bears Around the World*. "They build what observers call 'basking couches.' These are oval cushions made from twigs and branches, laid on sunny slopes in front of winter lairs."

"We find a bear's nest in a hackberry—our first sign of the Asiatic black bear," writes Peter Matthiessen in *The Snow Leopard*. "The bear sits in the branches and bends them toward him as he feeds on cherry-like fruits; the broken branches make a platform which the bear may then use as a bed."

BEAR HABITATS

Bears have adapted to various environments, including tropical forests, swamps, tundra and taiga, ice floes, deserts, the arctic, high mountains, and from sea level to nearly 14,000 feet (18,000 to 20,000 feet on some occasions).

The species—and individuals, too—have their primary (preferred) niches of varying habitat qualities that provide remoteness, food, cover, protection, mating opportunities, and denning sites. Bears' sizes may be influenced by habitat quality. Poor habitats normally produce relatively smaller bears, while an environment with an abundance of highly nutritional foods, such as major fish populations, produces large bears. "In the coastal areas of Alaska and British Columbia," notes Terry Domico in *Bears of the World*, "live the largest brown bears found on the North American continent."

	American Black	Brown	Polar	Asiatic Black	Giant Panda	Sloth	Sun	Andean
PRIMARY HABITATS								
Arctic/alpine tundra	X	X						
Arctic coastal regions			X					
Arctic (seas/ice)			X					
Bamboo thickets/mountain forest				X	X			
Brush savannahs/steppe						X		X
Cloud forests					X			
Coastal rainforest	X	X						
Coniferous forests	X			X				
Damp forests								X
Deciduous forests	X			X		X	X	
Deciduous monsoon forests						X		
Desert (open country)		X		X				X
Estuaries		X						
Forests (subtropical/tropical lowland)								X
Grasslands						X		X
Mixed forests	X	X		X				
Pine/broadleaf forests	X							
Plantations (agricultural areas)						X	X	
Swamps	X							
Thornbrush forests				X				
Thornbrush woodlands						X		X
Treeless/open tundra		X						
Treeless/scarcely forested		X						
Tropical rainforest/cloudforest				X			X	X

Polar bear along
Manitoba coast
©JOHNNY JOHNSON

Grizzly bears in their natural habitat of the Rocky Mountains
COURTESY YELLOWSTONE NATIONAL PARK

Bear Elevations

Individuals remain at the same general elevation but may range between elevations during day-to-day or week-to-week searches for food. They may also range between elevations seasonally, and normally move to a different elevation to den.

Representative elevations for each species:

American black bear	Sea level to 10,000 feet
Andean bear	820 to 15,000 feet in general
	1,900 to 6,400 feet (west, central, eastern Andes Mountains)
	Wide range of elevation in Peru
	An Andean bear climbed from 820 feet to 10,827 feet in twenty-four hours, an elevation gain that would take a human four to five days (Andean story)
Asiatic black bear	Sea level to 11,800 feet; occasionally to over 14,000 feet in the Himalayas (summer)
	Down to 4,920 feet during winter
	Occasionally near sea level in Japan
Brown bear	Most widely distributed species in elevation
	General range sea level to 10,000 feet
	Occasionally to 16,000 feet
	"Red Bear" of Asia is often in the yak pastures at 18,000 feet and in Bhundar at 20,000 feet
Giant panda	General range: 3,600 to 11,150 feet
	Primary summer range: 8,900 to 10,500 feet
	Known to have gone up to 13,250 feet during summer
	Ranges down to 2,600 feet during winter
	Lower elevations limited by cultivation and habitation
Polar bear	Sea level
Sloth bear	Sea level to base of the Himalayas
	Prefers low-elevation forests below 3,300 feet
Sun bear	Sea level to over 9,100 feet
	Prefers 1,600 to 4,600 feet

Bear Density

Bear densities vary seasonally throughout numerous habitats with food sources—such as streams congested with spawning fish and areas of poor food—being significant influences. Human populations and activities—urban and suburban sprawl, for example—also influence bear densities. Bears are displaced and crowded into the remaining undeveloped—and typically small—areas of inadequate quality for bear survival. The bears are forced upward into mountain ranges, as well as laterally. Populations are fragmented, and isolated groups may be so small they are unable to adequately reproduce for survival.

Bear Ranges

Bears have home ranges but are not territorial. They do not defend a territory from other bears, and the habitats of different species and individuals overlap. The ranges of males are normally three to five times larger than those of females. Adult female brown bears (in North America) have ranges two to five times larger than those of adult female American black bears.

Movement of bears is in response to available food sources, and hierarchy may dictate habitat niches for subadults or family groups that avoid dominant male bears. The poorer a bear's habitat in relation to food, the larger its range. Ranges

Giant panda in a "reserve" habitat
© SHUTTERSTOCK

"The two combatants were fighting at close quarters, the elk fighting for his life, the bear endeavoring to kill, probably for food," described park employee Lester Abbie in Paul Schullery's *Yellowstone Bear Tales*. "The bear [grizzly] had the elk gripped around the neck with his forepaws and was endeavoring to throw the elk, after the fashion of a rodeo performer bulldogging a steer. The elk in turn was endeavoring to get free and by so doing was shoving the bear around backward along the road."

". . . I followed a grizzly bear's trail through the snow," writes Tom Walker in *We Live in the Alaskan Bush*. "Twice I found places where the bear had made leaps of six feet or more and each time a small red splotch in the snow revealed that the grizzly—the biggest predator in North America—was effortlessly catching snowshoe hares."

"They will eat some of the lowliest crud in the world," relates Thomas McNamee in *The Grizzly Bear*, "but they still know a square meal when it comes along."

Giant Panda

- Bamboo approximately 99 percent of diet
- Has sixty species of bamboo available
- Has very low level of digestibility
- Intestines five to seven times body length (approximate size of a house cat's; horse's twenty times body length)
- Digestion aided by microbial action in intestines
- Must eat often and for long periods of time to gain the necessary nutrition; caloric intake only slightly more than calorie expenditure
- May consume 31 to 85 pounds of bamboo per day (97 feces droppings per day average)
- One giant panda ate parts of 2,232 bamboo stems in one day.
- Sits and brings food to its mouth with paws

"It has a good sense of taste and smell which seems unnecessary for an animal that eats only bamboo," notes Clive Roots in *The Bamboo Bears*.

Giant panda with bamboo, its nearly singular food
ISTOCKPHOTO.COM/BRYAN FAUST

Polar Bear

- Most carnivorous (approximately 99 percent) of the bears
- Only bear that spends more time in the water and eats more meat than the brown bear
- Ringed seals are the primary food (one ringed seal yields 60,000 calories).
- Utilizes bearded seals, marine mammal carcasses, seabirds, vegetation
- Stalks areas with open water and active movement of ice, where it is most apt to find seals
- Does not swim to catch seals, most often catching them at their breathing holes
- Stands to observe and locate a dark object (seal) on the ice
- Often synchronizes feeding on seals with the seal's patterns of sleeping alongside its breathing hole
- Catches prey one out of fifty attempts
- Stomach capacity is 154 pounds (large male).
- Able to eat 10 percent of bodyweight in thirty minutes
- Eats skin and blubber first (100 to 150 pounds of blubber per meal)
- One seal is energy for eleven days, though a bear typically kills and eats a seal once every four to five days.
- Will beg for blubber from whaling ships
- Eats berries during the summer (butt and muzzle stained bluish); digs puffins (birds) out of their burrows

Polar bears use a number of feeding strategies and tools, according to Feazel. They "push ice or snow blocks ahead of them as they slither close to the breathing holes . . . build walls of snow to hide behind and they use blocks of ice to smash through the icy crust that covers a [seal's] breathing hole."

Sloth Bear

- The "insectivore" of the bears, though a generalist feeder as well
- Expert termite hunter; discovers termites by smell (termites are the reliable year-round staple)
- Capable of locating a grub 3 feet deep in the ground
- Specialized snout for vacuuming termites and ants; lacks two incisor teeth; has long snout and lips that form a tube; closes nostrils by pressing down nose pad; tongue long and flat
- Noisy; sucking sound heard more than 200 yards away
- Does not meet in feeding groups like other bears, due to even food dispersal
- Supplements diet with dates, berries, and a variety of vegetation
- Fruits are important April through June.
- Rarely preys on other mammals or feeds on carrion

"To get them [termites] the bear smashes a

Sloth bear displaying elongated "sucking" snout
© SHUTTERSTOCK

rotten log or tears open a termite mound with its long claws," describe Paul Shepard and Barry Sanders in *The Sacred Paw.* "At the same time it alternately blows away the dirt and wood chips and sucks up termites. . . ."

Sloth bears in India utilize the fleshy flowers of the Mohwa tree and therefore are in competition with humans, who ferment the flowers to make an alcoholic beverage.

Sun Bear

- Uses exceptionally long tongue for specialized feeding
- Tongue probably evolved for eating honey
- A true "omnivore"; eats small vertebrates, invertebrates, fruits, and a variety of vegetation, too

The feeding antics of a bear may be quite amusing. "A six hundred pound grizzly bear may be seen leaping about in a meadow pouncing on grasshoppers, mice, ground squirrels, or licking up a line of ants," describes George Laycock in *The Wild Bears.*

Some feeding situations are ludicrous but quite serious for the hungry bear. "A polar bear jumped on the back of a surfacing whale, went down with it, and came up again still trying to bite a mouthful of blubber off the forty-ton behemoth," describes Frank Dufresne in *No Room for Bears.*

Other bear-feeding behaviors manifest themselves in different ways. An American black bear in British Columbia was observed sitting in a bald eagle nest, high in a tree. The actions of a pair of adult eagles nearby indicated they had lost eggs or young eaglets to the bear. Charles Darwin in *The Origin of Species* described a feeding behavior you might expect from an American black bear:

BENEFITS OF BEAR FEEDING BEHAVIOR

A bear's feeding activities:

- Prevent spread of diseases because it eats sick and dead animals (wild and domestic)
- Reduce rodent and insect populations
- Spread seeds via fecal material (a single feces was once found to contain 309 seeds of a plant)
- Prepare seedbeds for germination by its digging
- Fertilize riparian growth with fish remains
- May increase the soil's nitrogen content
- Provide other animals with scraps and remains of its own food

---

"In North America the black bear was seen by Hearne [English explorer] swimming for hours with widely open mouth, thus catching, almost like a whale, insects in the water." Andean bears will jump on the back of a cow, biting hunks from its shoulders; if the animal does not die from this action, the bear strikes it down and drags it into the forest.

The extremes in the use of vegetation (or meat) are the polar bear (at approximately 1 percent vegetation) and the giant panda (at approximately 99 percent vegetation), placing them at the very opposite ends of the scale from each other.

"It was digging out mice, and now and then a ground squirrel," wrote Charles Sheldon in *The Wilderness of Denali*, describing a feeding grizzly bear. "The mice had made tunnels under the snow leading from their holes. The bear, evidently scenting a mouse in a tunnel, would plunge its nose into the snow, its snout ploughing through, often as far as ten feet, until the mouse had gone down into its hole in the ground; then the bear would dig it out and catch it with a paw."

"If there were not considerable uncertainty in ground-squirrel hunting," relates Adolph Murie in *A Naturalist in Alaska*, "the bears would no doubt devote more time to it. But there is a limit to the amount of gambling they can indulge in, and even if successful they must return to foods, which are available in quantity to fill their rapidly emptying paunches. The ground squirrel has been referred to as the staff of life of the grizzly, but it is only a side dish." However, in some areas of the north, ground squirrels are an important source of protein. According to Ned Rozell in his article for Alaska Science Forum, "Farthest North Grizzlies Among Alaska's Most Adaptable" (Article #1350), "In a Canadian study of barren ground grizzlies, one bear dug up and ate 357 ground squirrels in six weeks."

Andean bear eating tall grass plant, Ecuador, South America
JIM CLARE/NATUREPL.COM

SEASONAL AVAILABILITY OF FOODS

"The different species of bears have characteristic food habits that depend in part on the environment and in part on adaptive food preferences," note Shepard and Sanders. "All bears are omnivorous, but the proportion of meat to plants in their diets varies, not only among different species but seasonally and with availability."

Food Sources

- Aquatic habitats
- Caches of other animals
- Dens of other animals
- Human sources (food and garbage that are easily digested)
- Ranging prey animals
- Natural food in the ground (vegetation, bulbs, animals, insects)
- Natural food above ground (vegetation, fruit, animals, insects)
- Nests
- Trees (fruits, birds, eggs)
- On the arctic ice

Bark Stripping

The sap and cambium layer of various trees (mostly conifers) are highly sought by bears in many areas. They grab the bark of a tree with their teeth and tear a strip, or even a sheet, down to the ground. Some bears bite large chunks from the trees. They then lick, pushing their nose and tongue up and down the exposed sapwood, enjoying the sweet sap. The major nutrient of the sap is sugar (5 percent), with minor elements of minerals and nitrogen.

". . . the bear was lapping at the trunk as if it were a candy stick," described Roger Conter in Paul Schullery's *Yellowstone Bear Tales*.

Stripping bark for sap is observed in the brown, American black, and Asiatic black bears. This activity may girdle and kill trees, resulting in a serious economic problem (millions of dollars lost annually) in the valuable timber forests of the Pacific Northwest and East Coast of North America and in Asia.

In the state of Washington, the species of trees preferred by bears (in order of preference) are Douglas fir, western hemlock, western red cedar, silver fir, Sitka spruce, lodgepole pine, and alpine fir.

Management programs have been developed in an attempt to reduce the stripping damage. Supplemental feeding during the spring and hunting by sportsmen and hired hunters to reduce the bear populations are major management actions.

Cannibalism

"Infanticide and cannibalism," according to Bettyann Kevles in *Females of the Species*, "may derive from different strategies to solve different problems. Male infanticide appears to be the deliberate elimination of a competitor's offspring. Cannibalism, on the other hand, seems to be simply a way of filling an empty belly."

The bear possesses "a gruesome and cannibal fondness for the flesh of his own kind," noted Theodore Roosevelt in *The Works of Theodore Roosevelt*. "A bear carcass will toll a brother bear to the ambushed hunter better than most any other bait."

Adult polar bears, not uncommonly, will resort to cannibalism to survive a summer, but "during a period [in the past] when heavy ice conditions made seals difficult for bears to obtain," relates J. W. Lentfer in "Polar Bear," his article in *Wild Mammals of North America* (Chapman and Feldhamer 1982), "an adult male [polar bear] had followed a female and two cubs approximately 3 km [1.9 miles] and then killed and nearly completely consumed both cubs." More recently, as the Arctic sea ice diminishes, hungry polar bears are resorting to cannibalism, seeking sows and cubs in their dens. An account by Ian R. Stone and Andrew E. Derocher in *Cambridge Journals*, 2007, relates, ". . . a cub of some 7 months was killed by an adult male bear, which was in poor condition, in the close proximity of the mother, which was also in poor condition. It seems probable that the attack was made for nutritional gain."

"Black bears occasionally kill and sometimes eat members of their own species," relates Cardoza. "Jonkel and Cowan . . . observed that some small bears . . . were killed [and eaten] by larger bears." An American black bear killed and consumed a smaller black bear in Yellowstone National Park during what was not necessarily a poor food year.

Accounts of bear cannibalism are common. The meat from old carcasses of bears, and those freshly killed, is consumed as bears, being omnivorous and opportunistic feeders, take advantage of the available foods. Some scientists believe cannibalism is a measure of population control among bears.

Salt Licks

Bears throughout the world use natural salt licks to supplement their mineral requirements and have also been observed at domestic livestock salt blocks.

Water

Bears drink water in a sucking and vacuuming manner, rather than lapping like a cat or dog. They prefer wading into the water if possible, so their heads are near water level. There is considerable slurping and gulping, and they must stop to breath. They drink several times a day, depending on the species and the individual bear's activities. However, the giant panda hardly drinks more than once a day, due to the high water content of its food. The sloth bear requires a considerable amount of water and drinks at least twice daily. In captivity bears drink between five and fifteen gallons of water a day.

Andean bears obtain considerable moisture from plants that act as natural basins to collect rain and comprise most of the Andean bear's food.

PERIODS OF ACTIVITY

Bears are more naturally diurnal than nocturnal, their primary activity period occurring during daylight hours; however, the amount of diurnal activity varies between species and individuals. They are adaptable, and their activities may become more nocturnal, with some geographic and seasonal variations, when human presence and impacts (recreation, development, and hunting) increase. "Another aspect of human contact," writes Paul Schullery in *American Bears*, is that "bears became nocturnal where they were hunted. This is entirely possible (though some bears are nocturnal under natural circumstances anyway), bears being remarkably adjustable animals."

The period when bears are active may be related to food requirements; however, activity periods for some bears are affected by temperature, weather, and lunar phases. One study, for example, indicated grizzly bears are:

- Active when the temperature is between 72°F and 12 degrees Fahrenheit
- Most active when the temperature is between 42 and 52 degrees Fahrenheit
- Active in the fog and a moderate rain
- Least active during the period of a full moon
- Most active during a new moon
- Seldom active on the night of the new moon

The giant panda, with a poor nutritional diet, must spend more time (day and night, though it is more active around dawn) seeking bamboo and eating and therefore is active 59 percent (on the average) of the day.

- Foraging (traveling/seeking and eating food) 55 percent
- Resting (sleeping, etc.) 40.9 percent
- Grooming, social activities, etc. 4.1 percent

Giant pandas actively move and feed over fourteen hours per day:

- 65 percent of the day during the spring
- 52 percent of the day during the summer
- 62 percent of the day during the winter
- 59 percent of the year

The bottom line could be that any bear may be active at any time.

ACTIVE PERIODS

American black bear	Crepuscular (twilight) in spring and fall
	Nocturnal in summer
	Nocturnal near human activity
Andean bear	Diurnal in heavy forest habitat
	Nocturnal in open-country habitat
	Some crepuscular (twilight) activity
Asiatic black bear	Primarily nocturnal; some bears diurnal
	Nocturnal near human activity
Brown bear	Diurnal
Giant panda	Diurnal
	Some nocturnal activity
Grizzly bear	Diurnal
	Nocturnal near human activity
Polar bear	Nocturnal and diurnal
Sloth bear	More nocturnal than other bears
	Sows with cubs are more diurnal
Sun bear	Primarily nocturnal
	Considerable diurnal activity

OTHER "BEAR" ANIMALS

Several animals throughout the world are referred to as bears due to their actions and appearance (but not necessarily total appearance) but in fact are not bears.

Aardvark (*Orycteropus afer*); Antbear

Piglike body, bulky, quite small, nearly naked, long tongue, insect eater (mostly termites) like the sloth bear. Noted for its burrowing powers. Africa (Sudan, Ethiopia to South Africa)

Beruang Rambai

In Jeffrey McNeely and Paul Wachtel's *Soul of the Tiger*, a biologist describes an unidentified, large primatelike animal of central Borneo: ". . . this 'hairy bear' was neither bear nor orangutan but probably a relict species of *something*."

A Big-Snouted Bearlike Beast; Karrai

The natives of Abyssinia claim to have hunted the beast to extinction (Dufresne).

Binturong (*Arctictis binturong*): Bearcat, Palawan Bearcat, Asian Bearcat

A carnivore of the civet family with the face of a cat, poor eyesight, the long tail of a monkey, and the body and slow, heavy gait of a bear. Vicious and mean when cornered. Southeast Asia rainforests

Giant Anteater (*Myrmecophohaga tridactyla*): Antbear

Not at all bearlike; a typical anteater with long claws; hugs (erroneously considered bearlike) attackers. Eats termites and ants. Central and South America

Kinkajou (*Potos flavus*): Honey Bear

An arboreal mammal of tropical Central and South America that has brownish fur and a long tail. The French word *quincajou* (Algonquian language) is associated with *quingwaage* (Ojibwa), meaning wolverine. Even with its questionable bearlike appearance, it was called honey bear and sugar bear because it sought bee trees and consumed the honey. Several of today's bears are referred to as honey bears.

Koala Bear (*Phascolarctos cinereus*)

An Australian marsupial (it has a pouch for its young) that originally was called a bear by the early English settlers of Australia due to its rotund, bearlike appearance. The koala has also been described as a fat bear cub and is sometimes called the Australian bear or Native bear. In 1925 Willard Colcord in *Animal Land* included the "Koala" as a bear: "The Australian bear is diminutive in size, and quite inoffensive." The status of the koala is considered "near threatened."

Lesser (Red) Panda (*Ailurus fulgens*): Red Cat-Bear, Cloud Bear, Fox Bear, Bear-Cat

Has characteristics of bears and raccoons, with 2-foot-long tail and long claws. The red panda is not a bear but is closely related to the raccoon. Himalayas, India, Nepal, China

Northern Fur Seal (*Callorhinus ursinus*): Sea-Bear

In no manner bearlike. Large, 300 to 600 pounds, more at home on land than true seals. Northern Pacific (California to Alaska) coasts. Arctic explorers and hunters in the 1800s called this fur seal the "sea bear," a name occasionally heard today.

Porcupine (*Erethizon dorsatum*)

The basic porcupine has occasionally been referred to as the prickly bear.

Raccoon (*Procyon lotor*)

The fur of the familiar Western Hemisphere raccoon was once known in the "trade" as Alaskan-Bear. North America and south to northern South America

Tree Hyrax (*Dendrohyrax arboreus*): Tree Bear

A rabbit-size tree dweller; not at all bearlike, though called a tree bear; actually more closely related to elephants. Eastern and southern Africa

Wassenbear

A European raccoon that is called a bear because it looks and acts like a little bear; the bear that washes its food (German: *wasser* means water).

Water Bear

An abundant (800-plus species) microscopic (1 mm or .04 inch long) invertebrate, with four pairs of legs and four to eight claws on each leg; crawls "bearlike" with a pawing motion; found in salt and fresh water, lichens, plant materials, moss, and soils occurring within tropical and arctic environments.

Wolverine (*Gulo luscus*): Skunk Bear, Devil Bear, Bearlike Weasel

The wolverine was called the "long-tailed mud bear" by Philetus Norris, the second superintendent of Yellowstone National Park, for reasons lost with time. Wolverines and bears are both often labeled "gluttons" due to their eating habits, and there exist some behavioral characteristics (tearing apart cabins, robbing traplines) similar to both animals.

Part II
Bears in the Human World

Bears and Indians have lived together on the continent of North America for thousands of years. Both walked the same trails, fished the same salmon streams, dug camas roots from the same fields, and year after year, harvested the same berries, seeds, and nuts. The relationship was one of mutual respect. But it went well beyond that. Bears were often central to the most basic rites of many tribes. . . .

—David Rockwell
Giving Voice to Bear

CHAPTER 5

The Influence of Bears on Humans

Bears in many ways remain in *their world*, in spite of us, who have placed them in the *human world*, interfering with, impacting, and influencing them and applying to them our anthropomorphic interpretations and attitudes.

ANTHROPOMORPHISM

For as long as humans and bears have lived together, the former have applied their images, perceptions, beliefs, and feelings to bears. And just possibly the bears have thought to them-

selves, *that "thing"* (or whatever a bear considers us) *acts just like a bear*. Therefore, this section is compiled without the slightest worry of appearing anthropomorphic—we *are* just that!

We anthropomorphize many animals, though few as often as bears, and maybe for a good

A curious black bear explores the human world. © SHUTTERSTOCK

reason—there are considerable anatomical and behavioral similarities. To begin with, bears and humans share mammalian traits, but also we judge bears by our own senses, abilities, and behavior. For instance, bears stand bipedally and even occasionally walk in that manner; sit on their tails (rumps), lean back against objects to rest, and may even fold a leg across their other leg; appear human when skinned; scratch their backs against stationary objects; snore; yawn; eat the same foods as humans; enjoy sweets; eat with paws (hands); use paws and claws with dexterity; leave human-like footprints; produce similar feces; nurse and discipline their young, even spank; display moods and obvious affection during courting (petting); and are inquisitive, curious, and inflexible. We describe them as intelligent, emotional, assertive, sensitive, aware, devious, cunning, and capable of reasoning (more than can be said of some humans), and their teenagers (the two- to three-year-olds) display the same "*look out, world—here I come*" attitude—all humanlike characteristics. And as Paul Schullery notes in his writings, bears may be "good" or "bad" depending on how they fit the "human plan."

"It is the bear's broad, searching, persistent openness that makes contact with us," note Paul Shepard and Barry Sanders in *The Sacred Paw*, "that flash of recognition in which men instantly perceive a fellow being whose questing provocation, whose garrulous, taciturn, lazy ways, even whose obligations and commitments to hunt, to hole up, and to dominate the space he lives in are familiar." Walt Disney in those wonderful movies and Ernest Thompson Seton in his descriptive writings attributed human traits to bears. According to David Rockwell in *Giving Voice to Bear*, ". . . the Yavapai of Arizona said, 'Bears are like people except that they can't make fire.'"

Our anthropomorphic interpretations are sometimes quite dangerous, as we perceive this wild animal to be amusing and bumbling. "By the time we reach grade school," writes George Laycock in *The Wild Bears*, "we already have a twisted idea of the character and behavior of the black bear. We are conditioned by children's books and television. Gentle Ben, Teddy Bears, Smokey Bear, we know and love them all and are sometimes shocked to learn that this roly-poly clown, or his mother, would do us bodily harm."

"Of the major carnivores that walk the wilderness trails of North America, three, the wolf, the mountain lion, and the bear, have cast an especially strong spell on human imagination and influenced substantially the lives of those who live where they are found," comments Ben East in *Bears*. "And of that somewhat mystifying trio, the bears have exercised by far the greatest influence."

Humanization terms include the following:

- Aggressive
- Lazy
- Cautious
- Mysterious
- Courageous
- Nasty
- Curious
- Shy
- Defiant
- Solitary
- Ferocious
- Strong
- Fun loving
- Unpredictable
- Funny
- Vicious
- Gluttonous
- "King of the American Wilderness"
- Intelligent

Shepard and Sanders note that the "combination of overall awareness and seeming nonchalance is among the bear's most manlike capacities: a taciturn, calculating mixture of knowing and blasé sophistication that can be unnerving to human observers."

American Indian legend relates that the grizzly bear is the ancestor of the race. "Him arms and him legs, jus like Indians." The Cree Indians, according to Harold McCracken in *The Beast That Walks Like Man*, describe the grizzly bear as "him stomach . . . him heart . . . him everything all-same. Him walk like Indian too."

BEAR—THE WORD

The word "bear" and its derivatives play an important and common part in our everyday conversations. Because it is a basic and versatile expression in the structure of our language, dictionaries devote numerous pages to the meaning of "bear" as a common noun but most prominently as a verb. Here is a sample lexicon:

Arctic *adj*: characteristic of the North Pole, the polar regions; "artik" derived from *articus* (Medieval Latin); Greek *arktikos*, from *arktos*, meaning bear

Arcturus *noun*: 1: The brightest star in the constellation Boötes, Arcturus is approximately thirty-six light-years from earth; 2: *Arktouros* (Greek); *Arcturus* is in a position behind the tail of Ursa Major, "guardian of the Bear"; *arktos*, bear plus *ouros*, a guard

Bear *noun*: 1: the variety of normally omnivorous mammals of the Ursidae family or any of the many animals that resemble bears; 2: A person who is crude, clumsy, awkward, or ill-mannered; 3: A hard-working, tough person of enormous endurance

Bear *verb* (bore, bare, borne, bearing, bears): 1: to carry, support, hold up; 2: to carry on one's person, convey; 3: to carry as if in the mind; maintain: <bearing love for others>; 4: to transmit at large <bearing glad tidings>; 5: to have as a visible characteristic <bearing a scar on his right arm>; 6: to carry oneself in a specific way; to conduct; 7: to have a tolerance for; endure; 8: to have a susceptibility to; admit to <the case will bear investigation>; 9: to produce; bring forth; yield; give birth; 10: to offer; render <bearing witness>; 11: to move by steady pressure; to push; 12: to attack with arms; wage war on <to bear arms>; 13: to prove right or justified; confirm; 14: to be patient or tolerant with

Bear *noun*: Old English *bear*; from Indo-European root "brown," "brown animal"

Bear-Baiting *noun*: the medieval "sport" of pitting dogs or bulls against a chained bear

Bearish *adj*: 1: considered to be like a bear; 2: characterization of falling stock market prices

Black Bear *noun*: the two black bear species, *Ursus americanus* of North America and *Ursus thibetanus* of Asia; brown (all shades) or black in color

Grisly *adj*: terrible; horrifying; gruesome

Grison *noun*: the two carnivorous mammals (*Grison vittatus* or *Grison cuja*) of Central and South America that have "grizzled" fur

Grizzle *verb*: to cause to be grizzly, grayish

Grizzly *adj*: 1: grayish; streaked, interspersed or flecked with gray 2: a grizzly bear

rkso- *noun*: an Indo-European word root; bear; *ursus* (Latin—bear, ursine); *arktos* (Greek—bear, arctic, Arcturus); *arto* (Celtic—bear, Arthur)

Ursa *noun*: Latin, meaning a she-bear; feminine of *ursus* (a bear); constellations Ursa Major and Ursa Minor

Ursine *adj*: pertaining to a bear; bear family; bearlike; *Ursinus* (Latin—bear, Ursus)

Ursuline *noun*: a member of an order of nuns of the Roman Catholic Church, founded approximately 1537 and faithful to girls' education. Named after Saint Ursula

"Bear" Origins

Bear	From the nickname bere, "bear"
Berg	Medieval; the mountain home of the bear people
Bruin	Nickname (Bruin the bear) given an animal character (beast) in a series of stories during the tenth century in France or Flanders
Grisly	Anglo-Saxon, *grislic*, meaning "horrible," as in monster, demon
Horribilus	How people perceived the grizzly bear
Bernard, Gilbert, Herbert, and **Roger**	Originate from "bear"

"BEAR" ELSEWHERE

The Eight Species in—	Spanish	French
American black bear	Oso negra de Americano	Ours noir
Andean bear (Spectacled)	Oso Andino	Ours a lunettes
Asiatic black bear	Oso negro de Asiatico	Ours a collier
Brown bear	Oso café (Oso grande)	Ours brun
Giant panda	Oso panda	Grand panda
Polar bear	Oso polar	Ours blanc
Sloth bear	Oso bezudo	Ours lippu
Sun bear	Oso Malayo	Ours des cocotiers

"BEAR" IN OTHER LANGUAGES

Albanian	*arush*
Belarusian	*miadzvedz*
Bulgarian	*mechok*
Canadian	bear; *ours* (French)
Chinese	*xiong*
Czech	*medved*
Danish	*bjorn*
Dutch	*beer*
English	*bear*
Estonian	*karu*
Farsi (Persian)	*khirs*
Finnish	*karhu*
French	*ours*
German	*bar*
Greek	*arctos*
Hebrew	*dob*
Hindu	*bhalu*
Hungarian	*medve*
Italian	*orso*
Japanese	*karma*
Korean	*kom*
Latin	*ursus*
Latvian	*lacis*
Lithuanian	*meska*
Nepalese	*bhaalu*
Norwegian	*bjorn*
Polish	*niedz'wiedz'*
Portuguese	*urso*
Russian	*medved*
Serbo-Croatian	*medvjed*
Slovakian	*medved*
Spanish	*oso*
Swedish	*bjorn*
Ukrainian	*vedmid*

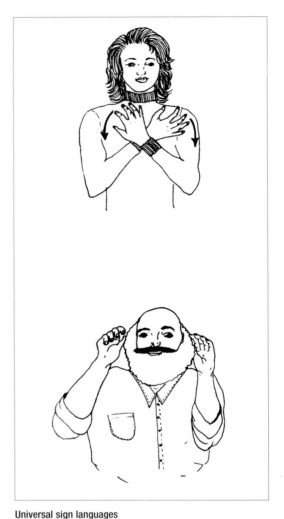

Universal sign languages
RENEE EVANOFF

"BEAR" SLANG

Vocabulary	Slang
Bear	A stock market term: speculate for a fall in prices
Bearish	Grumpy, rude behavior; boorish; stock market bear
Bear play	Rough, noisy behavior
If it were a bear . . .	It would bite; it would have bitten you (also: "If it had been a bear")
Play the bear	To behave roughly and rudely
Try like a bear	Try your hardest to attract a specific lady

"BEAR" IN THE WESTERN UNITED STATES

Vocabulary	Western Slang
Bear's ass	Common Mormon-country oath (actual meaning unknown)
Bear doctor	Medicine man whose animal guide is a bear (California Indian term)
Bear fighter	Man separating strips from boards in sawmill (logger term)
Bear jam	Berry jam (logger term); traffic "jam" caused by a bear
Bear sign (feces)	Doughnuts (cowboy term); berry jam (logger term)
Bear trap	A style of saddle (cowboy term); a severe horse bit (cowboy term); a section of movable dam capable of being raised or lowered to control water flow (river-boating term)

BEAR PLACE NAMES

Bear names have been used often for natural features and man-made developments, indicating the significance of bears and their impact on the early settlers of the United States. "Bear" most often became the name, or part of the name, when the animal was observed in the specific or general location such as a canyon, stream, ridge, or valley. Buildings such as cabins, churches, and schools, in those areas often adopted "bear" as a portion of their names. The U.S. Board on Geographic Names has officially listed more than 6,480 features reflecting the bear in all states except Hawaii.

BEAR NICKNAMES

U.S. College Athletic Teams

Adams State College; Alamosa, CO	*Grizzlies*
Alaska, University of; Fairbanks, AK	*Nanooks*
Athens State University; Athens, AL	*Bears*
Barclay College; Haviland, KS	*Bears*
Barnard College; New York, NY	*Bears*
Baruch College; New York, NY	*Bearcats*
Baylor University; Waco, TX	*Bears*
Bellevue University; Bellevue, NE	*Bruins*
Belmont University; Nashville, TN	*Bruins*
Bethany College; Scotts Valley, CA	*Bruins*
Binghamton University; Binghamton, NY	*Bearcats*
Bowdoin College; Brunswick, ME	*Polar Bears*
Brescia College; Owensboro, KY	*Bearcats*
Bridgewater State College; Bridgewater, MA	*Bears*
Brown University; Providence, RI	*Bears*
California, University of; Berkeley, CA	*Golden Bears*
California, University of; Los Angeles, CA	*Bruins*
California, University of; San Francisco, CA	*Bears*
Central Arkansas, University of; Conway, AR	*Bears*
Cincinnati, University of; Cincinnati, OH	*Bearcats*
Cincinnati (Raymond Walters College), University of; Blue Ash, OH	*Bearcats*
Concordia, University of; St. Paul, MN	*Golden Bears*
Franklin College; Franklin, IN	*Grizzlies*
George Fox College; Newberg, OR	*Bruins*
Golden State Baptist College; Santa Clara, CA	*Bears*
Kutztown University; Kutztown, PA	*Golden Bears*
Lander University; Greenwood, SC	*Bearcats*
Lenoir-Rhyne College; Hickory, NC	*Bears*
Livingstone College; Salisbury, NC	*Blue Bears*
Maine, University of; Orono, ME	*Black Bears*
McKendree College; Lebanon, IL	*Bearcats*
Mercer University (Macon); Macon, GA	*Bears*
Miles College; Fairfield, AL	*Golden Bears*
Missouri State University; Springfield, MO	*Bears*

Montana, University of; Missoula, MT	*Grizzlies*
Morgan State University; Baltimore, MD	*Golden Bears*
New York Institute of Technology; Old Westbury, NY	*Bears*
Northern Colorado, University of; Greeley, CO	*Bears*
Northwest Missouri State University; Maryville, MO	*Bearcats*
Oakland University; Rochester, MN	*Golden Grizzlies*
Ohio Northern University; Ada, OH	*Polar Bears*
Pikeville College; Pikeville, KY	*Bears*
Rocky Mountain College; Billings, MT	*Bears*
Rust College; Holly Springs, MS	*Bearcats*
St. Joseph's College (Brooklyn Campus); Brooklyn, NY	*Bears*
St. Vincent College; Latrobe, PA	*Bearcats*
Sam Houston State University; Huntsville, TX	*Bearkats*
Shaw University; Raleigh, NC	*Bears*
Shawnee State University; Portsmouth, OH	*Bears*
Southwest Baptist University; Bolivar, MO	*Bearcats*
State University of New York (College at Potsdam); Potsdam, NY	*Bears*
United States Coast Guard Academy; New London, CT	*Bears*
Ursinus College; Collegeville, PA	*Bears*
Washington University; St. Louis, MO	*Bears*
West Virginia Institute of Technology; Montgomery, WV	*Golden Bears*
Western New England College; Springfield, MA	*Golden Bears*
Willamette University; Salem, OR	*Bearcats*

Canadian Colleges and Universities

Alberta, University of; Edmonton, AB	*Golden Bears* (men) *Pandas* (women)
Columbia Bible College; Abbotsford, BC	*Bearcats*
Georgian College; Barrie, ON	*Grizzlies*
Lethbridge CC; Lethbridge, AB	*Kodiaks*
Sheridan College (Brampton Campus); Brampton, ON	*Bruins/Bearcats*
Sheridan College, Oakville, ON	*Bruins*

Source: National Association of Collegiate Directors of Athletics, The 2006–2007 National Directory of College Athletics (Cleveland: Collegiate Directories, Inc., 2006).

Major U.S. Professional Teams

Boston Bruins (National Hockey League)

Chicago Bears (National Football League)

Chicago Cubs (Major League Baseball, National League)

Memphis Grizzlies (National Basketball Association)

GOLF'S "GOLDEN BEAR"

Known as the greatest professional golfer in history, "The Golden Bear" earned his fame primarily due to his record of winning major championships. Born in Columbus, Ohio, in 1940, Jack Nicklaus was an outstanding golfer at age ten and began winning titles at twelve. He "broke" seventy at age *thirteen.* In high school he was given the nickname "Golden Bear," which was the school mascot.

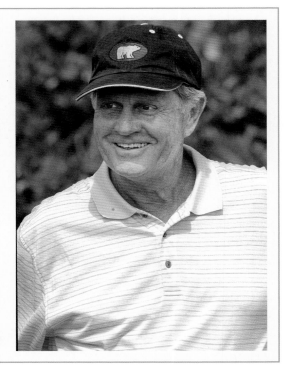

Golf's Golden Bear, Jack Nicklaus
JIM MANDEVILLE/NICKLAUS DESIGN

BEARS AND RELIGION

Bears have been considered spiritual by many cultures; they've been an element of religion since they first shared the earth with humans, being revered, feared, honored, worshipped, and sacrificed. Many myths, superstitions, and legends have followed bears through the centuries, with the performance of rites, festivals, dances, and other ceremonies centered around and within these sacred animals. Most early cultures believed them to be spirits, as well as accepted them as real animals. They were in the beginning thought to be the first Great Shaman. Bear cults (as early as the Pleistocene epoch) and fraternal organizations have existed in many societies and cultures. "Bears, large and powerful, have been important to people since man and bears first met," writes George Laycock in *The Wild Bears*. "Many cultures have assigned the bears religious roles in their societies and credited them with super-natural powers."

Bears are associated with puberty rites, initiation of shamans, shamanism, hunting, healing, and the initiation of women and men into secret societies. They have been considered immortal—entering the ground in the early winter but being reborn during the spring. Initiation rites are associated with hibernation. The ability of bears to hibernate plays a significant role in their association with religions. The importance of the bear in religion may be best illustrated by the Cult of the Bear, one of the earliest (Paleolithic) "faiths," which has survived for more than 20,000 years. Several biblical references to bears exist in the Old and New Testaments and *The Book of Mormon*.

Bears have been considered:

- A religious symbol
- To know the secrets of the plants
- Ancestors
- To possess mystical powers
- Able to cure the sick
- Able to tell the future
- Able to cause disease
- Half human
- Honorable
- To symbolize the ethics of maternity
- A spirit
- Able to impart immortality
- Able to determine patterns of life
- Able to die (hibernate) and be reborn (emerge from the den)
- Able to determine the circumstances of death
- Reincarnated family members
- To be like people
- Shamans of the animal world
- Messengers to the animal keeper

Bears in American Indian Cultures

"Bear has played a prominent role in many Native cultures and ceremonies," according to Gary Buffalo Horn Man and Sherry Firedancer in *Animal Energies*. "Many nations of Native people saw Bear as a powerful medicine person who was highly desirable as an ally and spirit helper. Some tribes prayed for medicine dreams . . . some sought Bear dreams as a way of locating them and receiving permission to hunt them in a sacred way. Other nations, such as the Navajo, felt that Bear was too powerful and fearsome a being to have contact with, and they would hunt Bear only if it meant not starving."

"The American Indians of the North Country respect the bear, looking upon it as a fellow citizen of the woods," notes Frederick Drimmer in *The Animal Kingdom*. "Many, when they kill a bear, are careful to apologize and to speed its spirit onward to the Happy Hunting Ground with prayers and sacrifices. In their belief, the animal's spirit is too powerful to be appeased by simple rituals—so they clean the skull and put it on top of a pole, where they hold it taboo."

AMERICAN INDIAN CEREMONIES

Group/Tribe	Ceremony/Ritual	Purpose
Acoma Pueblo	Bear with eagle plumes and a rattle painted on walls of a secret-society chamber	Initiation of a boy into society
Blackfeet	Men dressed in bear skins during a pipe-smoking ceremony	Intensifies the power of the pipe
Coos (Oregon)	Bear dance	Puberty rights of girls
Cree (Eastern)	The shaman fought the bear spirit, Memekwesiw; the shaman had to win	Bear hunts would be successful
	Respected the bears they killed	The bear keepers would provide more bears
	Drew with paint on a bear skull	Brought good dreams
	Placed a bear's kneecap on a hot rock to see if it would wobble	If the kneecap wobbled, bear hunts would be successful
	Threw a pinch of tobacco into the fire	In preparation to hunt bear
Crow	Ate the bear's heart	Provided the person with the heart of a bear, with courage
Dakota	Simulated death; died like bears, without fear; shared the bear's power of resurrection	Initiations
	Fasting, and being reborn; "making a bear"	Initiations into manhood
Delaware	Bear dance and other New Year activities	Rebirth of the earth
Inuit	Polar bear killed and its bladder inflated, dried (hung) indoors and offered food and water	The bear's soul (*innua*) was its bladder; the bear was being honored
Neanderthals	Ate the flesh of bears with reverence	The meat of bears provided them with immortality
Ojibwa	Bear dance	Celebrated puberty; identified girls with bears

Group/Tribe	Ceremony/Ritual	Purpose
Ojibwa (Midewiwin)	Imitated bears; good and bad bears were present	Initiations
Ojibwa (women)	Were called and treated as bears; associated with the dangerous aspect of bears	Initiations
Ostyak (Western Siberia)	Successful hunter shot an unaimed arrow at the lodge	The arrow hitting an upper beam meant future bear-hunting success; a lower beam, hard times
Pimi	Avoided bears	Thought they caused disease
Pomo	Dressed and imitated bears	Initiations
Pomo (eastern California)	Performed a bear dance; chased by persons dressed as bears	Initiation into manhood
Pomo (coastal California)	Grizzly bear impersonator frightened boys and girls; the "bear" dug a hole and the children collapsed into it	Initiations
Santa Clara Pueblo (NM)	Wore bear claws on wristlet or shirt	Gave power to fight like a bear
	Hunters blackened their faces after killing a bear	Protected them from attack by a bear on the homeward journey
Yokuts (a bear clan; CA)	Performed a bear dance	Honored the acorn crop
Many tribes	Sang a special song after they killed a bear	So the bears, who had control over other game animals, would allow future hunting success
Many tribes	Person brought into close contact with a bear so it was feared	Initiation; person is frightened so they would not be afraid in the future

The Shaman

Shamans were North American Indian medicine men. They sought to control bear magic and were messengers to the animal keeper. "An important role of the shaman was to assist in the hunt, especially when times were hard," relates David Rockwell in *Giving Voice to Bear*. "When hunters were unsuccessful and famine threatened, the shaman, in a trance, visited an Owner Of the Animals to ask for release of food animals."

Bears and shamans were thought to possess similar powers, and the shamans impersonated the bear and practiced its healing forces. "Shamans who had the bear as a spirit helper wrapped themselves in the skins of bears, wore necklaces of bear claws, painted bear signs on their faces and bodies, and smoked pipes carved in the shapes of bears," describes Rockwell. "In their medicine bundles they kept bear claws and teeth and other parts of the animal. They used bear claws and gall and bear grease in their ceremonies. They ate the plants bears ate and used them as their medicines. They danced as they thought bears danced, and they sang power songs to the animal . . . a grizzly bear song of the Tlingit [Indians of the Pacific Northwest area of North America], in which the shaman expresses sense of oneness with the bear."

Hon Kachina

The bear Kachina (Katchina, Katcina) of the Hopi Indians in the southwest United States is of such great strength that it is believed to cure the sick. It appears in the Kachina return, or Soyal of First Mesa, as the watchman or side dancer for the Chakwaina.

Bears and the Bible

The bear is often spoken of in the Bible, less often only than the lion, and has been considered a symbol of God's vengeance. In Lamentations Jeremiah sees God in His anger as a bear lying in wait, and in The Revelation the dragon gave power to a beast with the feet of a bear. Possibly the most well-remembered bear episode is in the Old Testament, 2 Kings, when the prophet Elisha is mocked for his baldness by some children. He curses them, whereupon two "she bears" rush out of the woods and kill forty-two of them. The bears of the Bible are Syrian brown bears (*Ursus arctos syriacus*).

Biblical References Old Testament

1 Sam. 17.34	And David said unto Saul, Thy servant kept his father's sheep, and there came a lion, and a bear, and took a lamb out of the flock.
1 Sam. 17.36	Thy servant slew both the lion and the bear.

1 Sam. 17.37	David said moreover, The Lord that delivered me out of the paw of the lion, and out of the paw of the bear, he will deliver me out of the hand of the Philistine.
2 Sam. 17.8	For, said Hushai, thou knowest thy father and his men, that they be mighty men, and they be chafed in their minds, as a bear robbed of her whelps in the field.
2 Kings 2.24	And he turned back, and looked on them, and cursed them in the name of the Lord. And there came forth two she bears out of the wood, and tare forty and two children of them.
Prov. 17.12	Let a bear robbed of her whelps meet a man, rather than a fool in his folly.
Prov. 28.15	As a roaring lion, and a ranging bear; so is a wicked ruler over the poor people.
Isa. 11.7	And the cow and the bear shall feed; their young ones shall lie down together: and the lion shall eat straw like the ox.
Isa. 59.11	We roar all like bears, and mourn sore like doves.
Lam. 3.10	He was unto me as a bear lying in wait, and as a lion in secret places.
Dan. 7.5	And behold another beast, a second, like to a bear, and it raised up itself on one side, and it had three ribs in the mouth of it between the teeth of it: and they said this unto it, Arise, devour much flesh.
Hos. 13.8	I will meet them as a bear that is bereaved of her whelps, and will rend the caul of their heart, and there will I devour them like a lion: the wild beast shall tear them.
Amos 5.19	As if a man did flee from a lion, and a bear met him; or went into the house, and leaned his hand on the wall, and a serpent bit him.

New Testament

Rev. 13.2	And the beast which I saw was like unto a leopard, and his feet were as the feet of a bear; and his mouth as the mouth of a lion.

Bears and Saints

Numerous saints had strong associations and influences with bears, with some deriving their name from *Ursus*.

Saint Augustine	Recommended eating the testicles of bears as a cure for epilepsy ("famous against the falling sickness")
Saint Blaise	Represents a pagan myth where Orpheus (most common example) appears as a bear
Saint Bonaventure	Described a monk who prayed for aid and a bear appeared, to serve this man of God
Saint Bridget	Celtic fire goddess; Christian saint; the name "Bridget" is a stem word for "bear"
Saint Columba	Depicted with a palm branch and a bear on a chain
Saint Gall	Exchanged bread with a wild bear for wood to build his house
Saint Korbinian	Depicted with a tame bear. While traveling to Rome, a bear killed his packhorse; thereupon, he forced the bear to carry his load.
Saint Peter Damian	Described a pope being transformed into a bear in the afterlife
Saint Sergius of Radonezh	Lived in a forest and shared his bread with a bear cub
Saint Ursula	A legendary British princess of the Christian faith who received her "bear" name when she reputedly died defending her 11,000 virgin maidens against the bear's onslaught. A variation of the legend claims the attack upon Ursula and her maidens was by the Huns in the fourth to fifth centuries AD.
Saint Ursus	Early Christian martyr
Saint Valentine	His twin brother was raised by a bear, and when later domesticated by Valentine, the bear was named Orson (meaning bear).

Bears and the *Book of Mormon*

2 Nephi 21:7 And the cow and the bear shall feed; their young ones shall
(2 Nephi 30:13) lie down together, and the lion shall eat straw like the ox.

Bears in Witchcraft

Bears are found in the writings of witchcraft throughout the world. *Ursus* ("orsus") in witchcraft was considered "a beginning." A sow produced a formless creature (the fetus) and sculptured her brood with her mouth, her licking shaping legs, head, and body.

Witches had the skill and ability to change shape and become a bear by means of the devil, a curse, or magic. A witch became the bear for a specific period of time, and the bear was occasionally a "familiar" spirit. They also transformed humans into beasts, including bears.

Centuries ago, in Northern Europe, humans were thought to become bears by wearing a bearskin or by anointing with a magic salve. Witches murdered, crippled, or harmed persons with "image magic," sometimes using a bear that would be tortured and killed, believing that the actions would be transferred and a person would also suffer and die.

A bear was the disguise of the devil, the Grand Devil of the celebration, the God, the Grand Master.

BEARS IN THE HEAVENS

Polaris, the North Star, which we are taught to locate when very young and which was for so long the navigational monument of the Northern Hemisphere, is also known as Alpha Ursae Minoris. Two constellations, Ursa Major (the Great Bear) and Ursa Minor (the Little Bear), move counterclockwise around the North Star. The first two stars in Ursa Major are pointing to Polaris, at the tip of Ursa Minor's tail.

The "bear constellations" never set, and since at least the beginning of recorded history the Great Bear and the Little Bear, with the North Star, have guided explorers, travelers, and navigators in the north.

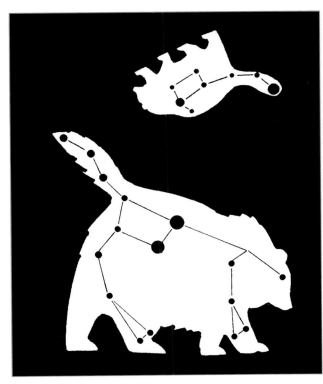

Little Dipper (Ursa Minor)
RENEE EVANOFF
Big Dipper (Ursa Major)
RENEE EVANOFF

Ursa Major

The Big Dipper, an asterism consisting of seven bright stars (six shine with extreme brightness) and seven fainter stars, forms only the hips (the cup) and the tail (the handle) but is the most conspicuous part of the Great Bear.

The British have long believed the Big Dipper to be the Plow, the Wain, or the Wagon. Some people believe the Great Bear more resembles a mouse, not a lumbering bear.

Arabians considered the four stars of the Big Dipper's bowl a coffin and the handle stars the mourners marching behind the coffin.

The stars of the Big Dipper are continually and very slowly changing position; the "dipper" will be a "frying pan" in a hundred thousand years.

Prominent Stars of Ursa Major
Bowl of the Dipper
- **Dubhe** (Alpha; the Bear), pointer star
- **Merak** (Beta; loins of the Bear), pointer star
- **Phecda** (Gamma; thigh of the Bear)
- **Megrez** (Delta; root of the tail)

Handle of the Dipper
- **Alioth** (Epsilon)
- **Mizar** (Zeta): Mizar has a companion star, Alcor, that has long been considered "The Test" of eyesight.
- **Alkaid** (Eta; end of the tail; also called Benetnash)

Paws of the Great Bear
- **Talitha** (front paws)
- **Tania Borealis** (hind paws)
- **Tania Australis** (hind paws)

Ursa Minor

The Little Bear is a constellation consisting of seven stars, with the Little Dipper comprising the major portion. Early peoples thought the Little Dipper resembled a dog's tail and called it Cynosure; others referred to it as a jackal or jewels. Today it is considered to appear as an old-fashioned cream ladle or gravy spoon.

The North Star, Alpha Ursae Minoris, is the brightest star in Ursa Minor and is at the end of the Little Dipper's handle (tail).

Many beliefs existed among ancient peoples as to the origin and influences of the Great Bear and the Little Bear. Some remain in a few of today's cultures and societies.

Prominent Stars of Ursa Minor
Bowl of the Dipper
- **Kochab** (Beta)
- **Pherkad** (Kochab and Pherkad are the guardians, or guards, of the Pole Star)

Handle of the Dipper
- **Yildun;** the Surpassing Star
- **Polaris** (Alpha); the North Star, the Pole Star

Origins of Ursa Major and Ursa Minor

Greek mythology: Jupiter fell in love with the nymph Callisto, and his jealous wife turned her into a bear. When Callisto approached her son, he did not recognize her and raised his spear to kill the "bear." Jupiter saved her by changing her son into a bear, and then placed them both in the sky. (Some writings relate similar origins but with Zeus placing the bears in the heavens.)

Another legend describes the bears as causing trouble on earth and Hercules swinging them by their tails into the sky.

Eskimo: According to Paul Shepard and Barry Sanders in *The Sacred Paw*, a woman betrays the "Bear" men and one kills her. Her husband's dogs attack the bear. "Suddenly, both bear and dogs burn wonderfully bright, and rise to the sky as stars. Bear and light merge for the Eskimo as a heavenly constellation."

Finns and Voguls: The bear of the earth originated from a cloud near the Great Bear.

Ostyaks (Siberians): The bear of the earth originated in the heavens, a combining of the Big Bear, the sun, and the moon, and descended to earth.

Beliefs (Bears in the Heavens)

The constellations have been integral entities in the beliefs and religions of many peoples. In mythology, both constellations were combined and called the Great Bear, and their turning has led to traditional symbols such as the "cross," "swastika," and "spiral."

Hindus: Called Ursa Major the Seven Bears or Seven Wisemen and placed red spirals on structures where a child was about to be born to aid the newborn into life.

Iroquois and Micmac Indians: The Great Bear was seen as four stars with seven hunters and the second hunter (Mizar) with a pot (the tiny companion star Alcor) to cook the bear. The bear's den was a group of stars above the bear. The hunters were seven birds (blue jay, Canada jay, chickadee, owl, pigeon, robin, saw-whet).

North American Indians: These peoples knew bears did not have long tails; therefore the "tail" stars were hunters pursuing the bears. The Great Bear rides low in the sky during the fall; it is looking for a place to bed down, preparing for winter (hibernation). Mizar and Alcor were horse and rider.

Greeks: The Hunter (Boötes) was pursuing the Great Bear and the Little Bear around Polaris—a celestial hunt.

Siberians: The Great Bear and the Little Bear together were the sacred elk Kheglen and were being chased by Mangi the bear spirit (Boötes).

The early watchers of the heavens found the bears to have long tails, which is probably based on their association or knowledge of the cave bear, *Ursus spelaeus*, which became extinct approximately 10,000 years ago.

During the early history of Western civilization, the "arctic" was thought to lie beneath the constellations. The Arktik'os, as it was referred to by the Greeks, was considered the country of the great bear.

The constellation Boötes (bo-O-tez), known as the bear guard, bear driver, bear keeper or herdsman, appears to be chasing the Great Bear. The star Arcturus (*arctos* = bear; *ouros* = keeper) is at the left knee area of Boötes.

Early cultures believed the constellations influenced many aspects of life and the environment, such as good health, strength and childbirth, climate, seasons and the weather, crop diseases, and animal behavior.

BEAR FESTIVALS AND HOLIDAYS

Bears are honored during annual holidays and festivals around the world. All of the events are festive, some are religious, and bears are the focus of the majority.

Ainu Bear Festival (Holiday—Japan)

The Festival of the Slain Bear is the bear feast of the Ainu, practiced in Japan each December to honor the bear, The Divine One Who Rules the Mountains. The Ainu annually capture and raise a bear cub (an Asiatic black bear) as an honored guest, being nursed by the Ainu women. The bear is sacrificed during the festival, with its soul returning home. "The Ainu believed that the manlike gods were garbed as animals only in the land of man, that meat and fur were gifts to men from them," write Shepard and Sanders, "and that the slain bear returned to its divine form. It is sent to the spirit world with festival dancing and feasting."

Bayou Teche Bear Festival (Louisiana)

An outreach program that highlights the peril of the endangered Louisiana black bear and features education, entertainment, and music; Franklin in April.

Bears of the Blue River Festival (Indiana)

An annual festival with arts and entertainment; Shelbyville in August.

Bear's Day

February second is Candlemas, the date of the Sacred marriage. Called Groundhog Day in America, it is considered Bear's Day in Austria, Hungary, and Poland, the day when bears emerge from their dens to look for their shadows.

Boggy Bayou Bear Festival (Mississippi)

An annual September pageant that includes educational bear seminars, bear material, a carnival, music, foods, and other outdoor events; Bears' Cove, Gulfport.

The Candlemas Bear Hunt (Holiday—France)

A celebration of the presentation of Jesus at the temple.

Celebrations in Oruro (Holiday—Bolivia)

A segment of the February "carnival" in which individuals costumed as condors and bears walk among dancers as they recall the days of worship and feast; Oruro.

Cesky Krumlov Castle Bear Festival (Czech Republic)

Each Christmas Eve a festival is held at the castle in the historic town of Krumlov to celebrate the bears of the castle's moat. Bears have occupied the castle moat since 1707, and Christmas Eve with the Bears is in their honor. The bears are fed festive sweets, and there is music, food, and bear-theme presents for the guests.

Festival of the Nine Imperial Gods (Holiday—Singapore)

An annual festival occurring during the first nine days of the ninth month (September) based on a centuries-old Chinese belief that the Nine Imperial Gods reside in the northern heavens. Seven gods are in each of the seven stars of Ursa Major, the Big Dipper; the other two are in two nearby stars visible only to immortals. The festival includes processions that seek the gods, inviting them to descend.

Florida Black Bear Festival

The festival is an annual educational event, with environmental presentations and field trips supporting the endangered Florida black bear. There is music, children's activities (with a bear theme), a fish fry, food (from bear-oriented vendors), and a dance; Umatilla in April.

Hugglets Teddy Bear Festival (London, England)

A festival featuring teddy bear exhibits, competitions, sales and supplies; Kensington Town Hall each September

Kentucky Black Bear Festival

Held annually in Cumberland (Black Bear Capital of Kentucky), the festival features education (bears), entertainment, food, and crafts; each May.

McCleary Second Growth and Bear Festival (Washington)

The City of McCleary's annual bear festival began in 1958, when an argument occurred as to whether Skamania County or Grays Harbor County had the tastiest bears. A tasting contest was held later that year in McCleary, and the annual Bear Festival was born. Every July approximately 12,000 persons attend this three-day celebration, where the American black bear is celebrated with arts and crafts shows, baseball,

the world-famous bear stew contest and feast, bingo, a children's play day, dances, a pancake breakfast, a queen's coronation, musical entertainment, parades, a 10-kilometer run (Ursa Major), a 2-mile run (Ursa Minor), and a salmon barbecue.

The festival is officially known as the Second Growth and Bear Festival. When the festival began, young trees, planted to replace the old-growth trees cut down for timber, were growing in the area surrounding McCleary (hence the "Second Growth"). Bears caused serious damage to the young forest by utilizing the bark as food. They were killed to protect the trees, and a bear hunt became an important aspect of the festival. Today a more effective system is in place—the bears are fed during the spring to protect the trees.

Teddy Bear Picnic (Colorado)

The annual Teddy Bear Picnic, in Estes Park, is a June event for all ages that features a drawing with proceeds benefiting the national organization Good Bears of the World. Musical entertainment and contests are included in this one-day function, including a contest rewarding the family that brings the most teddy bears.

Tori-No-Ichi (Japan)

The "bird fair" is a Shinto celebration that includes an activity in which the participants (influential members of the sect and wealthy merchants) have a market mascot—a "Kumade" (bear hand), which is an ordinary bamboo rake that resembles the clutching claws of a bear paw. The lore of the Kumade is that the possessor will have magic power to pull (rake) all desired treasure; November.

Vagabonds' New Years (Poland)

A New Year's festival with costumes, pantomime, and improvisations in which the devil and the bear frolic in the snow.

MYTHS AND LEGENDS

Many misconceptions and fallacies surround bears. Some are amusing tales, often obviously untrue, and several quite dangerous if taken as fact.

Black bears are not dangerous: All bears are wild, unpredictable, and potentially dangerous animals.

Bears are poor swimmers: Bears are excellent swimmers, often swimming for play and to cool off. They will swim across lakes, strong rivers, and open seas to reach a food source, to mate, or just to cross.

Grizzly (brown) bears can't climb trees: Mature grizzly bears normally do not climb like American black and other bears of the world due to the structure of their claws and their weight as adults. They do not have the sharply curved claws necessary to dig into tree bark but are quite capable of "laddering" up a tree utilizing available limbs to climb (as a person would). There are even a few observations of grizzly bears climbing in the same manner as black bears. Grizzly bear cubs and other worldwide species of bears climb quite well, some exceptionally.

Bears are large, cumbersome, and slow: Bears are large and *appear* cumbersome, but most are fast (some are capable of running 35 miles per hour for short distances), agile, able to leap long distances, and capable of climbing trees and scaling cliffs.

A companion dog keeps bears away while in bear country: Dogs may be of assistance in keeping bears away from a camp or providing a mutual warning of the bear's and your nearby presence. However, on many occasions, a dog has chased a bear, found too great an adversary, and retreated back to its master with the bear in hot pursuit.

Bears can't run well downhill: You cannot outrun a bear downhill. Bears run uphill, sideways on a hill, and definitely downhill nearly as well, always with speed, and are not known to stumble.

Bears do not eat human flesh: Bears do not normally prey on humans. However, when they do, or if they kill in a defensive action, their victims may be consumed.

Bears will not attack sleeping people: Bears have attacked people sleeping in tents and out in the open. More than once they have clawed or bitten a head protruding from a sleeping bag as the individual slept "under the stars."

Bears that approach or come in close contact with people are tame: Bears that are willing to be close to people are either conditioned to a nearby food source or are habituated to human activity. These bears are wild and dangerous animals—possibly more dangerous than the normally shy, retreating bears.

A repellent is protection from an aggressive bear: A repellent will "repel" most bears but may be false security, often replacing good sense and important precautionary actions necessary in bear country.

Bears hug their enemies to death (bear hug): A bear often appears to be hugging its prey, when actually it is standing to hold the victim and gain better advantage while using its powerful paws and jaws.

Grizzly bears always charge at first sight: Grizzly bears are normally shy and will retreat if at all possible. During the settling of North America, bears may have nearly always charged but probably not at first sight. The early explorers and pioneers were often aggressive, and the bear was threatened, often wounded. Today, many of those early "charges" would be considered defensive aggression.

Bears are hard to kill: Bears have thick skulls and considerable endurance, and many tales of difficulties in killing bears have saturated our early bear literature. However, the major problem the early explorers and pioneers had was inadequate firearms.

Bears hibernate: Bears are not true hibernators as are bats, squirrels, and woodchucks, though we normally utilize the word in describing the winter activity of many bears, as they do become quite lethargic and enter into a deep sleep.

Humans and bears have been crossed (interbred): There have been tales of bears being crossed with humans. However, all scientific investigations have found the reports of this interbreeding to be untrue. Early mythology led to many such stories.

Bears mate just before hibernation: The time between the beginning of hibernation and the birth of cubs is approximately the appropriate gestation period. However, bears mate several months before hibernation; the process of delayed implantation defers the development of the embryo until hibernation.

Bears suck their paws for sustenance: Early observers believed bears sucked nourishment from their paws during the long "fast of hibernation." The misconception was based on the fact that bears do on occasion suck their paws, and during the spring as bears emerge from their dens they slough the pads of their paws (a natural "shedding" of the skin).

Bears use the left front paw to eat honey: "The

THE YETI/SASQUATCH

Yeti and Sasquatch are names given to a large furry "being" that walks upright like a human (bipedally, with a similar stride). Its tracks are similar to a bear's, and it is more proportionally bearlike than apelike. Myth and reality most often include bears in the long-contested debate: *What are the Abominable Snowman (Yeti) of Asia and Bigfoot (Sasquatch) of northwestern North America?* Are they "beings" in themselves—an unknown, humanlike animal? Apes? Or bears? There appear to be habits and traditions of claiming Yeti is, and is not, "a bear." Some Yeti and Sasquatch sightings are without doubt bears. Bears may not have initiated the legends but definitely have perpetuated the stories.

---

meat of the bear's left front paw is said to be the sweetest and most tender part of the animal," relate Mills and Servheen in their project report, "The Asian Trade in Bears and Bear Parts," "because, according to myth, this is the paw used to [collect] honey from bees' nests." Actually, bears have been observed using either front paw while collecting and eating the contents of a beehive or nest.

Bears attack telegraph poles and wires: There are reports of bears climbing and damaging telegraph poles and wires in Siberia and telephone poles in Los Padres National Forest, California. It is theorized that the purpose for climbing the poles is that the humming wires sound like the buzzing of bees, and the bears are merely seeking bees and honey.

Bears have poor eyesight: This is a misleading belief. A bear's eyesight is not perfect—it is nearsighted—but it can detect form and movement at long distances, and its close-up vision is quite good.

An Ancient Myth

The saying "lick into shape" appears to be based on the ancient belief that a bear gave birth to an unformed, shapeless "ball of fur" that the sow licked into the proper shape of a bear. According to Aristotle there would be no mature bears without the sow's primal, maternal intervention, relate Shepard and Sanders. "Having produced them [cubs], by licking them with her tongue she completes their warming and concocts them, matures them." *Ours mal leche* (a badly licked bear) is a still-used French phrase and describes an incorrigible, ill-behaved child.

The Legend of Yosemite

"One morning a young chief of the tribe [Ah-wah-nee-chees], while on his way to Ah-wei-ya (Mirror Lake), where he intended spearing some fish, was suddenly confronted by an immense grizzly bear. The bear resented this intrusion upon his domain and made a fierce attack upon the young chief. The chief, who was weaponless, armed himself with the dead limb of a tree, which was lying near, and, after being sorely wounded, succeeded in killing the bear. Bleeding and exhausted he dragged himself back to the camp where he told his story to the admiring members of the tribe, who in acknowledgment of his bravery and skill, called him Yo-sem-i-te, their word for the fearless monarch of the forest, the grizzly bear. This name was transmitted to his children, and in time, because of their fearless and warlike natures, the entire tribe came to be known as the Yo-sem-i-tes" (Wilson 1923).

James Schoppert, *Sea Bear* 1980, Tlingit/Haida art, wood carving—polar bears
UNIVERSITY OF ALASKA MUSEUM OF THE NORTH (UA1981-3-152)
PHOTOGRAPHER: BARRY MCWAYNE

BEARS IN NORTH AMERICAN ART

The bears of North America have been creatively and realistically captured by numerous artists of the nineteenth, twentieth, and twenty-first centuries. The reader should visit art galleries and libraries to study these "stories" of the natural history and human/bear interactions. Bears are most often represented in paintings (oils, acrylics, watercolors) but also are represented in other art forms (sculptures, wood carvings, pen-and-ink drawings, lava rock sculptures, totems). All species of bears are represented in art worldwide.

BEARS IN LITERATURE

The earliest writings about bears may have occurred approximately 3,000 to 4,000 years ago in China.

Literature has long been saturated with books containing bear stories or publications devoted entirely to the animal. Bears have been addressed in folklore, fables, epics, technical writings, fiction and nonfiction, and mythical tales. Ballads, romances, fairy tales, poetry, religion, comedy, and historical narratives have all described bears and their behavior. They have been presented as evil, friendly, and heroes and are accounted for in the classics, comic books, textbooks, and the Bible. Writings have been for all ages.

"In literature it [the bear] is both smart and naïve, forgiving and vicious," describe Shepard and Sanders in *The Sacred Paw*. Some early authors who utilized the bear were William Shakespeare, the Grimm brothers, Aesop, and Charles Dickens. Shakespeare's works included more than 3,000 references to animals, including bears (live bears were occasionally used on stage in Shakespearean plays).

Some Early Bear Writings

- *Aesop's Fables*. Aesop, a Greek slave, 620–560 BC (English version, 1692)
- *Roman de Renart*. Evolved from Aesop's Fables, 1170–1250
- *The History of Four-Footed Beasts*. Edward Topsell, 1607
- *Beauty and the Beast*. W. R. S. Ralston, 1757 (classic version)
- *Kinder-und Hausmarchen*. Brothers Grimm, 1812–1815

- *Goldilocks and the Three Bears*. Robert Southey, 1837
- *A Bear's Christmas Carol*. Charles Dickens, 1843
- *Mother Goose's Fairy Tales of 1878*
- *The Willow-Wren and the Bear* (The Bear and the Kingbird). Brothers Grimm, (translated in 1884)
- *Snow White and Rose Red*. Brothers Grimm, 1889
- *Jungle Book*. Rudyard Kipling, 1894

Sherlock Holmes and Bears

Sir Arthur Conan Doyle included a reference to a bearskin hearth rug in "The Adventure of the Priory School" (in *The Return of Sherlock Holmes*). Dr. Thorneycroft Huxtable, MA, PhD, entered Holmes's Baker Street home, staggered against a table, slipped to the floor, and came to rest prostrate on a bearskin hearth rug.

Doyle's "A Study in Scarlet" refers to a large and savage grizzly bear on the Great Alkali Plain, a repulsive desert of North America (near the Great Salt Lake, Utah).

And Sir Arthur wrote of polar bears during the late 1800s, though without Sherlock Holmes. In *Life on a Greenland Whaler*, he refers to polar bears as ". . . poor harmless creatures, with the lurch and roll of a deep-sea mariner."

Naturalist John Muir and Bears

John Muir, born in Scotland, came to the United States and found the Sierra Nevada mountains of California and their bears. Wanderer, farmer, founder of the Sierra Club, activist, and naturalist extraordinaire, he was fortunately a prolific and descriptive writer. The thorough and detailed journals of his perceptions and thoughts are found in his numerous books. In *Trails of Wonder: Writings on Nature and Man* (a compilation of his work), Muir describes the bear:

> Magnificent bears of the Sierra are worthy of their magnificent homes. They are companions of men. . . .

> Bears are made of the same dust as we, and breathe the same winds and drink of the same waters. A bear's days are warmed by the same sun, his dwellings are over-domed by the same blue sky, and his life turns and ebbs with heart-pulsing like ours. . . .

A "READING LIST" OF BEAR BOOKS

The bibliography is extensive, and much of it might be deemed uninteresting "reading." However, it includes several books considered by bear authorities, enthusiasts, authors, and general readers as excellent writings—interesting, educational, practical, entertaining, inspirational, and enjoyable. Some may be entirely about bears, while a few only address them as a part of the story. Shown below is a list of books considered by a few bear enthusiasts as "special."

American Bears	Theodore Roosevelt (Paul Schullery, Ed.)
Arctic Dreams	Barry Lopez
"The Bear" (in *Go Down Moses*)	William Faulkner
Bear Attacks: Their Causes and Avoidance	Stephen Herrero
The Bear Hunter's Century	Paul Schullery
The Bears of Alaska in Life and Legend	Jeff Rennicke
The Bears of Blue River	Charles Major
Bears of the World	Terry Domico and Mark Newman
The Bears of Yellowstone	Paul Schullery
The Beast That Walks Like Man	Harold McCracken
Ben Lilly Legend	Frank J. Dobie
The Berenstain Bears (series)	Jan and Stan Berenstain
The Biography of a Grizzly	Ernest Thompson Seton
California Grizzly	Tracy Storer and Lloyd Tevis, Jr.
In the Presence of Grizzlies	Doug and Andrea Peacock
Giant Pandas	John Seidensticker and Susan Lumpkin
The Giant Pandas of Wolong	George Schaller, Hu Jinchu, Pan Wenshi, Zhu Jing
Giving Voice to Bears	David Rockwell

Goldilocks and the Three Bears	Robert Southey
The Great American Bear	Jeff Fair and Lynn Rogers
The Grizzlies of Mount McKinley	Adolph Murie
The Grizzly	Enos Mills
The Grizzly Bear	Bessie and Edgar Haynes
The Grizzly Bear	Thomas McNamee
The Grizzly Bear	William H. Wright
Grizzly Country	Andy Russell
The Grizzly in the Southwest	David Brown
Grizzly Years	Doug Peacock
The Last Grizzly	David Brown and John Murray (Eds.)
The Last Panda	George Schaller
Lewis and Clark among the Grizzlies	Paul Schullery
Meet Mr. Grizzly	Montague Stevens
Monarch of Deadman Bay	Roger Caras
Monster of God	David Quammen
Mountain Man & Grizzly	Fred Gowans
No Room for Bears	Frank Dufresne
Polar Bears	Ian Stirling
The Sacred Paw	Paul Shepard and Barry Sanders
Spirit Bear	Charles Russell
The Teddy Bear Book	Peter Bull
Three Little Bears	Max Bolliger
Touching Spirit Bear	Ben Mikaelsen
Track of the Grizzly	Frank Craighead, Jr.
True Bear Stories	Joaquin Miller
True Grizz	Douglas H. Chadwick
White Bear	Charles Feazel
The Wild Bears	George Laycock
Winnie the Pooh (series)	A. A. Milne
Yellowstone Bear	James Halfpenny
Yellowstone Bear Tales	Paul Schullery

Poetry

Bears have been included in poetry for centuries, and real and fictional bears appeared in more than a hundred modern items of poetry.

Robert Service, in *Ballads of a Bohemian*, penned "Teddy Bear," a tale not unusually sad for Service and the background that he describes. "There was one jolly little chap who used to play with a large white Teddy Bear," he explained. "He was always with his mother, a sweet-faced woman, who followed his every movement with delight. I used to watch them both and often spoke a few words. Then [after a month or more] this morning I saw the mother in the rue D'Assas. She was alone and in deep black. I wanted to ask after the boy, but there was a look in her face that stopped me."

TEDDY BEAR

O Teddy Bear! with your
head awry
And your comical twisted
smile,
You rub your eyes—do you
wonder why
You've slept such a long, long
while?
As you lay so still in the
cupboard dim,
And you heard on the roof
the rain,
Were you thinking . . . what
has become of him?

—Robert Service

Cartoon Bears (Newspapers, Books)

- "Barnstable" is the bear in the syndicated comic strip *Walt Kelly's Pogo*, by Doyle & Sternecky.
- "Woodruff" is the grizzly bear of *The Simple Beasts*, by Doug Hall.
- Park bears are the primary subjects of Phil Frank's *Travels with Farley*.
- Polar bears are found in *Mukluk*, by Robin Heller.
- Bears are not uncommon subjects of *The Far Side* cartoons by Gary Larson, and are often the characters of the political cartoons of other journalists.

Textbook

The California State Department of Education in 1966 published *Arctos the Grizzly*, by Rhoda Leonard (illustrations by Joseph Capozio). This book was utilized throughout the California school systems for several years.

Magazines

Outdoor Life, since the earliest issues in the late 1800s, has traditionally carried articles of bear adventures. In 1899 "Roping a Grizzly" established a standard, and was followed shortly by a story of capturing a polar bear with a rope in the arctic for placement in the New York Zoological Park (the author has no other details of this event, but it certainly sounds interesting).

War and Peace author Leo Tolstoy wrote a most notable article. His *Outdoor Life* story described a bear hunt in which he was seriously mauled by a bear (the bear had Tolstoy's head in his mouth) and was hospitalized for a month.

MUSIC AND BEARS

Music has been written and performed about and for bears. A few examples:

"Black Bear" is a traditional march for bagpipe bands, written for Scottish soldiers and to be played as the soldiers returned to their barracks at the end of the day. The music is often heard at "tattoos" (military pageants).

"Tiger Whitehead," a children's song by the late Johnny Cash, is about a locally famous Tennessee bear hunter of the 1800s and his wife. Their tombstones provide interesting epithets: The hunter's states he "killed 99 bears," and his wife Sally's notes she "nursed" (breast-fed) two bear cubs that Tiger brought to their home.

"Fight for California," written by Earl E. McCoy and Robert N. Fitch and arranged by Robert O. Briggs in 1909, is the University of California Golden Bears' (Berkeley) fight song. "Our sturdy Golden Bear/Is watching from the skies . . ." (UC Regents).

"The Bear *(L'Ours)*" is the nickname of Symphony no. 82, composed by Hayden in 1786. According to Ian Crofton in *Brewer's Curious Titles*, "The last movement is thought to sound like a bear dancing to the bagpipes, while others claim to have detected a growling in the bass line in this movement."

"BEAR MARKET" BEAR

As stock markets bound and rebound, there is a common and often frequent reference to the bear: a "bear market." Its opposite is a "bull market."

Stock Market Bear
GRAPHIC BY CLINT PORTER, SENIOR DESIGNER, D.A. DAVIDSON & CO.

"In stock market parlance," according to Charles Funk, *A Hog on Ice*, "a bear is a speculator who sells a stock that he does not own in the belief that before he must deliver the stock to its purchaser its price will have dropped so that he may make a profit on the transaction. A bull, on the other hand, is optimistic of future rises in the value of a stock. . . ."

The term "bear market" is based on Old English definitions:

- "To sell the bear skin before the bear is caught"
- To sell a bear: "To sell what one hath not"
- The stock sold: "A bear skin"
- The dealer: "The bear-skin jobber"
- The dealer (more recent): "The bear"

BATTLE BETWEEN BEARS AND APIARISTS

"There was reported by Demetrius Ambassador at Rome, from the King of Musco, that a neighbour of his going to seek Hony, fell into a hollow tree up to the brest in Hony, where he lay two days, being not heard by any man to complain;" describes Edward Topsell in *The History of Four-Footed Beasts*, "at length came a great Bear to this Hony; and putting his head into the tree, the poor man took hold there-of, whereat the Bear suddenly affrighted, drew the man out of that deadly danger, and so ran away for fear of a worse creature."

Honey is undoubtedly attractive to bears, since they and bees share the same habitats. Often fantasized as the only food of bears, honey is quite popular wherever a bear may find a natural beehive or commercial apiary. In reality, the bears are more interested in the brood (bee larvae) than the honey. The bear ". . . grasped the nest," wrote Ernest Thompson Seton in *Monarch the Big Bear*, "and leaping from the branch he plunged headlong into the pool below. . . . [H]is hind feet were seen tearing into the nest, kicking it to pieces; then he let it go and struck out for the shore, the nest floating in rags down-stream. . . . [H]e plunged in again; the wasps [bees] were drowned or too wet to be dangerous, and he carried his prize to the bank in triumph. No honey; of course, that was a disappointment, but there were lots of fat white grubs. . . ."

The sloth and sun bears are each known as the "honey bear"; however, all bears will take advantage of a beehive or swarms of bees. They will rip open bee trees, climbing to the highest limbs, or seek and destroy a commercial apiarist's hives.

During their honey (and larvae) collection endeavors, the bears are incessantly stung. They whine and squeal as their eyes and ears are stung and the bees are deep in their fur. But they are persistent and not at all deterred by the discomfort of stings. Topsell again writes of the relationship between bears and bees. "A Bear is much subject to blindness of the eyes, and for that cause they desire the Hives of Bees, not only for the Hony, but by sting of the Bees, their eyes are cured." An old tale? Maybe not! In today's world many people utilize the sting of bees as a "cure" for muscular sclerosis, cancer, arthritis, and other ailments.

"Like all other bears, the black bear is fond of honey. An experienced old bear will get the honey out of a tree with only a few stings;" explains Frederick Drimmer in *The Animal Kingdom*, but "the youngsters, more greedy than wise, get badly stung and bawl with pain—but they do not stop until they have eaten all the honey."

Bears, primarily the American black bear, inflict serious and costly damage to the broods as well as to the hives of commercial apiaries in North America, and eat the honey that was destined for the market. Bears are a major problem for the blueberry industry in Maine, as they destroy the hives of the necessary pollinator bees, resulting in significant protection costs as well as serious losses.

Annual loss of income from damaged equipment and lost honey production in North America today reaches between $500,000 and $750,000, and hundreds of American black bears are removed (mostly shot) due to their conflicts with the apiarists. Bear damage to beehives is of major importance in Europe, too.

Many apiarists attempt to discourage determined bears with a variety of methods, but once a bear obtains a reward of honey—or any food, for that matter—it will persist in returning to the source. Honey farmers in Europe and North America use costly electric fences around their hives and place the hives on rooftops, raised platforms, and poles and in buildings. Bears are relocated, but like any food-conditioned bears, they continue to return and, unfortunately for the honey industry, are successful in destroying honey, broods, hives, and equipment.

A few states and provinces, including Pennsylvania, Vermont, New Hampshire, and Minnesota provide compensation to the apiarist for bear damages.

The bears' special interest in beehives has not changed over time, for even four centuries ago Topsell wrote, ". . . [they] will break into Beehives sucking out the Hony."

WAR AND BEARS

Like other wild animals, bears have paid a price during civil and international wars fought in their habitats. They have died by direct mortality (shot, exploding mines, artillery), as a result of displacement from their habitat or through habitat destruction, and by being used as food during war-related economic decline. During World War I and World War II, bears were targets for soldiers behind the front lines as well as in battle, and displacement from their habitat caused significant indirect mortality. Bear research, protection, and other necessary management is minimal, if not nonexistent, during war. Wars and revolutions provide firearms for civilians who later use them to kill bears.

During the 1800s the Indian Army and Indian Civil Service slaughtered great numbers of sloth bears, which had been extremely numerous prior to that period. The soldiers were "trigger-happy," killing them for target practice and to pass the time.

War struck captive bears in 1940, when British RAF bombers attacked the train on which Albert Rix's entire bear act was traveling in southern Germany, destroying the bears.

Bears have been shot in more recent conflicts, and according to a Yugoslavian biologist, mines killed at least six brown bears during the war between Croatia and Serbia. Bears (and other animals) in the former Yugoslavia zoos also died from starvation during the conflict.

Army fences constructed along the disputed Pakistan/India border are presently diverting bears into villages where people are attacked and bears killed.

The drug wars of South America have resulted in indirect mortality of Andean bears, as their habitat is impacted when the drug cartel seeks more remote business locations and by the governments' programs of forest defoliation to locate and counter the cartel.

Though war is normally detrimental to bears, occasionally there is something positive. Since 1990 there has been an increase in the Asiatic black bear population in the Kashmir region (China, India, Pakistan). Poachers fearing capture or afraid of being shot by military or security forces (on both sides) are discouraged from entering bear habitat in the Himalayan forest areas. In 2007 U.S. military troops were being trained to prevent poaching in Afghanistan.

In Baghdad during the present Iraq War, a U.S. Army Reserve unit and a U.S. Army Medical Detachment are assisting in the upgrading of the Baghdad Zoo. According to U.S. Army Spc. Chad Wilkerson in an article for the Web site *Defend America*, "The main motivation for U.S. Army involvement at the zoo, . . . is the training of the staff and veterinarians who will be responsible for the animals and facilities there after the U.S. soldiers are gone." The U.S. Army Medical Detachment performed surgery on a thirty-two-year-old female brown bear that was found to have an infected and abscessed cancerous tumor on her abdomen. Wilkerson adds, ". . . Sadir [the bear] is on her way to a full recovery."

WILDFIRE AND BEARS

Bears have evolved with fire of various origins (volcanic, lightning, spontaneous combustion, and human). Fire (also flood, insects, disease, and drought) has altered the landscape, displaced bears, rejuvenated and improved habitats and food sources, created other foods, caused death, and triggered curiosity, fear, and flight. Wildfire has minimal negative impact on bears and is generally beneficial.

Twenty-one grizzly bears were monitored before, during, and following the Yellowstone fires of 1988. Of this group, thirteen moved into burned areas after the fire front passed, three remained within actively burning areas, three remained outside burning and burned areas, two may have perished in firestorms, and five bears denned within and eight outside burned areas (den sites of eight bears were not located, which is not unusual).

"The most important immediate effect of the fires on grizzly bears was the increased availability of ungulate carcasses during a fall otherwise offering few foraging opportunities," note Bonnie Blanchard and Richard Knight in their article "Reactions of Yellowstone Grizzly Bears . . . to Wildfire in Yellowstone National Park." "The fires had no apparent effects on overall choice of den sites, annual range sizes, or . . . [normal] movement."

"Bears were the most matter-of-fact fellows in the exodus," notes Enos Mills in *The Spell of the Rockies.* "Each loitered in the grass and occasionally looked toward the oncoming danger. Their actions showed curiosity and anger, but not alarm."

BEAR AUTOMOBILES

Stutz Bearcat

Harry C. Stutz, inventor and owner of the Stutz Motor Company of Indianapolis, Indiana, produced a series of "Bearcats," considered one of the greatest American sports cars, a true champion of the racecourse as well as the road. First built in 1919, the automobile was a technical anomaly for the time, the chassis and body light and quick, the engine with only four cylinders and side valves. It was considered the sports car of the Jazz Age, usually red, yellow, or blue.

Great Bear (Christie)

The Christie, produced in the early 1900s and entered in the second Vanderbilt Cup race in 1905, was the first front-wheel-drive racer. It moved in a zigzag manner due to a transversely mounted engine and a complex transmission system and was therefore deemed the "Great Bear."

Panda

A small, two-passenger automobile produced in 1955 and 1956 by Small Cars Incorporated of Kansas City. With a "roadster" chassis, it had a 70-inch wheelbase with a four-cylinder "Arrowjet" engine (the larger Kohler engine was optional). Critics claimed this $1,000 vehicle looked like a children's "peddle car" on a frame.

Bearcat

An unusual, small (120 inches long), two-cylinder-engine car produced in 1956 by The American Buckboard Corporation of Los Angeles. With a one-piece fiberglass "sports" body, it had a two-cycle engine, a 70-inch wheelbase, and five wheels. The fifth wheel was rear mounted and served as the drive (chain-drive) wheel. The manufacturer claimed 50 miles per gallon for the $1,000 vehicle.

Kodiak

A current, medium-duty, eight-cylinder Chevrolet truck, the Kodiak is designed for use as a tanker, dump, flatbed, high cube, or six-passenger crew cab. The engine is a V-8, gas or diesel, and the transmission comes in two- or four-wheel drive. The Kodiak is known for its extremely short turning diameter (equal to, if not better than, that of most sedans and small trucks).

BEAR BOATS (SHIPS)

Polar Bear

A trading schooner in the early 1900s that later served as a whaling ship in the Arctic Ocean, the *Polar Bear* was purchased by Vilhjalmur Stefansson in 1915 for arctic exploration.

Bear

A wooden-hull steam vessel, built for the U.S. Navy and launched in 1874, the *Bear* was a 198-foot cutter, displacing 1,700 tons. Acquired by the U.S. Revenue Cutter Service in April 1885, it served in the arctic, providing passenger service and transporting reindeer purchased from Siberia by the United States. A rugged ship designed for arctic ice fields, it handled the rough arctic seas and ice well. In 1929 the *Bear* became a merchant vessel, the *Bear of Oakland*, and prior to returning to the navy for service from 1939 to 1948, it was a floating courthouse as well as starring as the sealer *Macedonia* in the film *The Sea Wolf* (from a Jack London story). While being towed to Philadelphia in 1963 to become a floating restaurant, it floundered.

The U.S.R.C. *Bear* (Nome, Alaska)
THE CHARLES BUNNELL COLLECTION, ACCESSION #58-1026-1103, ARCHIVES OF ALASKA AND POLAR REGIONS DEPARTMENT, UNIVERSITY OF ALASKA, FAIRBANKS

Brown Bear

A patrol boat for the Aleutian Islands Wildlife Refuge during the 1930s, the *Brown Bear* was lost during World War II.

Hvidbjornen (Polar Bear)

The *Hvidbjornen* is a Danish navy patrol boat assigned to serve in the coastal waters of Greenland; it enforces fishing regulations and protects the polar bear populations.

Teddy Bear

A ship of the early 1900s used in Siberian trading, the *Teddy Bear* carried oil prospectors and passengers.

BEAR AIRPLANES

Tupolev TY-95 Bear

The Russian strategic bomber/missile carrier the Tupolev Bear (a four-engine turboprop) was put into service in 1955 during the Cold War; it remains in service today. A modified version to deliver nuclear bombs, the Bear-H, was put into service in 1979. Another version, the Tupolev TU-145 Bear, is in use in India.

Grumman F8F Bearcat

The Bearcat was a U.S. fighter (with a single-engine propeller) that was in service from 1946 to 1953. Developed for the Korean War, the Bearcat was possibly the finest piston-powered fighter ever built. However, it had little chance to display its prowess, as jet fighters came into being and the Bearcat was quickly overshadowed. The F8F Bearcat subsequently was used by the French in Indonesia.

BEARS AND MAIL

Stamps

The U.S. Postal Service has on occasion issued sheets, booklets, and blocks of wildlife postage stamps depicting bears.

Wildlife booklet, May 14, 1981

Wildlife, 18 cents—brown bear and polar bear

The brown bear and polar bear stamps are from a booklet of ten wildlife stamps engraved from photographs by Jim Brandenburg of Minnesota, a contract photographer for *National Geographic*.

©1981 REPRODUCED WITH PERMISSION OF
THE U.S. POSTAL SERVICE

©1987 REPRODUCED WITH PERMISSION OF THE U.S. POSTAL SERVICE

Preservation of Wildlife Habitats,
June 26, 1981

Save Mountain Habitats, 18 cents—grizzly bear

A grizzly bear approaching an evergreen forest with snow-covered mountains in the background is shown on this stamp. It is from a block of four commemorative stamps designed by Chuck Ripper, noted wildlife illustrator and author from Huntington, West Virginia. They were issued to enhance public awareness of the necessity of preserving the environment for native wildlife.

North American Wildlife,
June 13, 1987

Biological Diversity, 22 cents—brown bear, American black bear

These stamps show an Alaskan brown bear standing in the fall colors of dwarf birch and an American black bear climbing a tree. The stamps are from a sheet of fifty commemorative wildlife stamps also designed by Chuck Ripper. They were issued to depict the geographic and biological diversity of wildlife native to North America.

THE GREAT MAIL THEFT OF 1929

Naturalist Dorr Yeager relates a story in Paul Schullery's *Yellowstone Bear Tales* about an American black bear that stole the U.S. mail. An individual delivering mail in Yellowstone National Park stopped for a meal at a road camp in the park's interior. Upon returning to his vehicle (he had left at least one window down), he found the package of mail missing from the vehicle and now in a tree with a bear. The bundle was being thoroughly inspected by the bear, which eventually removed a box of chocolate cookies, consumed them, and again checked the mail. Finding no further rewards, the bear dropped the mail package to the mailman and settled in for an after-dinner nap on a tree limb.

Other Bear Stamps

- Polar Bear, 33 cents (1998–2003)
- Teddy Bears (four images), 37 cents (2002)
- Arctic Tundra; Nature of America Series—Brown Bear (single stamp in block of ten), 37 cents (2003)
- Northeast Deciduous Forest; Nature of America Series—American Black Bear (single stamp in block of ten), 37 cents (2005)

COMMEMORATIVE HALF-DOLLAR COINS (WITH CALIFORNIA GRIZZLY BEAR)

- California Diamond Jubilee; 1925 (San Francisco Mint)
- San Diego, California—Pacific Exposition; 1935 (San Francisco Mint); 1936 (Denver Mint)
- San Francisco—Oakland Bay Bridge; 1936 (San Francisco Mint)

BEARS IN HERALDRY

Heraldry is the profession or systematic use of an arrangement of charges or devices on a shield (coat of arms). Beginning with the crusades, animals (lions, dogs, stags, bears) have appeared in and have long been significant constituents—a common symbol—of heraldry.

"The Swiss canton and town of St. Gallen are named for St. Gallus, who, according to legend, tamed a bear to help him build a house," notes Marvin Grosswirth in *The Heraldry Book*. "It is not surprising therefore, that a bear appears in the arms of St. Gallen."

There was, however, an early problem with the use of bears in heraldry. In Switzerland the male organ of the bear had to be painted bright red, or the heraldist would be mocked for use of a she-bear. Such mockery led to a war in 1579 between the cantons of St. Gallen and Appenzell.

Numerous towns, cantons, cities, and other political units have adopted the bear as a symbol in their coats of arms.

Papal Arms

- The arms of Pope Benedict XVI includes a "saddled" bear, which Saint Corbinian tamed and used to carry his baggage.

Symbol

- Mother Russia
- Germany
- Koreas (considered an ancestor and symbolic animal)
- Finland (national animal)

Coats of Arms

- Appenzell Ausser-Rhoden (Switzerland)
- Appenzell Inner-Rhoden (Switzerland)
- Berlin (Germany)
- Bern (Switzerland)
- Bernhardt (Germany)
- Buskerud County (Norway)
- Dietingen (Germany)
- Freising (Germany)
- Greenland (Denmark)
- Lander (Germany)
- Portein (Switzerland)
- Rawa Coat of Arms (Poland)
- Zweisimmen (Switzerland)

BEAR FLAGS

The states of Alaska, California, and Missouri portray bears on their state flags. The Alaskan flag is the most mythical, but the California flag is the most famous, being the symbol of an armed revolt.

Alaska State Flag

The Big Dipper (Ursa Major—the Great Bear)

COURTESY STATE OF ALASKA DIVISION OF TOURISM

Missouri State Flag

Two grizzly bears, representing power and courage, support the state seal, which depicts a grizzly bear.

COURTESY SECRETARY OF STATE, STATE OF MISSOURI

California State Flag

The Bear Flag Revolt: On June 14, 1846, a group of Americans in central California rose in armed rebellion to secure California for the United States and prevent colonization by the British Empire. They seized the Sonoma garrison of Colonel Mariano Vallejo, the military commandant of the northern Mexican forces. The California Republic was formed as the Bear Flag was raised above the garrison at dawn the next day.

The flag had been hastily made of material from a bolt of cotton. A star was placed on the flag in the tradition of Texas. A red stripe was added at the bottom, and then William Todd, nephew of Mary Todd Lincoln (wife of Abraham Lincoln), drew a California grizzly bear. Todd was

Original "state" flag
COURTESY CALIFORNIA STATE LIBRARY

Present state flag
COURTESY OLD SACRAMENTO STAMP COMPANY, CALIFORNIA

a poor artist, and the bear better resembled a pig. The lettering "California Republic" was added below the "bear."

Within a few days Captain John Fremont deployed Edward Kern, an artist and map drawer, to Sonoma, where he made the flag's "pig" look like the appropriate and intended California grizzly bear. The bear adorning the present flag is from a painting by Charles Nahn and represents one of Grizzly Adams's bears.

BEAR LICENSE PLATES

A bear has historically and infrequently adorned the license plates of a few states and provinces:

- **Alaska:** Alaska flag with the Big Dipper (Ursa Major)
- **Montana:** ten different plates depicting an American black or grizzly bear
- **Louisiana:** Louisiana black bear; "Save the Louisiana Black Bear"
- **Maine:** American black bear
- **Washington:** American black bear
- **Northwest Territories:** polar bear; an imposing "bear" license plate (including a small version for motorcycles); first issued in 1970

COURTESY NORTHWEST TERRITORIES, TRANSPORTATION

BEARTRAP SADDLE

The "beartrap" saddle is exactly that—a trap for the rider. The saddle has a high, upright pommel, and the cantle, also high and upright, often hooks back toward the rider's thighs. It is good for breaking horses because the tightness keeps the rider in the saddle, but it is considered by many to be dangerous—if the horse falls, the rider is frequently injured or killed. A few beartrap saddles remain in use in the United States.

"BEAR" PLANTS

Bears have notably influenced the taxonomy of plants. The flora that have been named primarily because they are utilized by bears for food and healing include the following:

- bearbane
- bearberry (alpine)
- bearberry (evergreen)
- bearberry (red)
- bearbrush
- bear cabbage
- bear clover (mountain misery)
- bear corn
- bearfoot
- bear grape
- bear grass
- bear huckleberry
- bear-mat
- bear moss
- bear oak
- bearroot
- bear's breech
- bear's ear
- bear's foot
- bear's garlic
- bear's head
- bear's paw
- bear's tail
- bear's toes
- bear's weed
- bear's wort
- bear tongue
- bearwood
- berryberry (honeysuckle)

BEARS AS PETS

Bears have been harbored as pets in many different settings for centuries. Bears around the world are captured as orphans or taken from their mothers and become pets.

Theodore Roosevelt wrote of pet black bears in Yellowstone National Park during 1903: "Bears are tamed until they will feed out of the hand, and will come at once if called. Not only have some of the soldiers and scouts tamed bears in this fashion, but occasionally a chambermaid or waiter girl at one of the hotels has thus developed a bear as a pet," (Schullery, *Yellowstone Bear Tales*, 1991).

Grizzly Adams may well have had the most famous "pet" bears (see Grizzly Adams, this chapter).

"Pet" is defined as an object of affection, an animal kept for companionship. The long history of bears as pets has seen a variety of interpretations of the word—from playful companions inside the home to an animal caged outside for occasional viewing, a novelty to show guests. These interesting, delightful, and sometimes tragic relationships are normally quite short-lived. "A sun bear is easily tamed and makes an amusing household pet," notes Frederick Drimmer in *The Animal Kingdom*. "However, with age it is likely to grow bad tempered and become dangerous." This transition is also true with other bear species—they become undisciplined and dangerous as they grow older. Bears are wild animals born with wild traits. Unlike dogs, cats, and possibly some birds that have been domesticated during centuries of conditioning, a pet bear is a captured wild animal that is extremely dangerous. Too often, "pet" and "tamed" become synonymous, which is unfor-

tunate. "Tame" may mean merely conditioned to food, and when the edible reward is unavailable, wildness replaces tameness. Early behavioral adjustments may have occurred, but the bear remains a wild animal.

Bears definitely are amusing, especially as cubs, when they are small and many of their actions and antics are done with minimal strength and power. However, as they grow older, like humans they appear to become more irritable, and this, combined with their enormous strength, makes

---

CITY OF THE BEAR—BERNE, SWITZERLAND

German Duke Berchtold von Zahringen founded Berne in AD 1191 at a location where he had previously hunted and killed numerous brown bears. "Berne" is a corruption of the German word *baren* (bears).

Berne (Bern) is the capital of both Switzerland and the canton of Berne. The image of the bear adorned the city's first coat of arms as early as 1224, and today the city landmark is the Zeitglockenturm (a clock tower built in 1530), where a dancing bear, with other animals, appears as the clock strikes the hour. The bear is a decorative feature of the city, with figures on doorknockers, fountains, gates, and lampposts, and bear images adorn pastries, candies, pipes, and toilet articles.

An ancient statue of the Celtic bear goddess Dea Artio was unearthed in the city during 1832, another indication of the bear's longtime significance and association with Berne—"the city of the bear."

The Berne Bear Pits have been well-known exhibits since 1441, and during the French Revolution bears were "captured" at the pits and taken to Paris as prisoners. Today in Berne twelve or more bears exist in a 39-foot-wide and 11½-foot-deep fortified pit next to the Nydegg Bridge along the Aare River.

them quite capable of doing serious damage and harm wherever they choose to direct this attitude and power. A playful "pet" is capable of serious harm even if it "only" rolls its 300-plus pounds on a person.

When a bear is no longer wanted as a pet, it is nearly impossible to return to the wild and is most often destroyed. Though it may display wild traits and behavior, it has not been raised to fear humans and possibly did not learn to locate wild foods while it was with its mother. If returned to the wild, it would most likely seek foods from human sources, resulting in major conflict with people.

The sale of bears as pets in Southeast Asia is a major business; however, they are sold for their parts when they are no longer desired as pets.

There are positive "pet" stories. Montana author Ben Mikaelsen (*Rescue Josh McGuire*), has an American black bear (acquired from a research laboratory) he considers more a friend than a pet. However, Ben is quick to explain that Buffy, all 600-plus pounds of him, is not tame

THE BEAR AS A STATE OR PROVINCIAL ANIMAL

Several states and provinces of North America have American black or grizzly bears as "official" animals or mammals. The states of Mexico do not have "state animals."

State/Province	Bear
Alabama	Black bear
British Columbia	Spirit (Kermode) bear
California	California grizzly bear
Louisiana	Louisiana black bear
Montana	Grizzly bear
New Brunswick	Black bear
New Mexico	Black bear
Quebec	Black bear
West Virginia	Black bear

and is dangerous, unintentionally or otherwise, and would without doubt kill anyone other than Mikaelsen entering the bear's enclosure. He and Buffy have developed a trusting and total relationship—an understanding that includes closely followed rules that have been established between the two. The bear responds to specific demands, and Ben respects and meets the bear's requirements.

Ben identifies Buffy's displays of trust, honor, remorse, a very high level of pride (he is not to be laughed at), and emotions similar to humans. The bear expresses loneliness, jealousy, and an indication of being grief stricken when left alone. Buffy actually laughs (using lips and chest). And he understands a sense of justice and is protective of his friend Ben. Buffy and Ben conduct bear educational programs.

NATIONAL ANIMAL OF FINLAND— THE BROWN BEAR

The brown bear is respected and feared and, though hunted, is a sacred animal in the country of Finland. A historic emblem of the forests (king of the forests), along with the elk, the bear has since ancient times been an animal of rituals. It has long been considered unsafe to refer to a bear with the name "bear," so numerous nicknames are utilized, including mesikammen (honey-paw). Though respected, the bear is also at times quite unpopular, as the tax collector is considered "the bear."

TOURISM AND BEARS

Vacations and other travels to observe bears are increasing worldwide. Having long been popular attractions in national parks, bears have entered the true world of tourism. People travel independently or commercially to specific locations to view bears, and many family vacations often include bears as a priority. One of the first questions often asked as visitors enter some national parks is "Where are the bears?"

Several national and state parks, refuges, and forests of Japan, Canada, and the United States offer opportunities to view bears. A few areas are known for visitors' being able to readily observe bears, as many of the viewing areas are at food concentrations.

- Denali National Park (Alaska; grizzly bears)
- Glacier National Park (Montana; grizzly bears)
- Kamchatka Peninsula (Russia; brown bears)
- Katmai National Park and Preserve (Alaska; brown bears)
- Kodiak National Wildlife Refuge (Alaska; Kodiak brown bears)
- McNeil River State Game Refuge (Alaska; brown bears)
- Shiretoko National Park (Hokkaido, Japan; brown bears—one bear per square mile)
- Stan Price State Wildlife Sanctuary—Pack Creek (Admiralty Island, Alaska; grizzly bears)
- Tongass National Forest (Hyder, Alaska; grizzly and black bears)
- Wapusk National Park (Churchill, Manitoba; polar bears)
- Yellowstone National Park (Montana, Wyoming, Idaho; grizzly and black bears)

Elevated bear-viewing platform, Katmai National Park, Alaska
PETER HAMEL/COURTESY OF NATIONAL PARK SERVICE

Bear viewing areas may provide any or all of the following:

- Parking
- Interpretation
- Raised viewing platforms
- Signs
- Restrooms
- Boardwalks
- Trails
- Rangers
- Elevated paths (walkways)
- Safety (the viewing area near Hyder, Alaska, has a "guard")

Commercial bear-viewing tours provide a variety of services for travelers:

- Transportation
- Guides
- Lodging
- Interpretation
- Binoculars
- Meals

Many tours are general "wildlife adventures" and include "photo safaris." Tours are single day or long term and are conducted by any of the following:

- Auto
- Bus
- Airplane
- Hiking
- Boat and canoe
- Tundra Buggy

Churchill, Manitoba, the "Polar Bear Capital of the World," becomes a major tourism town during October and November. Polar bears congregate in the Churchill area as they await the development of the arctic ice. This is the "polar bear season" (10,000 visitors arrive each fall), and the Tundra Buggies are ready. These large

---

BEAR HATS AT BUCKINGHAM PALACE

Familiar to tourists visiting Buckingham Palace, London, is the Queen's Guard, a unit of the British Army that guards the "home Sovereign." The foot guards' uniforms basically have not changed since the mid-1800s and include the bright red tunic and, most importantly, the bearskin hat. The bearskin, on a wicker frame, 18 inches tall, weighing two pounds, and placed on a minimum-6-foot-tall guard, creates an imposing and respected figure.

The hats are made of Canadian brown bear hides, collected by the Inuits in an agreement with the government. More than 4,000 hats exist, and replacement is seldom necessary due to excellent care and refurbishing. Most hats have been in use a minimum of twenty years, and many are a hundred years old.

The cost of each hat is approximately $1,200. The bearskin hat is not to be confused with the busby, also made of bearskin, but considerably smaller and ornamented, and worn by nonguard units.

---

commercial vehicles were developed by a local resident to be used for safely viewing polar bears. They are a minimum of 7 feet off the ground, with large wheels, are heated (it is often -50 degrees Fahrenheit outside), and accommodate numerous passengers; e.g., families, individuals, professional photographers, or entire film crews.

The tourism associated with bear viewing provides considerable economic value to the communities adjacent to the viewing areas from the selling of associated gifts, literature, meals, lodging, gasoline, transportation, and other daily requirements. At the same time there is an unspecified amount of adverse impact on the bears. Habituation to humans occurs, as well as occasional displacement when some bears will not approach food sources in open areas with crowds of people nearby.

BEARS IN ENTERTAINMENT

Bears have long been utilized as performers in circuses, bear gardens, street acts, vaudeville, movies, and television.

The Romans considered bears a symbol of power and strength and included them in "circus" performances, with chariot races and warrior contests. The bears fought bloody battles with dogs, prisoners, or gladiators, performing in large outdoor arenas such as the Circus Maximus, which held 150,000 spectators.

The Roman emperor Caligula, who reigned from AD 37 to 41 and was one of the most depraved and monstrous rulers of all time, used 400 bears during a single "games," and Emperor Gordian, AD 238, used 1,000 bears in a single event. The fights were to the death with the men, alone or as a group, using bow and arrow, sword, or spear.

Competition was not always important, as there is evidence of a person with a spear facing six "snarling" bears, and prisoners were sometimes unarmed during the encounters. The disregard for fairness was at times reversed, as in the case of Emperor Commodus, AD 180 to 192, who shot one hundred bears with arrows in a single "event," while remaining out of their reach.

The bears performing in these activities were brown bears from the "known" world, and they often fought dogs, usually mastiffs often joined by Irish wolfhounds. Sometimes herds of bears fought packs of dogs. Roman circus battles also included polar bears that were placed in a flooded arena with seals.

Bearbaiting

Bearbaiting occurred as popular entertainment in "bear gardens" from the time of the Norman Conquest, AD 1066, into the eighteenth century, a period of approximately 700 years.

The bear-garden facilities initially consisted of a round building with three levels of seating (galleries) surrounding a 55-foot diameter ring. The gardens eventually contained several rings with protective stone walls and earthen floors. There were private and public playhouses with a variety of performances, such as gorillas riding on horses' backs.

"The primary activity," explain Lavahn Hoh and William Rough in *Step Right Up!*, "involved chaining a large bear, or perhaps a feisty young bull, to a stake in the center of a ring (by their neck or hind leg) where large mastiff dogs were encouraged to attack it. The dogs were particularly courageous, and they would continue to attack over and over again until they were too weak from the loss of blood to stand. Bets were taken on how many dogs would be killed before the bear or bull died."

Bulls were pitted against bears. A German playbill announced: "And lastly, a furious and hungry bear, which has had no food for eight days, will attack a wild bull and eat him alive on the spot; and if he is unable to complete the task, a wolf will be in readiness to help him" (*Harper's New Monthly Magazine*, October 1855).

Bear gardens (and bearbaiting) helped develop several major social innovations:

- They gathered an enormous variety of performers in one place.
- They established the tradition of audiences closely seated around a central arena or ring.

- They reestablished the tradition of audiences gathering at a fixed location for purposes of entertainment.

Similarly to the Roman circus, the London bear gardens were not "family entertainment," not only because of the brutal and gory scene but because the spectators were vulgar and unruly at best. According to Hoh and Rough, the bear gardens "were extremely popular with Londoners struggling through the filth of daily existence."

The gardens were notorious for noise and riotous disorder. There was chaos, tumult, confusion, and, in today's terms, disorderly conduct. Bear-baiting was also enjoyed by royalty, with one such event using thirteen bears for the entertainment of Queen Elizabeth I.

The gardens have been considered the beginning of the circus and "theaters," including the Elizabethan theater.

Bear gardens continue to exist today. According to the World Animal Foundation, "Although illegal in every country, bear baiting remains a popular past-time in Pakistan, where politicians and senior police officers can still be found watching the show. A series of dogs are set upon a chained bear [teeth and claws removed] who must fight for his or her life. The dogs and the bear sustain horrendous injuries."

Street Bears and Vaudeville

Bears have entertained in the streets for centuries. They were trained and led around on chains for public amusement during the Middle Ages, AD 476 to 1453. In Egypt during the thirteenth century, marketplace entertainment displayed trained animals, including bears that "danced" or went to sleep when instructed.

Asiatic black bear dances for handler and tourists, India
PETE OXFORD/NATUREPL.COM

Bears were utilized to amuse nobility and attract audiences to traveling musicians and jugglers. During the eighteenth and nineteenth centuries, itinerant musicians wandered throughout the countries of Eurasia, playing a musical instrument while exhibiting bears dressed in costumes. Brown bears from the Pyrenees Mountains were famous dancing performers. Vaudeville acts were using bears in the United States at the end of the nineteenth century, and a bear has been on a radio program in the United States, where it exchanged grunts with a comedian.

Bears are presently associated with traveling shows, street merchants, and wandering musicians in Asia. Wrestling matches are held between humans and bears, and they play basketball. Beggars in India use bears that ride bicycles and sit up.

More than 2,000 sloth and Asiatic black bears "dance" in Pakistan and India by standing on their hind legs, lifting their paws, and shaking their hips. Some gypsies and other itinerant entertainers wander with dancing bears that are seldom trained but forced by torture to perform up to twelve hours a day.

These performing bears are normally abducted as cubs to be trained at three to five weeks old. The abductor (who most likely killed the sow) receives $70 to $115 for a cub up to three months old. The cub may almost immediately be resold for $185. Bear schools (academies) have existed for decades; there, these performers learn tricks and are trained to "act." A trained adult is worth at least $650.

Brown bears and Asiatic black bears are trained for a variety of "performances." American black bears are used in U.S. exhibitions. The bears are usually muzzled while performing and are often declawed.

Bear and Bull Fights

Fights pitting a bear against a bull occurred in California between 1816 and the early 1880s. These extremely popular fights were festive occasions normally reserved for holidays, Sundays, and special religious days and were widely advertised with posters. The idea for these staged fights may have originated when ranchers and vaqueros observed violent fights out on the range between wild bulls and grizzly bears.

The fights were held in arenas, where spectators could witness the entire battle between the large California grizzly bear and the Spanish bull that had no fear, retreated from no enemy, and appeared to be born to fight.

The combatants were tied together with a cord approximately 20 yards in length, the front hoof of the bull to the rear paw of the bear. The bull would charge, attempting to gore the bear, and the grizzly would counter with paws and teeth. The grizzly often grasped the bull's snout with its teeth and would be in control and could break the bull's neck. "If the bull won, triumph usually came early in the struggle;" describe Tracy Storer and Lloyd Tevis in *California Grizzly*, "only with full fresh strength could he plunge his long, curving horns into the bear's body, toss his adversary high in the air, and then gore him to death as the bear lay prostrate on the ground."

The fights were vicious, with the bear the normal victor, but both fighters generally were injured, and the victor occasionally later died.

Bear and Lion Fights

Storer and Tevis relate the story of a staged mountain lion/grizzly bear fight in California in 1865. "The lion, which seemed to have no fear, leaped onto the bear's back and while clinging there and facing forward scratched the grizzly's eyes and nose with its claws. The bear repeatedly rolled over onto the ground to rid himself of his adversary; but as soon as the bear was upright, the cat would leap onto his back again. This agility finally decided the struggle in favor of the lion."

A fight was staged in Monterrey, Mexico, between a large California grizzly bear and a "man-killing" African lion. The grizzly bear, according to Storer and Tevis, handled the African king as a cat would a rat. The conflict was over so quickly that the spectators hardly realized how it was accomplished.

Circus Bears

The modern circus with bears originated in England during the mid- to late 1700s. Though bears appear to have given the early impetus to circus-type acts, they were late to arrive in the more modern circus.

"A bear had been introduced into plays at Astley's (Philip) in 1822," according to George Speaight in A History of the Circus, "but it proved incapable of performing the feats intended for it. Another appeared at Usher's benefit in 1837, but it was not until nearly the end of the century that there was much development in the training of these genial-looking but dangerous and untrustworthy animals."

Disposition, Temperament, and Training of Circus Bears

Circus bears of today most commonly consist of Siberian and European (Syrian) brown bears, polar bears, and Asiatic and American black bears. Some giant pandas and sloth bears are also performing. The polar bear is considered the most "eye-catching," while Syrian brown bears are the quickest to learn and the cleverest.

The Asiatic black bears are the comedians of the performing bears. They appear to appreciate applause and will intentionally move into their prescribed position late to attain laughter and attention.

Bears are ideal for training because of their personalities. They have humanlike mannerisms, are highly intelligent and curious, and will develop a very close rapport with their trainer. Physically they have excellent balance and eye/paw coordination. However, their most important trait in being highly responsive to training and learning specific functions may be that they enjoy playing.

David Jamieson and Sandy Davidson in The Colorful World of the Circus relate a wonderful

---

CIRCUS BEARS—A CHRONOLOGY

1888	Polar bears performed with Krone in Germany.
1889	A bear rode a horse, leapt through a balloon, and played with an English mastiff (a reversal from the Elizabethan bear gardens).
1890	Permane's Siberian bears were at a table and drank out of bottles, walked on a globe, and swung on a swing. "Bears have a good sense of balance," notes Speaight.
1904	Polar bears performed in England as part of Wombell's menagerie.
1909	Seventy polar bears, trained by Hagenbeck, performed at the London Hippodrome.
1911	The Hagenbeck bears performed at the Blackpool Tower Circus, where forty polar bears were in the water, occupying a ring only 42 feet in diameter.

example of rapport. "One evening when James Clubb was presenting his brown bears on Chipperfield's circus, the generator failed and the lights went out, leaving the ring in pitch darkness. One bear immediately rushed to James and hugged him. To begin with, he thought he was being attacked but then he noticed the bear was shaking with fright and he realized she had run to her trainer for reassurance."

Circus bear handlers have found that bears should never be taken for granted during training and performance. According to Hoh, bears "look

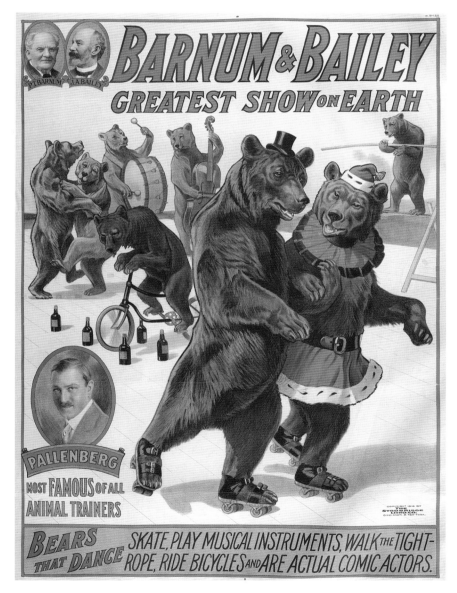

Strobridge Lithograph Co., 1916
BARNUM & BAILEY: PALLENBERG MOST FAMOUS OF ALL ANIMAL TRAINERS
COURTESY OF THE JOHN AND MABLE RINGLING MUSEUM OF ART TIBBALS DIGITAL COLLECTION

BEAR ACTS

Historically, bear performances have included:

- Riding a bicycle
- Pulling a rickshaw or wagon with another bear on the seat
- Balancing on the rola bola
- Standing on and rolling a ball
- Foot-juggling a burning pole
- Walking on its forefeet around the ring
- Pedaling a small car
- Performing a handstand on another bear's back
- Roller skating
- Dancing the pas de quatre from Swan Lake
- Sitting in a chair at a table
- Wrestling with each other

- Skipping rope
- Riding motorcycles
- Balancing on a tightrope
- Playing the harmonica
- Playing the concertina (accordion)
- Somersaulting
- Eating with knife and fork
- Dunking a basketball
- Pushing a cart with another bear as a passenger
- Somersaulting
- Marching to band music
- Performing handstands on wooden tubs
- Juggling items

- Making a hoop with their bodies and tumbling
- Rolling
- Sliding down slide into water
- Diving
- Riding horseback
- Walking bipedally on two tightropes
- Wrestling with people
- Dancing in a set with a woman
- Simulating the pursuit of an enemy
- Playing the drums
- Falling dead when "shot"
- Going through the manual exercise of a soldier with a musket
- Ringing bells

much more harmless and cuddly than they really are." They show no emotion or facial expressions, are not affectionate, will hold a grudge, and will attack out of instinct with no warning or obvious provocation. They must perform in cages, on leads or muzzled and must be handled with rewards, loving care, and infinite patience. The bears must recognize the trainer as the master. Performances are better if their required action has meaning to them and is a natural role, not a new and difficult skill.

There is an ominous saying in the circus world, according to Hoh, "that bear trainers never retire." The "armless wonder" Jack Hubert lost one arm to a bear and the other to a lion; Chubby Guilfoyle was maimed by his bears, and one trainer suffered a seriously broken leg when a bear fell on him. Polar bears, though the most versatile, are also the most dangerous of circus

bears. Trainer Captain Jack Bonavita (née John F. Gentner) was killed in 1917 while working with a group of polar bears.

Through the years nearly all trainers have found that reward, not punishment, is the only effective way to train a bear for performance. Gentle methods of wild animal training are favored over the threat.

Mixed Animal Acts

Bears have been occasionally mixed with other animals in various acts, though these performances are difficult and extremely dangerous. A bear's expression is poorly developed; therefore there is suspicion and a lack of rapport between the bears and other animals. Bears have been mixed with tigers, lions, leopards, cougars, jaguars, panthers, mastiff dogs, hyenas, and other species of bears.

Bear Troupes and Handlers

Bear acts are rare today, with circuses generally not owning their own acts. Troupes and handlers work under contract with the various circuses.

Bears in the Movies

Movies with a bear as the star have been relatively few. Many short animated cartoons have highlighted bears, but less than two dozen full-length films featuring a bear have been in movie theaters of the United States.

- Numerous movie cartoons, 1939–1949, Universal Studios, animated; featured Andy Panda
- *Song of the South*, 1947, Disney, animated; featured Br'er Bear
- *Bear Country*, 1953, Disney
- *The Two Little Bears*, 1961
- *Hey There, It's Yogi Bear*, 1964
- *Night of the Grizzly*, 1966
- *The Jungle Book*, 1967, Disney, animated; featured Baloo, the only bear to sing an Oscar-nominated song, "Bare Necessities" (vocalist, Phil Harris); Baloo is a sloth bear in Rudyard Kipling's book, *Jungle Tales*.
- *Gentle Giant*, 1967; black bear; from the novel *Gentle Ben*
- *King of the Grizzlies*, 1970, Disney
- *Man in the Wilderness*, 1971
- *The Bears and I*, 1974, Disney
- *Grizzly* (a.k.a. *Killer Grizzly*), 1976
- *The Life and Times of Grizzly Adams*, 1976
- *Day of the Animals*, 1977
- *The Many Adventures of Winnie the Pooh*, 1977, Disney, animated
- *Prophecy*, 1979; a mutant animal, most likely a bear

- *The Bear*, 1989
- *Amazing Panda Adventure*, 1995
- *Grizzly Falls*, 1999
- *The Country Bears*, 2002, Disney
- *The Jungle Book 2*, 2003
- *Brother Bear*, 2003, Disney
- *Brother Bear 2*, 2006, Disney

BEARS IN ZOOS

Bears were the first zoo animals, probably due to being the easiest to keep. The queen of Egypt, Hatshepsut, had a bear facility in 1500 BC that possibly could be considered the earliest zoo. Early Chinese rulers also had zoos, and King Ptolemy II of Egypt (285 to 246 BC) had a polar bear in a private zoo in Alexandria.

Menageries—small traveling exhibits—became popular and were the forerunner of the present-day zoo. The first U.S. zoo was established in Philadelphia during 1859, with a polar bear as the first North American "zoo bear."

The sources of today's zoo and wildlife park bears are those bred and raised in zoos, those captured specifically (legally and illegally) for sale to zoos, and those that are problems and have been removed from conflicts with people. Zoos have paid thousands of dollars for bears, with giant pandas being the most expensive (see Giant Pandas, this section).

Zoos serve as laboratories, and much knowledge of certain species has been learned only from zoo animals, while some zoos have breeding programs to perpetuate a species. Zoos offer visitors an opportunity for a better understanding of bears. A visit to the zoo has been described as "serious fun."

Humans often, in their anthropomorphic manner, interpret a zoo bear's actions to indicate

Sun bear in zoo displays coloration and claws
© SHUTTERSTOCK

for enrichment. Food is hidden, and they must "work" for it. There is "furniture" (trees, rocks, logs, pools, areas to dig) for their exploration and play. They have objects to handle. Bear habitats are cleaned daily.

Quality and amount of health care for captive bears varies considerably throughout the world, from virtually none to daily high-level attention. Many zoos and wildlife parks provide regular preventive and responsive veterinarian health care, including periodic scheduled physical examinations. Care may include the following:

- X-rays
- Parasite control
- Blood chemistry
- Antibiotics when necessary
- Dental cleaning and necessary maintenance
- Surgery when necessary

Zoo Foods

Foods are not what would be considered "wild" but are carefully regulated for the nutrition of the zoo bear. Dietitians specifically prepare omnivore food:

- Vegetables (carrots, sweet potatoes)
- Dry food mixtures
- Chicken, fish, and other meats
- Vitamins and minerals
- Fruits (oranges, apples, grapes)

unhappiness. Zoologists claim zoo bears are "happier than wild bears," though some people challenge that claim. Life is without question easier, and many bears, having been born in captivity, know no other life than a zoo or wildlife park. Present-day zoos are improving the environment for bears, with space, caves, streams, trees and other vegetation, and boulders, and wildlife parks offer larger, more diverse, and interesting habitats. Bears are offered an opportunity

Bears are fed one to four times daily, usually with a main evening meal and "snacks" during the day. In wildlife parks the morning snack is often hidden outside where the bears must search, as if in the wild. Many bears receive an individual daily diet based on body condition, behavior, and season. A common daily diet for

DAILY CALORIE REQUIREMENT	
American black bear, juvenile, 155 pounds	3,876
Grizzly bear, adult, 704 pounds	10,592
Grizzly bear, adult, 374 pounds	6,591
Grizzly bear, cub, 110 pounds	4,611

American black bears and grizzly bears may consist of the following:

- Omnivore chow (UNIZOO, commercially prepared)
- Apples
- Bread (white)
- Dry dog food (commercially prepared)
- Chicken heads (fresh)
- Fish (substituted for dog food)
- Carrots
- Eggs (hard boiled)

A giant panda's diet may consist of the following:

- Bamboo
- Apples
- Carrots
- Sweet potatoes
- Sugarcane
- Rice "gruel"
- Special high-fiber biscuit

In some zoos the daily polar bear diet consists of the following:

- One-third fish (usually trout)
- One-third meat (ground beef with crude proteins and fats)
- One-third polar bear chow biscuits (dry pellet food designed for polar bears)

Zoo bears often develop "cage fat" and are fatter and heavier than wild bears. A thirty-month-old giant panda at a zoo weighed 176 pounds, whereas wild thirty- to thirty-three-month-olds are 110 to 121 pounds.

Feeding and habitat maintenance is accomplished with the bears in auxiliary compounds, as bear keepers are continually alert to avoid conflicts, injury, or death. The escape of a bear *must* be prevented. Security is maintained at the bear facilities to protect the bears, visitors, and bear keepers, during open and closed hours.

Visitors must be prevented from feeding bears or gaining access to the bear habitat. In one case an intoxicated youth, having sneaked into a New York zoo during the night, entered a polar bear area and was killed by the bears. The polar bear is considered by many zoo keepers as the most dangerous zoo bear, though some zoos consider elephants and leopards the most dangerous zoo animals.

Zoos with Bears

The International Species Information System (tracking and coordination) lists more than 172 participating zoos worldwide (there are other zoos with bears) with more than a thousand bears. Bears are transferred between zoos by loan and sale, and cubs are occasionally born, so numbers and species often change. All eight species of bears are represented in the zoos throughout the world, ranging from a single to seven species in each zoo.

Giant Pandas

Giant pandas are the most popular bear for the zoo public. Giant pandas are found in zoos, parks, a breeding center, "gardens," reserves, an animal world, a giant panda "base," and a research center:

ATTACKS BY CAPTIVE BEARS

A sampling (31) of attacks in Eurasia, 1991–2002

Location

Zoo	19
Circus	8
Preserve/park	3
Street (dancing bear)	1

Visitor/Handler

Visitor	23
Bear handler*	7
President of a circus	1

Age of Person Attacked

3 (years)	1 (number of victims)
4	2
5	2
7	3
9	3
10	2
11	3
12	1
27	1
Unknown	13

Injuries

Mauled/serious injuries	17
Mauled/death	14 (includes 5 handlers)

Cause

Visitor too close	14
Escaped bear	4
Visitor feeding	6
Petting and feeding	1
Handler feeding	6

* *"Handler" refers to any animal handler, keeper, and attendant.*

- North America (as of 2007)
  Five facilities; fourteen giant pandas
  Chapultepec Zoo, Mexico City, MX (3)
  National Zoological Park, Washington, DC (3)
  Memphis Zoological Garden, Memphis, TN (2)
  Zoo Atlanta, Atlanta, GA (2)
  San Diego Zoological Garden, San Diego, CA (4)
- Europe (as of 2005)
  Two facilities; four giant pandas
- Asia (excluding China; as of 2005)
  Four facilities; eleven giant pandas
- China (as of 2005)
  Twenty-five facilities; 158 giant pandas

The cost of keeping a giant panda in a zoo (non-Chinese) is more than five times that of the next most expensive animal (elephant). The Chinese government charges $1 to $2 million *a year* for the loan of a giant panda (normally a ten-year contract).

"FAMOUS" BEARS

Grizzly Adams

Born John Capen Adams, on October 22, 1812, in Medway, Massachusetts, "Grizzly" Adams became one of the most colorful characters in bear fact and fiction. He worked as a circus hand (where he was mauled by a tiger he was handling), shoemaker, farmer, rancher, and trapper, as well as attempted several other businesses. The gold rush lured him to California in 1849, where he became a mountain man.

While hunting and exploring the Oregon and Washington country, he captured a grizzly bear cub that he named "Lady Washington." She was the first of his trained captive grizzly bears that accompanied him on the streets of San Francisco. Ben Franklin, captured as a cub, became Lady Washington's companion. Samson was taken as an adult and, being "unreliable," was kept caged. Adams captured other bears and established the Mountaineer's Museum in San Francisco, where he displayed his bears with a jaguar, deer, mountain lion, and other small animals. Lady Washington and Ben Franklin were more than displayed—they wandered freely through the museum.

Grizzly Adams was extremely knowledgeable about bears but often unreliable in relating the facts. He did not keep a journal, and his memory often did him injustice. More of a hunter and trapper than a scientist, but also a naturalist, he was a keen observer. For example, he was aware—in the 1850s—that rings are added to the bear's teeth each year; growth rings have much more recently become a valid indication of a bear's age.

He loved bears but hunted and captured them relentlessly and may have been the most famous California bear hunter. Naturalist A. Starker Leopold claimed Grizzly Adams was one of the persons most responsible for the elimination of the grizzly bear in California.

Adams died in Massachusetts in 1860. His many skirmishes with grizzly bears, a tiger, and the mountains of the West had finally done him in.

Ben Franklin with Grizzly Adams
AN ENGRAVING FROM THEODORE HITTELL'S THE ADVENTURES OF JAMES CAPEN ADAMS, MOUNTAINEER AND GRIZZLY BEAR HUNTER OF CALIFORNIA (1860) UNIVERSITY OF CALIFORNIA, BERKELEY

The Teddy Bear

This lovable bear has been a most popular American and international "toy" since the early 1900s, loved by adults and children alike. Basing it on a cartoon drawing of a bear, Morris Michtom, of Brooklyn, New York, created the Teddy Bear as a Christmas item. Patterned after the koala bear, the toy bear with shoe-button eyes was originally named "Teddy" after and with the permission of Theodore Roosevelt.

Michtom had observed the 1902 "Drawing the Line" cartoon by Clifford Berryman of the *Washington Post*. The cartoonist was expressing President Theodore Roosevelt's reaction to a request to shoot a "roped" bear provided for him so his Mississippi bear hunt would be successful. The cartoon was not only about drawing the line between good and bad sportsmanship but was thought to also reflect a sensitive racial issue (the "color line") and a boundary dispute between Mississippi and Louisiana. Though the cartoon depicts a cub,

Theodore Roosevelt drawing the line in the 1902 Clifford Berryman cartoon that led to the "Teddy Bear."
ARCHIVES OF AMERICAN ART, SMITHSONIAN INSTITUTE

the Louisiana black bear in the actual occurrence was an adult weighing 230 pounds.

The Teddy Bear has evolved during its one-hundred-plus years, becoming more portly, and though other toy bears have come onto the scene, Michtom's remains a fixture of American childhood.

Winnie-the-Pooh

In 1914, during World War I, Captain Harry Colebourn was leaving his Winnipeg, Manitoba, Canada, home by train to join his regiment, the Royal Winnipeg Rifles of the Canadian Infantry, at Eal Cardier, Quebec. During a stop at the White River in Ontario, he bought an American black bear cub for $20 from a hunter who had killed the mother.

Colebourn, a veterinarian caring for army horses who loved animals and provided them with affection and care, named the cub "Winnipeg" (Winnie). The "tame" bear became his companion and would sleep under the Canadian soldier's cot.

When his brigade began preparing to ship out from England to the bloody battlefields of France, he realized his bear could not accompany him to the front line. Therefore, he donated Winnie to the London Zoo, where she became one of its most popular attractions. Being tame and gentle—even eating out of a person's hand—she would give youngsters rides around the zoo grounds.

Author A. A. Milne regularly visited Winnie at the zoo, and she was the inspiration for his 1926 creation Winnie-the-Pooh; he gave the world the honey-loving bear, a bear of very little brain that has enchanted children around the globe. Milne's books, *Winnie-the-Pooh* and *The House at Pooh Corner*, have been translated into more than twenty languages, including Latin, Esperanto, and Serbo-Croat.

Winnie is the subject of a feature-length animated film by Walt Disney, and in Russia, Winnie-the-Pooh is a popular children's character known as Vinni Pukh.

When Winnipeg died at the zoo in 1934, her popularity prompted a London newspaper to run an obituary as though she were prominent royalty.

Smokey Bear

The famous guardian of the forests for more than sixty-four years is an American black bear. In August 1944 the U.S. Forest Service and the Advertising Council developed their forest-fire-prevention symbol—Smokey Bear—issuing posters of the now-famous bear pouring water from a bucket onto a campfire. Smokey's popularity rapidly spread, and in 1947 he began to use his eventually equally famous fire-prevention slogan, "Remember, Only YOU Can Prevent Forest Fires." (In 2001 Smokey recognized that fire was necessary for the health of public lands and adjusted his slogan to "Only YOU Can Prevent Wildfires.")

Firefighters in the Lincoln National Forest of New Mexico during the spring of 1950 observed a bear cub along the fire lines. Later, following a blowup of the fire, the cub was found with seriously burned paws and hind legs. Rescued by the firefighters and assisted by a local rancher and a New Mexico Game and Fish ranger, the cub was flown to Santa Fe for veterinary aid.

The young bear recovered, and the New Mexico state game warden presented it to the U.S. Forest Service to be utilized in its fire-prevention program; thus the living symbol of Smokey Bear. "Smokey" lived his life at the National Zoo in the nation's capital. He passed away on November 9, 1976, but the symbol—the bear dressed in blue jeans with a belt, carrying a shovel—continues to remind us to "prevent wildfires." This American icon has been recognized by an Act of Congress, was placed on a U.S. postage stamp, had a radio show, and has his own zip code.

Bodyguard Bears

Roman emperor Valentinian I (AD 321 to 375; became emperor in AD 365) used two quite large brown bears in the capacity of "bodyguards," chaining them nightly in front of his sleeping chamber. His bodyguards were apparently effective at their home post, as the emperor died during a battle in Moravia.

CHAPTER 6

Bear Hunting

Bear hunting has occurred since early "humans" and bears shared the same areas of the Eurasian continent. Bears were sources of food and clothing—and they were enemies. Humans undoubtedly were occasional bear food. In the days of chivalry, the Spanish kings held the bear hunt in high order, pursuing the quarry with select hounds and their finest horses. The Norsemen of Norway, Denmark, and Finland would seek no advantage in a hunt, meeting the bear alone, fighting and killing with only a sword or spear.

Bear hunting on the North American continent was little different. "When the Indians hunt it [grizzly bear] they generally go six or eight in a band," Indian interpreter and trader John Long observed in 1778 (Gowans 1986). "The instant they see one, they endeavour to surround it, by forming a large circle: if it is on the march they fire at it." Gowans adds that Lewis and Clark were told by the Mandan Indians that "they 'hunted [the grizzly] in parties of eight to ten men,' and that 'the warriors wore war paint as they would when going to war against enemies.'"

"The Eskimo who brings down a polar bear is respected by his folk as a master hunter," writes Frederick Drimmer in *The Animal Kingdom*.

When early explorers reached North America, they began killing bears, and hunting became an important element in colonial settlement. Hunting to bring the bear to justice, without a conservation ethic, colonists and pioneers killed enormous numbers of bears, and populations quickly diminished. A Pennsylvania hunter killed 400 in his lifetime, and a New York settler 96 in three years. Fur companies sold 18,000 skins annually in the early years of North American settlement. During one three-year period, over 8,000 bearskins were shipped from Ohio alone.

An illustration from a nineteenth-century magazine depicting a Russian hunter with an espatoon and a brown bear.

Bears were eliminated from Ohio, and only during the past few years have they started to return to the state, immigrating from Pennsylvania and West Virginia.

Hunting for bears provided entertainment as well as sport for the New England colonists during the 1700s. They conducted bear and turkey shoots in which a bear was pursued and killed, with the carcass going to the best marksman.

PRESENT-DAY BEAR HUNTING

The populations and distribution of bears has drastically changed in most countries. There are fewer bears in many areas; populations and even species have been extirpated in many regions and in some countries entirely. Some populations have increased, and others are reestablishing. Bear hunting in much of Asia is prohibited, but illegal hunting continues at an alarming rate, with the expected population declines.

Bears are hunted today, as they were historically, for a myriad of cultural, personal, and economic purposes that include the following:

- Major element of bear management
- Control population size
- Eliminate problem bears
- Practice for war
- Defense of property
- Record book
- Eliminate "vermin"
- Religious reasons
- Family tradition
- Self-defense
- Food
- Sport
- Hired for another person's reasons
- Status in the community
- Manhood rites (machismo)
- Thrill of the hunt
- Parts for the market
- Pleasure
- Trophies
- Support family
- Bring the bear to justice

North America

Bear hunting today is in many respects quite different from what it has been historically. There are improvements in firearms, ammunition, and transportation. Hunting philosophies are somewhat different, as is the *need* to kill bears.

Hunters kill bears for sport and trophy, and game wardens and other government hunters "remove" bears for management purposes (population control and reduction of nuisance bears). Guided hunts are very common, and bear-hunting licenses and tags are a major revenue source for states and provinces, as are hunting's general expenditures (equipment, transportation, food, lodging, guiding) for the local economies.

HUNTING EXPENDITURES—ANNUAL AVERAGE BLACK BEAR HUNTS (TEN-YEAR PERIOD—MONTANA)	
Residents	$3 Million
Nonresidents	$1 Million

Sport hunting occurs mostly during weekends and special vacations, and the day-to-day, relentless pursuit of bears by an individual is rare if not nonexistent. However, "the thrill of the hunt" remains for those seeking a bear.

ANNUAL HUNTING HARVEST NORTH AMERICA**

American Black Bear

United States

Alaska	2,580	New Mexico	335
Arizona	250	New York	959
Arkansas	339	North Carolina	1,693
California	1,692	Oregon	1,056
Colorado	466	Pennsylvania	3,419
Georgia	293	South Carolina	38
Idaho	1,880	Tennessee	262
Maine	3,531	Utah	92
Maryland	38	Vermont	497
Massachusetts	136	Virginia	1,454
Michigan	2,219	Washington	1,228
Minnesota	4,151	West Virginia	1,524
Montana	1,724	Wisconsin	2,925
New Hampshire	488	Wyoming	247
New Jersey	328		

Canada

Alberta	1,076	Nova Scotia	851 (b)
British Columbia	4,463	Nunavut	(c)
Manitoba	1,976	Ontario	5,590
New Brunswick	2,004	Quebec	3,502
Newfoundland/Labrador	325	Saskatchewan	2,158
Northwest Territories	(a)	Yukon Territory	96

Mexico (c)

Grizzly/Brown Bear

United States

Alaska   1,691 bears

Idaho, Montana, Washington, and Wyoming: No hunting seasons

Canada

Nunavut   24 bears (annual quota: 30)

Yukon   100 bears

Alberta, British Columbia, and Northwest Territories: Information unavailable

Polar Bear

Alaska, Manitoba, Quebec

No sport hunting; may be taken by Native Americans

Ontario

No sport hunting; may be taken by Native Americans (quota: 30; < 9 harvested)

Newfoundland/Labrador

No sport hunting: (quota: 6 for nuisance bears; 6 harvested)

Northwest Territories, Yukon

Limited sport hunting (quotas); may be taken by Native Americans

Nunavut

Bears harvested: 498; includes harvest (all mortality) in 12 populations (other provinces/territories)

Yukon

None (despite legal harvest)

** *Data based on 3- or 4- year average*
(a) *Information unavailable*
(b) *Includes snare trapping*
(c) *No hunting season*

Professional bear hunter Bernard Paque, in a 1991 *Wall Street Journal* article, perhaps best described present-day bear hunts. "Hunting with friends, two rigs and CB radios is fun, but when I'm chasing through the woods, just me and the bear and the dogs, now that's a bear hunt." This description remains appropriate today, though ATVs and cell phones have dramatically joined, if not replaced, the "rigs" and "CB radios."

Weapons

Early weapons were crude, and hunters lacked an advantage, until about one hundred years ago. "Traditionally, the Eskimo has hunted the polar bear with a lance," according to Thomas Koch in *The Year of the Polar Bear*. "It was not until recently that guns were introduced to the Eskimo's culture."

"During the days of muzzle-loading rifles, its [the grizzly bear's] name and fame inspired terror throughout the mountains and foothills of the wild western domain which constituted its home," writes naturalist/zoologist William Hornaday in *The American Natural History*. "For many years it held the old-fashioned Kentucky rifle of the pioneer in profound contempt, and frequently when it was used to annoy him, the user met a tragic fate. I believe that Grizzlies have killed and maimed a larger number of hunters than all other bears of the world combined."

Hunters worldwide have killed or captured bears with an assortment of weapons and "tools," from various firearms and traps to arrows, knives, rocks, clubs, and poisons. Weapons have ranged in size from pocketknives to whaling (harpoon) guns.

The early bear trap was developed in Europe but perfected in the United States. Powerful and extremely difficult to escape from, it was used throughout the frontier West although rarely in recent times. "The [bear] trap," relates Carl P. Russell, *Firearms, Traps, & Tools of the Mountain Men,* "is credited to Mr. D. Crossett, pioneer craftsman of Kenosha, Wisconsin, in the 1840s and 1850s."

The Spaniards and Indians in the early 1800s killed bears with a box trap, "a large, strong box made of rails and having a doorway," as Tracy Storer and Lloyd Tevis describe in *California Grizzly.* "A riata [lariat] was coiled on the floor round a hunk of meat. When a grizzly stepped within, the rope was yanked to snare him and the door was slammed shut. Then the Indians attacked with spears."

Spear-traps, popular in Eurasia, were constructed of ". . . a spear with an iron head wedged horizontally in the ground between two upright sticks," describe Desmond Morris and Ramona Morris, *Men and Pandas,* "the tip of the weapons being set at an appropriate height to pierce the heart region. . . ." The trap was automatic, with a sapling as a spring, and a cord attached to a trigger that was sprung by the bear.

Set guns consisted of an anchored double-barreled shotgun directed at bait, with trigger wires or strings attached to the bait. When the bear pulled the bait, the wires pulled the trigger, firing the gun. Pistols were also used in this fashion. Trip wires across a trail triggered anchored muskets.

One aggressive, or foolish, hunter sat in a baited pit with logs over it and shot the bear on the logs overhead.

Those without a firearm or the willingness to build a trap resorted to innovative methods. Bait was laid in the path of a bear. A bent sapling was anchored, and a knife was attached to the loose end of the sapling. The bait and sapling were set with a figure-four trigger, and when the bait was moved, the sapling drove the knife at the bear.

In California, one of the most noble and thrilling means of taking a bear was with the riata,

Cowboys Roping a Bear
PAINTING BY JAMES WALKER/
DENVER ART MUSEUM

or lariat. "The vaqueros would never dream of hunting a grizzly with a gun, but solely with their rawhide reatas, which were between sixty and eighty feet in length," notes Thomas McIntyre in his article for *Sports Afield*, "American History—Grizzly." According to "Bears and Bear-Hunting" in *Harper's New Monthly Magazine*, 1855, "The native population . . . Mexicans, are excellent horsemen, and throw the lasso with the precision of the rifle-ball." And Storer and Tevis in *California Grizzly* quote the common saying, *La reata es el rifle del ranchero*—the lasso is the rifle of the rancher. They also relate a description of this exciting method: "The animals were lassoed by the throat and also by the hind leg, a horseman at each end, and the two pulling in opposite direction till the poor beast succumbed." (W. H. Davis, *Sixty Years in California*, 1889).

Bear hunters around the world have pursued bears by numerous means, including on foot, horseback, mule back, and elephant back; in trucks, cars, boats, dugout canoes, airplanes, and helicopters and on snow machines (and in armor during the medieval period).

They have shot from roads, trees, scaffolds, trails, and blinds; used dogs and bait; hunted in wild areas, in developments, on the ocean, and on ice floes; and they have hunted and trapped alone, in groups, and in masses. Thousands have taken the quarry, but also at times the hunter has returned empty-handed, and many hunters have been killed or mauled.

Firearms

The early firearms used to hunt bears were without question inadequate. Theodore Roosevelt described them in Paul Schullery's *American Bears* as "the long-barrelled, small-bored pea-rifle, whose bullets ran seventy to the pound, the amount of powder and lead being a little less than that contained in the cartridge of a thirty-two calibre Winchester." Roosevelt also subscribed to the fact that if you had a "thoroughly trustworthy weapon and a fairly cool head," you could follow a bear "into its own haunts and slay grim Old Ephraim."

Some additional old advice was that in order to gain an advantage, you should hunt "close-um," meaning to hunt at close range, saving ammunition and being more accurate. Nothing was mentioned about "close-um" being more vulnerable to an attack.

Bear hunting is and always has been life threatening, but the firearms of today provide the killing power hunters lacked during the period of continental settlement, and there is no question of the improved ability to kill over the prehistoric days.

The "best firearm" to hunt bears is continually debated but may be best described by Clyde Ormand in his *Complete Book of Hunting*. "The 'best' grizzly rifle is the most powerful rifle the hunter can shoot well." He further comments that for the Alaskan brown bear "the right rifle-cartridge combination is the most powerful the hunter can handle within reason."

TROPHY AND RECORD BEARS

Trophies are an important product of bear hunting, with a full mount or head, skull, and hide popular with the individual hunter. "The black bear is among the most coveted trophies in the United States," relates hunting authority Ben East in *The Ben East Hunting Book*. The "largest" is important to many trophy-bear hunters. However, "largest" is often difficult to determine.

The Boone and Crockett Club

The club, started by Theodore Roosevelt in 1887 as a "Big Game" conservation organization, ascribes to strong ethical hunting, such as fair chase and sportsmanship, and several North American states and provinces have adopted many of its standards. Roosevelt aptly named the club after frontiersmen Daniel Boone and Davy Crockett, who represented the hunting standards prescribed.

In 1950 the club adopted a scoring system that provides "objective" measurements and scores of big-game animals, thus "Big Game Records" of North America. The club manages an official scoring system meant to record skull size.

Official Boone and Crockett Scoring System

Recorded skulls normally originate from a fair-chase hunt, though a few were discovered and "picked up." The recorded score is the total (in inches) of the skull length and width. Records are maintained by species of bear.

BOONE AND CROCKETT CLUB BEAR RECORDS (NORTH AMERICA)

World Record Skulls (Length plus Width in Inches)

Species	Score	Year	Hunter	Location
Brown bear	30^{12}/$_{16}$	1952	Roy Lindsley	Kodiak Island, AK
Polar bear	29^{15}/$_{16}$	1963	Shelby Longoria	Kotzebue, AK
Grizzly bear	27^{13}/$_{16}$	1976	(Picked up)	Lone Mountain, AK
Black bear	23^{10}/$_{16}$	1975	(Picked up)	Sanpete, UT

Longest Skulls

Species	Length (Inches)	Year	Location
Brown bear	19^{13}/$_{16}$	1961	Port Heiden, AK
Polar bear	18^{8}/$_{16}$	1963	Kotzebue, AK
Grizzly bear	17^{6}/$_{16}$	1970	Bella Coola Valley, BC
Black bear	14^{12}/$_{16}$	1975	Sanpete, UT

Widest Skulls

Species	Width (Inches)	Year	Location
Brown bear	17^{14}/$_{16}$	2006	Uganik Lake, AK
Polar bear	11^{7}/$_{16}$	1963	Kotzebue, AK
Grizzly bear	10^{9}/$_{16}$	1976	Lone Mountain, AK
Black bear	9^{4}/$_{16}$	1993	Mendocino, CA

Sources of Largest Bears (Skull Size—North America)

Brown Bear

- 12 of the 16 largest from Kodiak Island, AK
- 18 of the 26 largest from Kodiak Island, AK
- 25 of the 43 largest from Kodiak Island, AK
- 2 of the 27 largest from Aliulik Peninsula, AK
- 5 of the 46 largest from the Alaska Peninsula, AK

Polar Bear

- 6 of the 9 largest from Kotzebue, AK
- 25 of the 48 largest from Kotzebue, AK
- 8 of the 47 largest from Point Hope, AK (Point Hope is 150 miles north of Kotzebue, AK)

Grizzly Bear

- 3 of the 5 largest from British Columbia
- 10 of the 14 largest from Alaska
- 23 of the 33 largest from Alaska
- 15 of the 50 largest from British Columbia
- 32 of the 49 largest from Alaska
- 3 of the 44 largest from Alberta

American Black Bear

- 6 of the 11 largest from Pennsylvania
- 15 of the 41 largest from Pennsylvania
- 6 of the 23 largest from Wisconsin
- 2 of the 12 largest from California
- 6 of the 47 largest from Arizona

BEAR HUNTERS

The author finds it tempting to categorize the bear hunters as "great," "famous," "an incidental hunter," or whatever. However, the criteria for great, or any category, are debatable. The hunters killed by bears may be considered famous—or were they just foolish and careless? The hunters who eliminated all bears from an area—are they famous or notorious? The hunters of the 1800s, a wide-ranging type of people, were famous due to their strange personalities or, in the case of Theodore Roosevelt, because they were prominent individuals (or president of the United States). David Brown notes in *The Grizzly in the Southwest* that you must be "fanatical" to be a famous hunter.

"Famous" Bear Hunters

The list of "famous" hunters is compiled from historical and present-day literature. Few hunters of today make the list, probably because they are considerably more rational than early hunters, but they are also better equipped, have less necessity to hunt, and have minimal opportunity for notoriety—today's North American hunter lives in a considerably different world.

The list provides considerable information about some, with little about others, but they were all "bear hunters"—notorious, legendary, famous across the continent or in their community. They hunted as a profession, for subsistence, to help a friend, incidental to another occupation, or for sport or shot a bear only at an opportune moment and even occasionally "in self-defense." Some hunters, such as Ben Lilly, hunted with an obsession. And keep in mind that an anonymous source noted that bear stories "are like fine wine, they improve with age."

John Adams (John Capen Adams; Grizzly Adams)

- *Occupation*: wilderness traveler, miner, oxen drover, storekeeper, hunter/trapper, mountaineer, shoemaker, frontiersman
- *Period*: mid-1800s
- *Location*: California
- *Species hunted*: grizzly bear, black bear

Robert Eager Bobo

- *Occupation*: soldier, farmer
- *Period*: late 1800s
- *Location*: Mississippi
- *Species hunted*: black bear
- *Number of bears killed*: 150 to 300 a season (27 on a single day); killed a bear with a knife; largest bear killed: 711 pounds

Jake Borah

- *Occupation*: hunter, guide
- *Location*: Colorado
- *Species hunted*: black bear, grizzly bear

James Bridger

- *Occupation*: hunter, trapper, guide, legendary frontiersman
- *Period*: early to mid-1800s
- *Location*: Rocky Mountains
- *Species hunted*: grizzly bear, some black bear

Nicolae Ceausescu, An Infamous Bear Hunter

- *Occupation*: harsh dictator/ruler of Romania
- *Period*: 1960s–1989
- *Location*: Romania; protected "game/hunting" areas where only he and his friends hunted
- *Species hunted*: brown bear

- *Number of bears killed*: approximately 400 in his 25 years of reign; killed 22 in a day in 1974
- *Demise of Ceausescu*: overthrown and executed in 1989 by a junta (for political/tyranny reasons, not necessarily bear hunting)

Holt Collier

- *Occupation*: slave, valet, Confederate soldier
- *Period*: mid-1800s to early 1900s
- *Location*: Louisiana, Mississippi
- *Species hunted*: black bear
- *Number of bears killed*: directly responsible for or assisted in killing over 3,000 bears

David (Davy) Crockett

- *Occupation*: soldier, scout, congressman, pipe-stave maker, hunter
- *Period*: late 1700s to mid-1800s
- *Location*: Tennessee
- *Species hunted*: black bear
- *Number of bears killed*: total unknown; 105 during winter of 1825–1826 (6 months); killed 17 in a week; killed a bear with a butcher knife; largest bear killed: 617 pounds

Grancel Fitz

- *Occupation*: hunter, writer, photographer
- *Period*: 1923–1955
- *Species hunted*: black bear, Alaskan brown bear, grizzly bear, polar bear

Ralph Flowers

- *Occupation*: professional hunter for the Washington Forest Protection Association
- *Period*: mid-1900s
- *Location*: Olympic Peninsula and western Washington

- *Species hunted*: black bear that were damaging harvestable trees (timber industry)
- *Number of bears killed*: 1,125 in a 38-year period

Edwin Grimes
- *Occupation*: hunter
- *Location*: Pennsylvania
- *Species hunted*: black bear
- *Number of bears killed*: over 200; killed his 200th on his 80th birthday

Wade Hampton III
- *Occupation*: soldier/patriot, Confederate general, governor of South Carolina, U.S. senator (South Carolina)
- *Period*: 1800s
- *Location*: eastern Tennessee, western North Carolina, South Carolina, Mississippi to eastern Texas
- *Species hunted*: black bear
- *Number of bears killed*: involved with killing 500 (directly responsible for two-thirds of those); killed 68 in 5 months; killed 30 to 40 with a knife

Allen Hasselborg
- *Occupation*: hunter
- *Period*: early 1900s
- *Location*: Admiralty Island, Alaska
- *Species hunted*: brown bear
- *Number of bears killed*: numerous

"Bear" Howard
- *Occupation*: hunter, rancher-farmer, Mexican War soldier; marketed bear meat and sold gallbladders to Chinese apothecary shops

- *Period*: 1800s
- *Location*: Arizona
- *Species hunted*: grizzly bear

"Old Ike"
- *Period*: late 1800s
- *Species hunted*: grizzly bear
- *Number of bears killed*: nearly 100; Theodore Roosevelt considered him one of the most successful bear hunters.

Benjamin "Ben" Vernon Lilly
- *Occupation*: blacksmith, farmer, cowboy, logger; a fanatical bear hunter (market hunter, hunt master, government hunter, folk figure, and legendary character)
- *Period*: late 1800s to early 1900s
- *Location*: Louisiana, Mississippi, Texas, Mexico, New Mexico
- *Species hunted*: grizzly bear, black bear
- *Number of bears killed*: 300 to 400 (48 in a year); used up to 25 dogs; killed many bears with a knife

James A. "Bear" Moore
- *Occupation*: hunter, farmer
- *Period*: late 1800s to early 1900s
- *Location*: New Mexico
- *Species hunted*: grizzly bear; killed a bear with a knife

George Nidever
- *Period*: early to mid 1800s
- *Location*: San Luis Obispo County, California
- *Species hunted*: grizzly bear
- *Number of bears killed*: 200; 45 in 1837

A Norwegian Hunter (name unknown)
- *Period*: over many years
- *Location*: arctic
- *Species hunted*: polar bears
- *Number of bears killed*: approximately 700

Ramon Ortega
- *Period*: late 1800s
- *Location*: mountainous Ventura County, California
- *Species hunted*: grizzly bear
- *Number of bears killed*: over 200; 70 in 5 years; 15 in a day

Bernard Paque
- *Occupation*: hunter for the Washington Forest Protection Association
- *Period*: late 1960s to early 1990s (23 years)
- *Location*: Washington
- *Species hunted*: black bear
- *Number of bears killed*: over 2,300

William Pickett
- *Occupation*: Confederate army colonel, civil engineer, Wyoming representative of the Boone and Crockett Club, artist, rancher (subject in Ernest Thompson Seton's *The Biography of a Grizzly*)
- *Period*: 1876–1882
- *Location*: Wyoming, Yellowstone National Park (hunting legal at that time) and adjacent areas
- *Species hunted*: grizzly bear
- *Number of bears killed*: more than 70

Theodore Roosevelt
- *Occupation*: rancher, soldier, writer, president of the Untied States
- *Period*: mid-1800s to early 1900s
- *Location*: Colorado, Idaho, Louisiana, Mississippi, Montana, North Dakota, Wyoming
- *Species hunted*: grizzly bear (his favorite big-game animal), black bear

Isaac Slover
- *Occupation*: trapper; killing grizzly bears was his great ambition, but he considered it his pastime
- *Period*: 1842–1854
- *Location*: southeastern California
- *Species hunted*: grizzly bear
- *Number of bears killed*: "many"

Vic Smith
- *Occupation*: guide, scout, whiskey smuggler, machinist, trapper, mail carrier, fugitive, hunter
- *Period*: 1870–1890
- *Location*: primarily Montana
- *Species hunted*: grizzly bear, black bear
- *Number of bears killed*: 700 to 800

Andy Sublette
- *Occupation*: guide, mountain man, miner, fought in Mexican War
- *Period*: mid-1800s
- *Location*: across the United States
- *Species hunted*: grizzly bear, black bear
- *Number of bears killed*: "many"

Wilburn Waters

- *Occupation*: apprentice saddler, sheriff, artist, hunter
- *Period*: mid-1800s
- *Location*: southwestern Virginia, east Tennessee
- *Species hunted*: black bear; killed bears with a knife

James St. Clair Willburn

- *Occupation*: school principal, meat hunter
- *Period*: mid-1800s
- *Location*: Trinity County, California
- *Species hunted*: black bear, grizzly bear; killed a grizzly with a knife

Tazewell Woody

- *Occupation*: hunter
- *Location*: Rocky Mountains and Great Plains
- *Species hunted*: black bear, grizzly bear
- *Number of bears killed*: many, according to Theodore Roosevelt

Dick "Uncle" Wootton

- *Occupation*: trapper, scout, Indian fighter, wagoner, guide, stagecoach station operator, rancher, buffalo hunter, innkeeper, infamous mountain man in the pre–Civil War West
- *Period*: mid-1800s
- *Location*: Kentucky, Colorado
- *Species hunted*: black bear, grizzly bear
- *Number of bears killed*: considered to have "killed his share"; killed a grizzly with a knife

William Wright

- *Occupation*: blacksmith, mailman, carpenter, hunter, naturalist, author (*The Grizzly Bear*)

MULTIPLE KILLS IN MINIMAL TIME

Enos Mills in *The Grizzly* relates the following:
- "William H. Wright once killed five bears with five shots in rapid succession."
- "I was with a hunter in a berry-patch when four grizzlies fell with four lightning-like shots."
- "George McClelland in Wyoming killed nine bears inside of a minute."

- *Period*: late 1800s to early 1900s
- *Location*: Idaho, Montana, Washington, British Columbia, Alberta
- *Species hunted*: grizzly bear, black bear; used a 12-pound, single-shot .45-100 Winchester; killed a grizzly with a pocketknife

George Yount

- *Occupation*: one of the first pioneers in California, arriving at Napa Valley in February 1831
- *Period*: mid-1800s
- *Species hunted*: grizzly bear, black bear
- *Number of bears killed*: total unknown; claimed to have often killed 5 or 6 in a day

Other Frontiersmen and Hunters Who Killed Bears with a Knife

A frontiersman might occasionally be without a firearm but never without a knife, and too often it came forth as the weapon of the moment. Out of necessity when a gun failed, or for sport or excitement, knives were used to killed bears. The use of the knife to kill a bear was described by one frontiersman as "cold steel, with blade as slick as silk."

Jim Baker

While a scout for General Fremont, he attacked and killed a grizzly bear using a "butcher" knife, with minimal injury to himself; a second grizzly (wounded) attacked him, all within a few minutes; he also killed the second bear, though he was badly mauled.

Colonel William Butts

He killed a wounded 2,100-pound grizzly bear in San Luis Obispo County, California, March 29, 1853, with an 8-inch blade knife; badly mauled, he survived to later become editor of the *Southern Californian* newspaper.

John Farney

Farney's gun failed as a black bear charged while he was hunting in Jackson County, Ohio. He threw his tomahawk, which glanced off the bear's head, then used his knife to kill the bear.

John Hugh Glass

A trapper in the 1820s, Glass killed a wounded sow grizzly bear (with two cubs) with his knife as it seriously mauled him.

Bob Nichols

This "modern-day" hunter killed a bear with a knife. The charge of the grizzly sow protecting her cubs was so rapid Nichols could not fire his rifle; the 880-pound bear was mauling him when he managed to use his knife to stab it in the throat (in its jugular vein) (Fort St. James area of British Columbia).

William Parenteau

In Colorado in 1890 Parenteau killed a wounded sow grizzly bear (with a cub) with his "long-bladed" knife.

Takumik

". . . an Eskimo named Takumik who did combat with a polar bear; the man armed only with a knife [prerifle days], but he killed the bear, earning himself the fame of the greatest of the old-time hunters" (from *Hunters of the Northern Ice*); a quotation in Larry Kaniut's *Alaska Bear Tales*.

Spanish Vaqueros

W. P. Hubbard in *Notorious Grizzly Bears* describes the death of a "stock-killer" by vaqueros on horseback: ". . . was overtaken and stretched out with a *reata* around his [bear] neck and each foot. Then one of the riders, . . . would dismount, and with his knife dispatch the . . . bear."

Frontiersmen Who Killed Bears with Other Weapons

Bears were killed with a variety of weapons, for sport and out of necessity. "In 1754 [in Connecticut] . . . Israel Putnam, later a famed Revolutionary soldier," according to James Cardoza in *The Black Bear in Massachusetts*, "lost a hog to a hungry bear. Tracking the bear to its den, Putnam reputedly entered the lair and dispatched the bear and its two cubs with a club, and recovered the carcass of his pig."

Robert Bobo

When his gun did not fire, Bobo stabbed a black bear to death with a sharpened cane (large stick) and the assistance of his dogs fighting the bear.

Don Jose Ramon Carrillo

Carrillo dueled grizzly bears with a light-handled sword.

W. H. (William) Eddy

A member of the ill-fated Donner Party, snowbound in the Sierra Nevada of California in November 1846, faint from starvation, Eddy followed the tracks of a large grizzly bear. He wounded the bear with his gun, and it charged. Impeded by its wound, the bear could not catch Eddy. After using his only two bullets, he killed the bear by striking it in the head with a club.

Indians (Asia)

Sloth bears were readily speared from horseback on the Indian subcontinent during the 1900s.

General William "Red" Jackson

Jackson chased down a large grizzly bear and split its skull with a saber while on horseback in the Southwest during a pre–Civil War excursion.

Joseph Lapoint

He stabbed to death a grizzly bear using a bayonet fixed on a gun (death by bayonet uncertain; possibly also shot).

Joseph Meek

Meek used his tomahawk to kill a wounded grizzly bear with cubs.

Samuel Pope

Pope killed an already wounded grizzly bear with his tomahawk.

James Samuel

Samuel, believing his dogs had treed a possum in a tree hollow, was unarmed except for a pole ax. When a bear instead of a possum appeared, he killed the bear with the pole ax.

A Shawnee Indian (Name Unknown)

In the Rocky Mountains the Shawnee, according to Gowans's *Mountain Man & Grizzly*, ". . . has acquired much fame by attacking and destroying numbers of them (grizzly bears), with an old rusty sword, which he flourishes about their ears with no little dexterity and effect."

Ed Wiseman

He killed possibly the last grizzly bear in Colorado, in September 1979, with a handheld arrow, as he was being mauled.

Frontiersmen Killed by Bears

Most fatalities involved a combination of being inadequately armed or unarmed, using inadequate caution, and meeting a wounded bear. According to Gowans, "the hunter who took any unnecessary chances in dealing with a 'Grizzly' always regretted it."

In addition to those on the deceased list, many others were obviously killed by bears, but their stories have been lost with time, were never recorded, or were unknown to others. Bears continue to kill people in today's world (see Human Injuries and Deaths, Chapter 8).

Jim Boggs

One story of Boggs's death tells us that while hunting in the Russian River country of California in 1850, he approached within 12 feet of a lair, where a grizzly sow with cubs attacked and killed him. Another account of the incident says that while hunting, a companion roped a large grizzly bear and was attacked. Boggs approached and shot the bear, who released the companion. The wounded bear then attacked and killed Boggs.

Fred Fritz

A rancher in eastern Arizona around the turn of the century, Fritz surprised a grizzly bear while on horseback and armed only with a pistol. The bear attacked him, and during the mauling he shot the bear six times, broke the pistol over its head, and attempted to use his pocketknife. His dogs chased the bear away. Badly mauled, he became an "authority" on how it feels to be attacked by a bear. Though he survived for about five years, the primary cause of his death was considered to be the mauling.

Dr. Monroe Hamberlin

Hamberlin, a physician, was hunting at Lake George near Vicksburg, Mississippi. After commenting that "I never saw one [bear] that I was afraid to tackle," he shot at a 640-pound black bear, and the ball glanced off the bear's head. Attacked, Hamberlin fought with his knife. His dogs pulled the bear from him, but they were beaten, and the bear returned to the doctor. Subsequently his companions shot the bear, but Hamberlin died after three days of suffering.

"Old Ike"

Old Ike was killed by a grizzly bear in the spring or early summer of 1886 at the headwaters of the Salmon River in Idaho. An experienced bear hunter but considered somewhat careless, he was hurriedly following the bear and pursued it to a dense stand of trees, where it charged him. "He fired one hasty shot, evidently wounding the animal, but not seriously enough to stop or cripple it; and as his two companions ran forward they saw the bear seize him with its wide-spread jaws, forcing him to the ground," described Theodore Roosevelt in Paul Schullery's *American Bears*. "They shouted and fired, and the beast abandoned the fallen man on the instant and sullenly retreated into the spruce thicket, wither they dared not follow it. Their friend was at his last gasp; for the whole side of the chest had been crushed in by the one bite."

Peter Lebec

Lebec was killed by a grizzly bear on October 17, 1837, at the site that became Fort Tejon, Kern County, California. His companions buried him at the site. The Indians of the area related a story during the late 1800s of a person (assumed to be Lebec) who pursued a grizzly bear and shot it. He approached the bear, believing it to be dead, and it killed him.

Hyrum Naegle

Hyrum and his brother George were following a grizzly bear they had wounded near Colonia Pacheco, Chihuahua, Mexico, around 1885. "They had been briefly separated while George repaired a malfunctioning rifle," relates David Brown in *The Grizzly in the Southwest*. "Then George heard a shot and went to investigate.

He found Hyrum under the bear's forefeet, the animal 'tearing at his head.' On seeing George, the bear released his victim, only to be felled by George's repaired rifle." His brother managed to get Hyrum on his horse, tied to the saddle and home alive, but he died of his dreadful wounds after two days.

Isaac Slover

A trapper and hunter who was considered durable and stubborn and had a great ambition to kill grizzly bears, Slover shot one on October 14, 1854, on Mount San Antonio, California. The large wounded bear crawled into the brush, and Slover reloaded and followed, where he was attacked, torn to pieces, and died. He was approximately eighty-one.

Andy Sublette

Sublette, a mountaineer, trapper, and guide, was badly mauled by a grizzly bear in 1853. While separated from his party, on December 18 or 19, 1854, in Malibu Canyon near the present-day area of Santa Monica, California, Sublette shot and wounded a grizzly bear. Apparently he was then attacked and fought the bear with his knife and the aid of his dog. His dog survived. The bear died, and after several days Sublette died at the age of forty-six.

Richard Wilson

Wilson, a hunter, and partner of "Bear" Howard, shot a grizzly bear with an inadequate rifle in Oak Creek Canyon, Sedona, Arizona, during mid-1885. Alone, he followed the wounded bear into a thicket, where he was attacked. He attempted to climb a small tree but was dragged down and killed.

Name Unknown

Ernest Thompson Seton, in *Lives of Game Animals*, describes a trapper who was killed in Ontario, Canada, in November 1929 by a "monstrous" black bear with face and neck laden with festering porcupine quills.

Name Unknown

A man was killed in the "early days" by a grizzly bear in Strawberry Canyon, now part of the University of California campus, Berkeley, California, according to M. T. Carleton in *The Byrnes of Berkeley*.

Name Unknown

"Near Bodega, Sonoma County [California, mid-1800s], a young man armed only with pistols, followed a mortally wounded bear into a thicket and was literally torn to pieces," according to Tracy Storer and Lloyd Tevis in *California Grizzly*.

Eskimos Killed by Polar Bears

"Many Eskimos have been killed by polar bears," writes Richard Perry in *Bears*. "[T]he great majority of them have been hunters killed while lancing or knifing bears at close-quarters."

CHAPTER 7

The Use of Bears and Bear Parts

BEAR PARTS

Ever since man has been sharing his habitat with bears, there have been tangible and material uses made of the bear, as well as spiritual and ceremonial influences. Food, clothing, medicine, heat, light, shelter, ornaments, and tools have been provided by all species and used by many different cultures, including native inhabitants, explorers, pioneers, and early settlers. Parts were not only for individual uses but were traded, used as gifts, bartered, and sold. Many of these traditional uses continue today.

The meat of a bear was considered an excellent food. In 1784 one colonist noted, according to Cardoza, "all who have tasted the flesh of this animal say that it is most delicious eating; a young Bear, fattened with the autumnal fruits, is a dish fit for the nicest epicure. It is wholesome and nourishing, and resembles pork more than any other meat." The meat was prepared like ham, as bears in some situations were used in place of hogs. The light oil of the fat was pure white. "All of the Indians of the Upper Missouri," relates Fred Gowans in *Mountain Man & Grizzly*, describing Prince Maximilian's story, "often wear the handsome necklace made of the claws of the grizzly bear. These claws are very large in the spring, frequently three inches long, and the points are tinged of a white colour, which is much esteemed; only the claws of the fore feet are used for necklaces, which are fastened to a strip of otter skin, lined with red cloth, and embroidered with glass beads, which hangs down the back like a long tail."

Traditional Uses of Parts

Baculum
- Aphrodisiac
- Magic potency

A mark of distinction; an Indian chief with a claw necklace—a symbol of the bear's power

Bones

- Ceremonial
- Hand tools (many were carved)
- Weapons (dagger)

Claws

- Belts
- Bracelets
- Headbands
- Jewelry
- Necklaces (sometimes 40 claws)
- Ornaments
- Wristlets

Fat (Bear Grease)

- Cooking (pies, cakes, biscuits, doughnuts)
- Hair pomades
- Hair restorer
- Healing salve
- In place of butter
- Lamp oil
- Leather softener
- Medicine (rheumatism and other infirmities)
- Miracle drug
- Ointment
- Olive oil substitute
- Perfume
- Salad oil
- Salves for human and animal wounds
- Source of dietary fat
- To fry fish
- Tonic
- Waterproofing (shoes, boots)

The fat of bears was used as a medicine for a variety of ailments. Cardoza relates a colonist's story: "One Mr. Purchase cured himself of the Sciatica with Bear-grease, keeping some of it continually in his groine. It is good too for Swell'd Cheeks upon cold, for Rupture of the hands in winter, for limbs taken suddenly with Sciatica, Gout, or other diseases that cannot stand upright nor go, bedred. . . ." And another colonist claimed it was quite popular for use against baldness.

Not only was the fat a home remedy, but Cardoza quotes physician John Josselyn, who apparently prescribed "bear fat" and recorded in the 1800s that "grease is very good for Aches and Cold Swellings, the Indians anoint themselves wherewith from top to toe, which hardens them against the cold weather." Cardoza also relates an individual's story that the Canadian Indians smeared their bodies with bear oil "when they are excessively cold, tired with labour, hurt and in other cases. They believe it softens the skin, and makes the body more pliant, and is very serviceable to old age."

Feces

- Cure for constipation, taken frozen (The author imagines this remedy would certainly *solve* the problem, while possibly creating a few more.)

Hides

- Altar coverings
- Bedding
- Boot bottoms
- Boot covers
- Boot laces
- Burial robes
- Busbies (towering caps like those worn by the royal guard at Buckingham Palace)
- Caps (winter)
- Clothing
- Controls menstrual period (giant panda skin)

- Coverings
- Decoration
- Dog traces and harness reins
- Doors (house)
- Fragments (polish sled runners)
- Ground mat
- Hats (drum major and other headwear)
- Hunting blinds
- Linings for expensive sleeping bags
- Louse mops
- Mantles (clothing)
- Muffs
- Overcoats
- Pants (waterproof)
- Parlor rugs
- Pay taxes (giant panda; ancient China)
- Robes (clothing; carriage and sleigh)
- Sled (rolled and frozen)
- Sled covers
- Sleeping mats
- Sleeping robes
- Souvenirs for visitors
- Status symbols
- Trophies and wall hangings

Gall Bladders
- Aphrodisiac
- Medicine

A FEW USES OF PARTS IN THE SEVENTEENTH CENTURY

In *The History of Four-footed Beasts*, Edward Topsell describes several uses of bear parts. Mythical or factual, these were applications of physical or psychological medicine.

Blood: "If the blood or grease of a Bear be set under a bed, it Will draw unto it all the fleas, and so kill them by cleaving thereunto."

Eyes: "The right eye of a Bear dryed to powder, and hung about childrens necks in a little bag, driveth away the terror of dreams, and both the eyes whole, bound to a mans left arm, easeth aquartian Ague."

Fat: "They are exceedingly full of fat or large-grease, which some use superstitiously beaten with Oyl, wherewith they anoynt their Grape-sickles when they go to vintage, perswading themselves that if no body thereof, their tender Vine-branches shall never be consumed by Caterpillars."

"... cure, confused and distracted parts, spots, and tumors in the body."

"... helpeth pain in the loyns, if the sick part be anointed ..."

Cures "... all Ulcers of the legs or shins ... feet ..."

"... it is soveraign against the falling of the hair ..."

Liver: The liver is "... trod to ("*gall*") powder under ones shooes easeth and defendeth Cripples from inflammation ..."

A remedy when "... bitten by a mad dog ..."

"... against the Palsie, the Kings Evill, the Falling-sickness, and Old Cough, the Inflammation of the Eyes, the running of the Ears, the difficulty of Urine, and delivery in Childbirth, the Hemorrhoides, the weakness of the Back."

"The stones in a Perfume are good against the Falling evill, and the Palsie ..."

Head

- Food (a delicacy)

Intestines

- Thongs (cords)
- Window "glazing" (stretched over window; translucent covering)

Meat

- Dog food
- People food

Paws

- Boots (included some of leg skin)
- Ceremonial; part of a necklace
- Food (delicacy)
- Gloves
- Medicine bag (shaman)
- Religious gloves
- Souvenirs for visitors

Sinews

- Sewing "thread"

Skulls

- Ceremonial
- Ritual magic
- Trophies

Teeth

- Amulets
- Jewelry
- Necklaces
- Ornaments

Furs/Hides

Though present-day North American bear hides have little commercial value as "fur" and are mostly used as "bear rugs" and wall hangings (trophies), early Native Americans possessed different opinions and values. "The only Bears of this country, are the small black Bear, with a chance Yellow Bear," Bessie Haynes and Edgar Haynes in *The Grizzly Bear* quote the "Old Indians" as saying. "This latter has a fine furr and trades for three beavers in barter, when full grown."

James E. Cardoza, in *The Black Bear in Massachusetts*, includes a comment by E. Emmonds ("A report on the quadrupeds of Massachusetts," 1840). Emmonds wrote: "These robes [bear] wear much longer than those of the Buffalo, being in texture much stronger, and more impervious to rain; and, besides, they are considered much handsomer and richer in appearance."

"Nanook's fur also might be tied on the end of a long caribou bone to make a kumak-sheun, a louse map," writes Charles Feazel in *White Bear*, referring to a use by the Eskimos. "When drawn through the hair of the family . . . the fur would attract the little pests. . . ."

Thousands of bear furs have been shipped from North America since the 1700s. In 1702 bearskins were of equal value to beaver pelts; 16,512 furs arrived in the French port of Rochelle in 1743, and 8,340 were exported from the East Coast of the United States in 1763. However, the majority of pelts stayed in the United States, as bear hides sold in the general range of $2 to $20 each during the 1860s.

ASIAN USES OF BEARS AND THEIR PARTS

The early subsistence use of bears has evolved, and now the taking, trading, and use of bear parts are an important international business in many countries, with major economic benefits for all involved—bears have a high market value. Thousands of bears are killed annually, and their populations are unfortunately rapidly declining due to this trade. The trade is primarily Asian, and most bears and bear parts originate in China, Malaysia, and Thailand; however, the supply is decreasing as the bear populations in those countries diminish. The United States (40,000-plus bears a year) and Canada also are significant suppliers. All eight species of bears are utilized, with parts used for clothing, decoration, food, and medicine.

MAJOR BEAR PARTS TRADE COUNTRIES

Major Suppliers	Major Consumers
Bangladesh	China
Bhutan	Hong Kong
Cambodia	Japan
Canada	Philippines
China	Singapore
India	South Korea
Indonesia	Taiwan
Japan	
Laos	
Malaysia	
Myanmar	
Nepal	
North Korea	
Sri Lanka	
Thailand	
United States	
Vietnam	

More than three billion people in the Orient practice "Chinese medicine," with over a billion Chinese consumers alone. There are millions of other users in non-Orient countries.

A Siamese prescription in the nineteenth century for "morbific fever" was an exotic cocktail, according to Jeffrey McNeely and Paul Wachtel in *Soul of the Tiger.*

> *One portion of rhinoceros horn, one of elephant's tusk, one of tiger's, and the same of crocodile's teeth; one of bear's tooth; one portion composed of three parts bones of vulture, raven, and goose; one portion of bison and another of stag's horn, one portion of sandalwood. These ingredients to be mixed together on a stone with pure water; one half of the mixture to be swallowed, the rest to be rubbed into the body; after which the morbific fever will depart.*

"Use of bears and bear parts in folk medicine is common with the fat being used for bone bruises, and claws and baculi used for strength and fertility [also as an aphrodisiac]," notes Chris Servheen in his article, "The Status and Conservation of the Bears of the World." China and South Korea are the leading consumers of bear parts.

Bears

Whole bears, most often Asiatic black bears, dead *and* alive, are sought for various purposes, such as for their parts (including the meat), as pets, in zoos and circuses, as performers, in bear farms, and to attract customers to businesses. A buyer may purchase a whole bear, with resale value as parts five to twelve times the cost. Bear cubs sell for $70 to $4,000 and adult bears for $650 to $9,400 each. A large trophy grizzly bear in North America sells for more than $14,000.

Blood and Bones

Strength is enhanced by the consumption of bear blood, while bone products are purchased as souvenirs in the tourist trade and used as food supplements—including a pulverized form that is added to baby formula in the belief that the child will grow up strong as a bear. Tools are made from bones; for example, scythes for cutting grass are made from shoulder bones (sharp blades).

Claws

Bear claws bring good health, including strength and fertility. They are worn in Sri Lanka as protection from evil; in other countries they are often sewn on infant backpacks for good luck. Pendants and souvenirs are made of claws, popular with tourists. Claws sell for $15 to $60 each.

Fat

Bear fat is used for maladies, including rheumatism, and may be found bottled in liquid form. Records of bear fat as a medicine in China date back as early as 3494 BC.

Gallbladders

Bear gallbladders are the most dominant and prized bear part—the mainstay—in the parts trade. A gallbladder is the size of an average human thumb and looks like a fig when dried. The dried bile of the bladder, the gall, is most often found on the market in a crystalline form

Sloth bear as a business attraction in India
PETE OXFORD/NATUREPL.COM

ranging in color from golden brown to near black. Golden gall is considered superior to dark colored. Dried gallbladders weigh between 50 and 150 grams (1.76 and 5.29 ounces).

Bear gallbladder has been part of Chinese medicine for more than 3,000 years. Gall is considered a cure for most anything and is even a

- Colic
- Coughs
- Diabetes
- Excessive drinking (alcohol) and smoking
- Fatigue
- Fever
- Flu
- Fractures
- Hemorrhoids
- Infection
- Internal parasites
- Pain
- Poor appetite

registered medicine in Japan, where more than fifty pharmaceutical companies sell some form of gall. It is also used in Japan as a poison (but used elsewhere as a poison antidote). Koreans are avid users of gall, where it is available at thousands of clinics. Worldwide it is an ingredient of over a hundred heart medicines, more than twenty stomach medicines, digestive aids, and several children's medicines.

Bear gallbladder, in its many forms, is a treatment for a vast number of ailments, including conditions of the following:

- Bladder
- Blood
- Heart
- Intestines
- Liver
- Lungs
- Skin
- Spleen
- Throat

Gall is a remedy for the following:

- Asthma
- Burns
- Cancer

"Bile salts are taken in chunks melted on the tongue or downed with water, dissolved in liquor, mixed with other traditional ingredients such as musk and pearl, stuffed in capsules, molded into manufactured tablets, and blended into ointments and creams," write Judy Mills and Chris Servheen in their project report, "The Asian Trade in Bears and Bear Parts." Gall is also found as a powder and in suppositories, oil compounds, tinctures, and wine mixtures. Gallbladders in some situations are soaked in a clear alcohol (vodka, gin), and then the alcohol is consumed. More than seven factories in China alone produce over sixty different medicines containing gall.

Gall is derived from bears worldwide. Some pressure has been removed from the wild bear populations as "bear farms" are developed to raise and maintain bears to "milk" gall. More than 16,000 "bile bears" exist in South Korea, China, and Vietnam. The cruel and unhealthy conditions in which the bears are housed are a major concern. Each bear lives in a cage (2.6 feet by 4.2 feet by 6.5 feet) where it is nearly incapable of turning around, developing "cage" sores. The small cages facilitate the ease of milking.

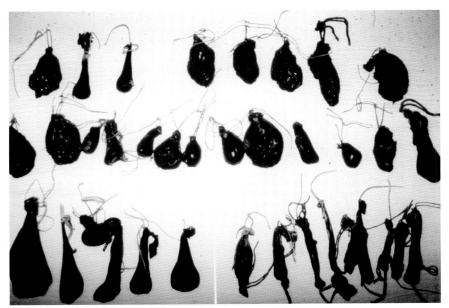

Gallbladders taken from American black bears illegally killed in southeastern United States
COURTESY WILLIAM COOK, NATIONAL PARK SERVICE

A bear may produce 300 to 700 ounces of bile each milking and more than 6,000 kilograms (211,644 ounces) each year. Supposedly, one bear milked for five years will save 220 wild bears. Still, tens of thousands of wild bears are killed annually for their gallbladders, as the gall of a wild bear is prized and sells for six to seven times that of "farmed" gall.

The price of gall from street sources varies considerably among different countries and within each country, depending on the specific source, color (golden or dark), quality, and other circumstances of the transaction. A low-end price may mean the gall is from a pig or other animal. Some extreme-case prices are approximately eighteen times the price of gold (gold: $900+ per ounce). The street value of gall (in powder form) is greater than that of cocaine.

The price of gall bladders ranges from $150 in Ecuador to $64,000 in South Korea. A gram of gall generally ranges from $2 to $590 worldwide.

In San Francisco, bottles of bile crystals sell for $50 and gallbladders for approximately $135.

Hides

Bear hides (furs) have several uses, including coverings and decorations for floors, wall hangings, and furniture. They are worn in traditional dances, and pieces of hide are ground up and placed in pouches that are worn around the neck as black magic to ensure good health. Hides sell for anywhere from $1,000 to $5,000; those with paws and head attached bring the highest prices.

One million dollars was offered for a single hide in South Korea (the owner retained the hide and had it mounted), and $10,000 was paid for a giant panda hide in Southeast Asia, where with resales, it finally sold for more than $100,000. Another giant panda hide upon resale(s) brought several hundred thousand dollars.

Meat

Bear meat is considered medicinal—a tonic food. It strengthens the body, fights weakness, enhances health and vigor, and provides energy for a person's general mental and physical well-being. "For the 1988 Olympics . . . thirty Thai bears were illegally shipped to South Korea to fortify Korean athletes with their meat and galls," according to Mills and Servheen. The meat of the Andean bear is highly prized in Peru. There are hundreds of bear-meat recipes, including spare ribs, steaks, stews, and preparation by grilling. Bear liver is eaten raw with spices and is a novelty dish in many restaurants in Japan. It is also used as dog food. The meat of a full bear may sell for more than $4,000, while a steak dinner exceeds $25, and a can of meat is more than $15.

Paws

Paws, like the meat of a bear, are also considered medicinal tonic food to prevent various ailments, such as the common cold, and to provide strength.

A BEAR PAW BUSINESS TRANSACTION FROM "BEAR TO BOWL"

- A bear *pays* with its life, providing four paws.
- Hunter with a "single" bear paw for sale.
- Middle-handler *pays* hunter: $60.
- Wholesaler *pays* middle-handler: $100.
- Restaurant *pays* wholesaler: $200.
- Customer *pays* restaurant for a bowl of bear paw soup: $850.

However, they are mostly prized as a delicacy, a restaurant cuisine, and a banquet food.

In Bangkok, notes Servheen, ". . . restaurants procure bears for . . . meals using the paws and meat and sometimes reportedly killing the bear in front of the guests to assure them the meal is authentic and fresh."

The primary source of market paws is Asiatic black bears. The paws are used in soup or stew, braised and served with vegetables, and soft fried, as in a restaurant in the Beijing, China, zoo.

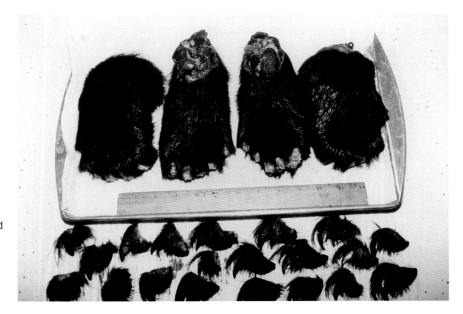

Paws and claws removed from American black bears illegally killed in southeastern United States
COURTESY WILLIAM COOK, NATIONAL PARK SERVICE

". . . Korean tourists come in groups to Thailand to eat bear paw soup and meat," according to Servheen. A single paw sells for $80 to $160 at markets, while a single serving of bear paw soup in a restaurant in Asia is $700 to $1,400, and in Asian restaurants in the United States more than $90 a bowl.

Teeth

Bear skulls and teeth are sold as souvenirs and ceremonial items. Teeth are sewn on infant backpacks in the same manner as bear claws, for good luck. Skulls sell for $40 to $375 and canine teeth for more than $60 each.

PETS AND PERFORMERS

Sun bears and Asiatic black bears are the species typically used where live bears are performers or pets or otherwise live in a domestic situation. Some are street performers, and several performing bear troupes exist and appear in circuses worldwide. "Captive bears are taught to wrestle and dance for groups of 'gypsies' who earn their sole living from the bears," notes Servheen. "Pet keeping also affects bears by creating a market for live bears, especially cubs, that are sold in local markets."

Bears are used in a promotional capacity, attracting customers to gasoline stations, restaurants, brothels, and stores. As pets, bears are sometimes taught to assist with household chores and serve as watch "dogs." The British military in Malaysia has used bears as mascots. Thai Buddhists harbor and care for bears as a "good deed" that will provide them credit after death. And when performance and pet bears become too old and difficult to manage, they are sold to restaurants and other businesses for medicine and food.

EATING BEAR MEAT

Bear meat has been used as food since humans and bears shared common areas. The North American settlers often sought bears as a desirable and reliable source of meat.

When their crops failed in 1772, the California colonists at the missions established by Gaspar de Portola slaughtered their cattle. When supply galleons did not arrive, a hunting party spent three months hunting grizzly bears, jerking the meat, and providing over 9,000 pounds to northern settlements. A story in an 1855 edition of *Harper's New Monthly Magazine* describes bear meat: "Bar meat is best . . . in the fall. Cotch a bar, then when he has had a cornfield to hid in, and his spar ribs taste like rostin' ears."

"A steak cut from the haunch of the grisly bear, and roasted on a stick by a camp fire, is by no means despicable fare . . ." relates T. J. Farnham in *Life, Adventures and Travels in California*.

"Roast grizzly and bear steaks were always prominent features of the bills-of-fare in mining camp restaurants [California goldrush period]," commented B. F. Herrick in his article "Grade-School Grizzly," "selling at a dollar a share, payable in gold dust."

". . . Our Camp Keeper had prepared an elegant supper of Grizzly Bear meat . . . ," noted mountain man Osborne Russell in *Journal of a Trapper*, on August 10, 1837, while camped along the Stinking River in present-day Wyoming. John Muir also enjoyed grizzly bear, commenting that it was the "best meat in the mountains."

Bear meat is not now the popular meal or the necessity it was then, though many hunters and their families worldwide consume it.

- Flavor is between pork and beef (varies with bear's diet; tastiest if from two-year-olds that are feeding on berries or roots rather than on fish).

- Texture like coarse pork
- High in fat; quite greasy (pork recipes are good guides for cooking)
- Polar bear cub meat similar to veal
- High level of *Trichinella* worm (trichinosis); cook very well
- Polar bear liver has high (toxic) levels of Vitamin A; do not eat
- Seldom eaten by Indians

CHAPTER 8

Bears and People

The interactions between people and bears have long been high-intensity conflicts, and most have included dramatic and varied reactions by both parties. Though the Lewis and Clark expedition believed the grizzly bear would rather attack than avoid humans, most evidence indicates that bears will typically flee at the sound or smell of people. In India, villagers fear the aggressive sloth bears more than tigers. However, to rely on each individual bear to be "typical" would be quite foolish.

INTERACTIONS

A bear's interactions with people may include any of the following:

- Approaching for a better view
- Avoidance—secretively move away; remain in location allowing people to pass; visibly and/or noisily, rapidly flee
- Curiousness—approach or watch from a distance
- Aggression—bluff charge to closer distance; depart
- Attacks—to lessen the threat to cubs or the perceived threat to itself; to protect a food source; predation (departs without persistence; persists in attack, then departs; persists in attack, consumes victim)
- Food conditioning—with repeated exposure, bears come to associate people with food; consequently bears seek and eat people's food and garbage
- Habituation—bears are accustomed to people and willing to approach

A study of brown bears in Kamchatka (eastern peninsula of Russia) analyzed the response of bears to 230 encounters with humans. The results:

- 70.7 percent avoided humans.
- 18.8 percent identified humans and moved away.
- 12.1 percent were indifferent.
- 2.2 percent reacted with a threat demonstration.
- 1.2 percent attacked.

Bears' impacts on people may be described in three basic ways:

- They have direct contact with people, inflicting injury or death.
- They damage crops and property and kill domestic livestock.
- They are nuisances (habituated and conditioned to human foods; unafraid and will approach; not tame).

"Foolhardy settlers, contemptuous of the bear's abilities or puffed up with self-righteous bravado," writes James Cardoza in *The Black Bear in Massachusetts*, "attempted to overcome bears with such varied instruments as jack-knives, axes, oxgoads, pitchforks, and hoes."

Sources and Causes of Interactions and Conflicts

Agriculture

Bears seek crops such as carrots, corn (maize), melons, strawberries, raspberries, cranberries, and grains (oats), and they trample crops. Orchards are damaged as bears eat apples, coconuts, pears, and plums, often inflicting more serious damage by tearing limbs from the trees. Beehives are a common attraction to bears, and serious economic losses are sustained annually. In Southeast Asia, plantations are being developed in bear habitat to grow crops for the rapidly increasing human population, resulting in bears conflicting with livelihoods.

Begging

People feed bears, conditioning them to human foods and developing beggars. Injuries occur when a bear becomes persistent while in close contact with people or when the person stops feeding them. Begging has long existed in parks and near developments. Bears begging along roads are often killed when struck by vehicles. "When pressed to find food in the summer," writes Koch, "polar bears have been known to swim to the sides of ships and beg for scraps of blubber." Most begging bears are eventually destroyed when they threaten or injure someone.

Bicycling

Bicyclists are sometimes chased by bears, who perhaps perceive them as prey, while traveling on roads and have virtually pedaled into bears on roads and backcountry trails. Bicyclists move rapidly and encounter bears at a close distance without warning.

Birdfeeders

Bears are attracted to the variety of foods (seeds, suet, fruit) provided in feeders for birds. Birdfeeders may be the *most* common residential bear attractant.

Camping

Campers in the front- or backcountry may be confronted with bears because of unsecured food and garbage or because previous campers provided bears with food rewards (by feeding them or because of poor food storage or a dirty camp), and the bear is now habituated and food conditioned.

Dogs

Dogs, hunting or pet, conflict with bears by chasing them or barking, drawing a reaction from the bear. The dog normally retreats to its master, bringing along his newfound "friend." Dog food is an attractant when outside at a residence or cabin and sometimes when inside. In a remote area of Alaska, a bear broke into a storage shed where 450 pounds of dog food were stored for sled dogs. The entire supply was consumed, according to a park ranger, with slightly less than that many pounds deposited only a few feet away on the porch in the form of feces.

Dumps

Garbage in the quantities found in dumps will provide bears with a long-term source of unnatural foods. Livestock carcasses in dumps or ranch "carcass pits" provide an additional attractant.

Feeding Bears

Foods are placed outside residences to attract bears for viewing and photography. The owners

(management) of some hotels and other lodging facilities at times put out foods to attract bears for the viewing pleasure of their guests.

Fishing

Bears challenge fishermen for their catch and compete with commercial fishermen (for fish and fish eggs) at their nets, also sometimes damaging the nets. They also compete with persons who legally and illegally take fish and fish eggs at salmon spawning streams.

Forest Industry

Bears damage and kill trees by biting, stripping the bark, and eating the sapwood (which is 5 percent sugars). Such damage may result in major economic impacts on the timber industry. The state of Washington estimates an economic loss of $5,000,000 per year. Frank Dufresne in *No*

Room for Bears relates a comment by bear hunter "Bear" Bill Hulet, in Washington State. "I've knowed a single b'ar to wreck five hundred firs [Douglas] in a season." Forestry workers in North America and firewood collectors in Southeast Asia are brought into contact with bears by the nature of where they work. Forestry roads provide people with access to bear habitat.

Garbage

Commercial or household garbage is a major attractant, sought by many bears throughout the world. Bears have access to the majority of the worldwide garbage.

Human Foods

Human foods at private residences, camps, lodges, hotels, ranches, and villages may provide an attractant for bears if not properly stored. Such

foods are normally high in protein, and bears become conditioned to them, seeking comparable foods from similar sources.

Hunting

Though hunting is an accepted and valuable bear-management tool, the activity often leads to conflicts. Hunters are often not as careful in bear country because they have protection—their guns. They move stealthily and therefore have surprise encounters. Hunting dogs attract unwanted bears. Wounded bears are a major problem (nearly all hunters killed by bears in Alaska were pursuing a wounded bear). Gut piles resulting from harvest of game are a major attractant for bears.

Livestock

"The most potential contributing factor in the destruction of the grizzly in the United States," writes Harold McCracken in *The Beast That Walks Like Man*, "was the introduction of domestic cattle and farm stock into the grassy mountain valleys and more open ranges west of the Great Plains."

"Although comparatively few bears become stock killers . . . the habit apparently persists in those individuals acquiring it . . . ," notes Cardoza. "Claimed losses, however, may greatly exceed the actual damage caused by bears . . . discrepancies . . . arise from the bear's habit of feeding on carrion" (see Bears and Livestock Conflicts, this chapter).

Present-day livestock losses are primarily sheep. "in Norway," notes Linnell, et al., in the *European Brown Bear Compendium*, "A total of 15–30 bears kill 3,000–4,000 sheep each year. . . ." Bears directly kill many sheep, but in North America the majority of the loss is from stampeding sheep that are "piled up" in fence corners, injured and dead.

Sloth bears often encounter livestock herders in Southeast Asia, resulting in the death of the bears. Andean bears prey upon livestock in South America, resulting in dead cattle, dead bears, and injured and dead ranchers.

Mining and Petroleum
Gas and oil and other mineral exploration and extraction often take place in bear habitat, providing opportunities for humans to encounter bears, with resulting conflicts.

Parks
National parks in the United States and Canada have long been sources of human/bear conflicts, as bears have been fed in feeding grounds and at roadsides and have raided unsecured human food and garbage. Conversely, parks provide refuge and protection for bears.

Photography
Photographers attempting to attain the perfect close-up often invade a bear's "space" and are attacked, mauled, and killed.

Population Growth
As the world population rapidly increases, each of the sources and causes of this list correspondingly increases (more bear habitat used for agriculture, recreation, dumps, forest products, livestock, etc.).

Urban/Suburban Sprawl
Town, village, and city growth are spreading into bear habitat, bringing humans and bears more frequently into contact and confrontation. More recreational homes and facilities are encroaching on bear habitat. Every day, human activities spread across the landscape, resulting in more direct conflict with bears and increasing loss of bear habitat.

Actions of Bears (by Species)

American Black Bear
- Damages beehives and honey production
- Damages gardens
- Kills domestic livestock
- Seeks human food and garbage
- Strips bark from trees
- Is suspicious of any intruder
- Enters residential areas
- Breaks into buildings seeking food. "They are diabolically clever at gaining entry to locked buildings," notes Roger Caras in *North American Mammals.*

Andean Bear
- Damages young palm trees; eats new leaves
- Kills young llamas
- Kills cattle and other domestic animals
- Damages crops

Asiatic black bear
- Seeks garbage
- Conflicts with farmers/herders
- Kills livestock
- Damages crops and beehives

"This was one of the 'spoiled' bears that had become accustomed to people and were unafraid. Up and down the road he had been breaking into . . ."

Adolph Murie
A Naturalist in Alaska

Trunk of a tree stripped of bark by a bear
COURTESY YELLOWSTONE
NATIONAL PARK

Brown Bear

- Challenges fishermen for their catch
- Damages beehives and honey production
- Damages commercial fishing nets and catches
- Kills domestic livestock
- Damages sunflower crops (in Iran)
- Seeks game harvests of hunts
- Seeks human food and garbage
- Enters residential areas
- Lives in peaceful coexistence with people and their animals in the Caucasus and Carpathian Mountains of Romania
- Powerful; breaks into buildings (tears out windows, doors, walls)
- Attacks when startled

Giant Panda

- Enters camps for food
- Damages crops
- Conflicts with firewood gatherers

Polar Bear

- Enters towns and villages
- Less afraid of people than other bears
- Considers people to be prey
- Seeks garbage

Sloth Bear

- Conflicts with farmers and herders
- Conflicts with firewood gatherers
- Viciously attacks when startled
- Damages crops
- Kills cattle and goats

Sun Bear

- Conflicts with farmers and loggers
- Enters settlements
- Damages banana, coconut, and palm oil plantations
- Damages crops
- Viciously attacks when startled

Bears and Livestock Conflicts

Conflicts between bears and cattle have occurred for centuries. Edward Topsell in *The History of Four-Footed Beasts* wrote about the problem in 1607: ". . . kill their Cattel left at large in the field in the day time; They likewise shoot them with guns, giving a good sum of money to them that can bring them a slain Bear."

History records several grizzly bears that were considered infamous stock killers—"outlaws." They killed thousands of cattle, sheep, horses, mules, and hogs. Unfortunately the dastardly deeds of a few outlaws led to the deaths of thousands of bears who were guilty only by association.

The outlaw grizzly bears became addicted to the domestic animals that were introduced to their natural habitat. The cattle were abundant, congregated, and relatively easy to kill.

During the "cattle boom" of the late 1800s and early 1900s, the West was open range with considerable grass, and the transcontinental railroad became available for market shipping. The ranges were overstocked; hence, large herds of cattle were easy pickings for the predators—bears, mountain lions, and rustlers.

The bears were persecuted. Ranchers responded to the loss of their stock by hunting down and killing any bear they could find—war was declared against grizzly bears, and by the 1880s the very large #6 bear trap was available (the "Bear Tamer"). Strychnine was placed in many cattle carcasses, and firearms were improved. Government hunters were used, and in 1914 the U.S. Department of Agriculture formed the Predatory Animal and Rodent Control (PARC), hiring numerous professional hunters, some of whom are listed in Chapter 6, Bear Hunting.

Most of the outlaws had an identifying physical feature. There were several "clubfoots" and "toes," without doubt explained by having been in leg/foot traps. Navajos called the stock killers The Phantom or The Ghost Bear. The Paiutes in Nevada referred to an outlaw as The-Evil-Spirit-Bear-Who-Lives-in-the-Rocks, while in Nevada (and southern Idaho) there was a "Slaughterhouse."

A DRASTIC CONTROL MEASURE

In 1953 a cattle rancher established a herd of 600 cattle on Kodiak Island, Alaska, in the midst of the Kodiak bears. Predictably, conflicts were numerous: cattle and rancher vs. bears, Department of Fish & Game vs. citizens, and citizens vs. the rancher. The department attempted to control the bears with a most extreme measure. Larry Kaniut in *Alaska Bear Tales* provides a description of that bizarre situation. "The shooting of bears on Kodiak was sanctioned by the Fish & Game. We requested it and was a long time getting their permission. They hired a P-51 World War II fighter pilot, mounted an M-1 Garand, eight-shot rifle on a Cub [Piper] airplane, and shot bears with it on the leased grazing areas." Several bears were killed, but the action was short-lived, as the pilot strayed from the permitted area, illegally killed several bears, and was grounded. The rancher quit ranching after fifteen years of battle with the Kodiaks.

The Bandit	Oregon; 1899–1904; 1,000 pounds; shot by Charlie Logue; the Bandit was barbequed at a barn dance in Charlie's honor
Big Blue	Washington; 1897–1900
Big Foot Wallace	Wyoming; characteristic track—two toes of left front paw missing; shot in 1885
Bloody Paws	Wyoming; characteristic—silvery white in color; best-known outlaw bear in the state; rampaged for twelve years; shot by rancher Jack Madden
Crippler (Old Crip)	Washington; 1900–1903
El Casador	California; 1800s; characteristic track—part of paw missing due to a bullet; shot and killed by Juan Francisco Dana
Moccasin Foot	Montana; late 1890s; 1,300 pounds; characteristic track—all toes missing from a hind foot; shot by Vic Smith
Old Club Foot	New Mexico; late 1800s; shot by Ben Lilly, with his incredible excursion tracking the bear into Mexico and back
Old Ephraim	Utah; early 1920s; 1,100 pounds; shot by sheepherder Frank Clark (last observed grizzly in Utah)
Old Mose	Colorado; late 1800s–early 1900s; characteristic track—two missing toes on left hind foot; pursued for nearly thirty-five years; Enos Mills in *The Grizzly* wrote, ". . . he was often seen and constantly hunted . . . ;" shot in 1904 at forty-plus years of age
Old Silver	Idaho; 1898–1901; 984 pounds; characteristic—very silver-tipped fur; shot by homesteader Swenson
Old Two Toes	Montana; 1902–1906; 1,100 pounds
Pegtrack Grizzly	California, Feather River country; cunning and seldom observed
Red Robber	Utah; 1880–1885; 900-plus pounds; characteristic—rusty red fur (Red); lived in the Butch Cassidy/Sundance Kid country (Robber); shot in 1885
Reel Foot	California; characteristic track—two toes missing; shot in 1890
Susie	New Mexico; aka The Lady Outlaw; very large female; 1,200-plus pounds; shot
Three Toes	Wyoming; characteristic track—two toes missing (trap); shot about 1914

CHAPTER 9

Today's Bears
THE STATUS OF BEARS

Bears are in a time of rapid change and are disappearing from today's world. Because of their interacting with humans, six of the eight bear species are threatened with extinction. The future of bears in many countries is uncertain, and some populations are assured of disappearing. Many populations remain only in reserves and parks, where their status is localized. The most threatened species occur in tropical mountains and islands. Southeast Asia and South American bears are rapidly declining.

BEAR SPECIES AT GREATEST RISK
(IUCN 2006 STATUS)

Andean bear	South America; threatened
Asiatic black bear	Asia; threatened to endangered
Giant panda	China; endangered
Sloth bear	Indian subcontinent; threatened
Sun bear	Southeast Asia; endangered

BEAR POPULATIONS AT GREATEST RISK
(IUCN 2006)

Andean bear	Columbia; Peru; Venezuela
Asiatic black bear	Baluchistan; Southeast Asia (several areas); Taiwan
Brown bear	Italy; France; Mongolia; Spain; Tibet
Giant panda	All populations
Sloth bear	Several population fragments
Sun bear	Entire range

"Man and bears are direct competitors for space and resources worldwide," explains Christopher Servheen in "The Status and Conservation of the Bears of the World." "This competition is mediated by resource availability and the adaptability of both species. Man is certainly more adaptable and effective at resource exploitation when in competition with bears. Man continues to develop new and effective mechanized resource use strategies while bears continue to attempt to use resources in 'natural' ways. Under such a system of interaction, **the efficient adaptable species will eventually eliminate the competitor.**" (Bold added by author for emphasis.)

By the year 2025 the world's human population is projected to be double what it is now (January 2009: 6,750,800,000), primarily in Southeast Asia. All species of bears will be highly impacted, and three species may have vanished. If global warming is not controlled, the polar bear may be gone as well.

The importance people have placed upon bears has not always been beneficial for the animals. Today, as well as in the past, bears are viewed in a broad range, from being elements of the wilderness to their tangible benefits in the form of subsistence and commercial value. There are nontangible benefits as well, as they provide enjoyment and excitement and serve as religious symbols.

The 1889 Annual Report of Yellowstone National Park's Superintendent Captain F. A. Boutelle recommended control of predators

AMERICAN BLACK BEAR STATUS AND TREND

United States	Status	Trend		Status	Trend
Alabama	Game	Stable	New Hampshire	Game	Stable
Alaska	Game	Unknown	New Jersey	Game	Increasing
Arizona	Game	Stable	New Mexico	Game	Increasing
Arkansas	Game	Increasing	New York	Game	Increasing
California	Game	Increasing	North Carolina	Game	Increasing
Colorado	Game	Increasing	North Dakota	(a)	(a)
Connecticut	Protected	(a)	Ohio	Endangered	Increasing
Florida	Threatened	Increasing	Oklahoma	Game	Stable
Georgia	Game	Increasing	Oregon	Game	(a)
Idaho	Game	(a)	Pennsylvania	Game	Increasing
Kentucky	Protected	Increasing	Rhode Island	Protected	Increasing
Louisiana	Threatened	Stable	South Carolina	Game	Increasing
Maine	Game	Increasing	Tennessee	Game	Increasing
Maryland	Game	Increasing	Texas	Threatened	Increasing
Massachusetts	Game	Increasing	Utah	Game	Increasing
Michigan	Game	Increasing	Vermont	Game	Stable
Minnesota	Game	Stable	Virginia	Game	Increasing
Mississippi	Endangered	Increasing	Washington	Game	(a)
Missouri	Protected	Increasing	West Virginia	Game	Increasing
Montana	Game	Stable	Wisconsin	Game	Stable
Nevada	Game	Stable	Wyoming	Game	(a)

Canada	Status	Trend		Status	Trend
Alberta	Game	(a)	Nova Scotia	Game	Increasing
British Columbia	Game	(a)	Nunavut	Game	Increasing
Manitoba	Game	Increasing	Ontario	Game	Stable
New Brunswick	Game	Increasing	Quebec	Game	Increasing
Newfoundland/Labrador	Game	Increasing	Saskatchewan	Game	(a)
Northwest Territories	Game	(a)	Yukon	Game	Stable

Mexico	Status	Trend		Status	Trend
Baja California Norte	Threatened	Decreasing	Nuevo Leon	Threatened	Stable (b)
Chihuahua	Threatened	Stable (b)	San Luis Potosi	Threatened	Decreasing
Coahuila	Threatened	Stable (b)	Sinaloa	Threatened	Decreasing
Durango	Threatened	Decreasing	Sonora	Threatened	Stable (b)
Jalisco	Threatened	Decreasing	Tamaulipas	Threatened	Stable (b)
Nayarit	Extinct		Zacatecas	Threatened	Decreasing

(a) Information unavailable   *(b) Stable in protected areas*

because they were plentiful, like the other animals. "I am more than ever convinced that the bear and puma do a great deal of mischief and ought to be reduced in numbers. While they may be something of a curiosity to visitors to the park, I hardly think them an agreeable surprise. Very few who come here 'have lost any bear.'"

Nearly all countries where bears live have at some time placed bounties on them. "As long as bears and men have shared the earth," writes George Laycock in *The Wild Bears*, "there has existed between them a special adversary condition. Although we sometimes ignore the small wild animals around us and let them go their way, the bear is a special case. Until recent years we have, almost universally, looked upon these animals as if they somehow threaten our territorial dominance." Some people continue to view bears in this light. As human development and activities spread, the large carnivores are the first to die due to loss of habitat and direct killing.

Status and Trend of Bears in Mexico

Minimal reliable information is available, though scientific efforts are currently attempting to identify the population and status of the American black bear in Mexico. The grizzly bear (brown bear) in Mexico is considered extinct.

Status of Grizzly Bears (United States—Greater Yellowstone Ecosystem)

In the mid-1970s the grizzly bear population in the Lower 48 states had continued its decline, prompting the U.S. Congress to place the *Ursus*

arctos horribilis on the Endangered Species List as Threatened. Species recovery is the responsibility of the U.S. Fish and Wildlife Service. The chronology:

- July 1975: listed on the Endangered Species List as Threatened in the Lower 48 states
- 1981: U.S. Fish and Wildlife Service grizzly bear recovery coordinator established
- 1982: Grizzly Bear Recovery Plan is implemented
- 27 years of interagency grizzly bear recovery efforts
- March 2007: the Yellowstone Distinct Population Segment (Greater Yellowstone Ecosystem grizzly bears) is a recovered population, no longer threatened; removed from the Endangered Species List (delisted)
- April 2007: initiation of a five-year program to review accuracy of delisting determination
- The Greater Yellowstone Ecosystem population managed under a Conservation Strategy program
- Other Lower 48 populations remain threatened

Worldwide Status of Bears

American Black Bear

Survival ensured; on International Union for Conservation of Nature and Natural Resources (IUCN) Red List (see Appendix B) as Least Concern; international trade regulated by CITES, Appendix II; flexible to human pressures; most populations relatively secure (stable or increasing); some populations endangered by fragmentation, lack of food, and overall habitat loss

Alaska and British Columbia: glacier bear (isolated subspecies/bluish gray color phases) at risk due to interbreeding resulting in "black" offspring; Kermodei bear threatened by human habitat destruction

Canada: protected; game species; increasing in six of seven provinces

Mexico: endangered; limited harvest in Serranias del Burro under special protection status; managed under the Black Bear Action Plan; trends in each state range from increasing to decreasing depending on specific population; major concern is lack of information

United States: protected; game species; increasing in twenty-five of thirty-four states (known trend); listed as Endangered by state of Ohio; Louisiana black bear (subspecies *luteolus*) in Louisiana, Mississippi, and Texas listed as Threatened under the U.S. Endangered Species Act; Louisiana black bear listed as Endangered by state of Mississippi; Florida black bear (subspecies *floridanus*) listed as Threatened (protected) by state of Florida

Andean Bear

Overall population disappearing and endangered; considered endangered in northern Bolivia, Columbia, Venezuela; undisturbed environment in eastern Ecuador and Peru and northern Bolivia; protected by national legislation in each country; killing continues; numerous protected areas; 2 to 4 percent habitat loss per year; lack of knowledge prevents adequate management; international trade regulated by CITES, Appendix I; on IUCN Red List as Vulnerable; captive breeding programs in place; numerous parks and other sanctuaries providing protection

Argentina: Vulnerable

Bolivia: Endangered

Columbia: Endangered

Ecuador: Vulnerable

Panama: existence questionable

Peru: hunted extensively; two-thirds of habitat lost in last thirty years (1,000 feet of lower elevation every three years due to elimination of food sources); at great risk

Venezuela: Endangered

Asiatic Black Bear

Threatened to Endangered and generally declining; highly fragmented populations; uncertain future in most of range; on IUCN Red List as Vulnerable; international trade regulated under CITES, Appendix I

Afghanistan: Threatened; impacted by war

Bangladesh: protected under Bangladesh Wild Life Preservation Act, 1974, but fast perishing

Bhutan: protected

Cambodia: protected; specific status data unavailable; considering reintroduction

China: decreasing; protected as a conserved animal under Chinese Wildlife Protection Law of the People's Republic of China; listed as a Vulnerable species under China Data Book of Endangered Animals; *U. thibetanus mupinenis* threatened

India: regulated as a special game animal; protected under Wildlife Protection Act

Iran and Pakistan: *U. thibetanus gedrosianus* (Baluchistan bear) critically Endangered (IUCN Red List); high risk of extinction

Japan: population considered safe, possibly increasing (highly questionable); no protection; sport hunting harvest (500 per year); considered pests (4,000 nuisance bears killed each year)

Laos: protected under Decree of the Council

of Ministers, in Relation to the Prohibition of Wildlife Trade

Myanmar: protected under Burma Wild Life Protection Act (minimal protection; may be killed with special license)

Nepal: protected

North Korea: protected

Russia: protected; sport hunting harvests (seventy to one hundred per year)

South Korea: protected by Authority of the Wildlife Protection and Hunting Law (endangered wild animal); considered a "National Monument" within the Cultural Properties Protection Law; near extinction; six bears (two male, four female) from Russia added to population in 2004 as part of "restoration project"

Taiwan: protected by Wildlife Conservation Law

Thailand: protected under Wild Animals Reservation and Protection Act; at great risk; considering reintroduction

Vietnam: no protection or management; many taken for bile farms; at great risk

Brown Bear

Survival ensured; on IUCN Red List as Least Concern; subspecies and individual populations extirpated and others threatened with extirpation; low numbers in Europe; international trade regulated by CITES, Appendix II

Afghanistan: protected; declining; critically endangered; poorly studied; extinct in some areas; war impacted

Albania: protected*; stable**

Andora: recent reoccupation

Armenia (southeast): Caucasian bear (trans-Caucasian grey bear); 150-year debate whether a separate subspecies; population critically low; registered in Armenian Red Book; hunting prohibited

Austria: protected; increasing

Azerbaijan: minimal data available

Belarus: population status unknown

Bhutan: possibly extinct

Bosnia/Herzegovina: game species; decreasing

Bulgaria: protected; decreasing

Canada: game species; special concern/stable population (Yukon); presently secure in remaining areas that have minimal access to humans; population precariously low in Alberta

China: protected as a conserved animal under the Wildlife Protection Law of the People's Republic of China

Croatia: game species; stable

Czech Republic: protected; population status unknown; possibly only transients

Estonia: game species; stable

Finland: game species; stable; some populations protected

France: protected; small perilous population in Pyrenees Mountains

Georgia: minimal data available

Germany: extinct; recent minimal reintroduction failed

Greece: protected; decreasing

India: protected under Wildlife Protection Act; on IUCN Red List as Vulnerable

Iran: serious threats to survival; little ecological data

Iraq: minimal data available; war impacted

Italy: protected; very few; two populations increasing; one population status unknown

Japan: vulnerable; game species; killed as pests; hunted

Kazakhstan: minimal data available

Kyrgyzstan: minimal data available

Latvia: protected; very few; stable

Macedonia: game species; stable

Mongolia: Gobi bear; protected (Great Gobi Strictly Protected Area); very rare; at great risk; listed in Mongolian Red Book

Nepal: protected under the National Parks and Wildlife Conservation Act

Norway: protected; stable (northeast); increasing (Europe)

Pakistan: critically endangered (IUCN); declining; protected in preserves/parks; locally persecuted; hunted; war impacted; possibly more on street as dancing bears than in wild

Poland: protected; stable

Romania: protected; population decreasing; limited harvest as part of management plan to attain a lower population

Russia: game species; increasing

Serbia/Montenegro: minimal data available

Slovakia: protected (limited harvest); increasing

Slovenia: protected (limited harvest, one hundred taken in 2007); increasing

South Korea: minimal data available

Spain: protected; decreasing

Sweden: game species; increasing

Tajikistan: minimal data available

Turkey: IUCN—Least Concern

Turkmenistan: minimal data available

Ukraine: protected; decreasing

United States: protected; under Endangered Species Act in Lower-48 states (Greater Yellowstone population removed from the Threatened and Endangered Species List in 2007; managed under a Conservation Strategy, with monitoring and a system review); Northern Continental Divide Ecosystem population listed as Threatened; game species in Alaska

Uzbekistan: minimal data available

Giant Panda

Rare (probably always has been); most endangered bear; highly fragmented population; survival outside preserves doubtful due to Chinese population expansion (more than one hundred million people nearby); protected but with few protective measures; presently sixty preserves; 185-plus pandas in zoos; captive breeding programs in place; international trade regulated under CITES, Appendix I; on IUCN Red List as Endangered; protected as a second-class conserved animal under the Chinese Wildlife Protection Law of the People's Republic of China; penalties for poaching—two years to life imprisonment to death (at least three poachers have been put to death)

Polar Bear

Occupies most of original habitat (more than any other world bear species); listed under the U.S. Endangered Species Act as Threatened; on IUCN Red List as Vulnerable; protected under the International Agreement on the Conservation of Polar Bears and Their Habitat (Canada, Denmark-Greenland, Norway, Russia, United

States–Alaska); major international management cooperation exists through the IUCN (Polar Bear Specialist Group); international trade regulated under CITES, Appendix II; United States and Russia entered an agreement in 2007 on the Conservation and Management of the Alaska-Chukotka Polar Bear Population; listed as Threatened by the World Conservation Union (2006); major habitat loss is occurring as polar ice decreases (climate change); five of the nineteen populations stable, two increasing, five decreasing; seven unknown trend

Canada: protected; designated Special Concern by COSEWIC; designated Special Concern (Species at Risk in Ontario—SARO); population declining (Yukon); hunting limited to Eskimos and other Native Americans for subsistence and sale of skins; harvests regulated by quota

Denmark (Greenland): protected; hunting limited to Eskimos and other longtime residents for subsistence and sale of skins

Norway: hunting prohibited unless in defense of life and property

Russia: completely protected in Russian arctic; hunting prohibited; laws poorly enforced in some areas

United States (Alaska): protected under U.S. Endangered Species Act (Threatened) and U.S. Marine Mammals Protection Act; Native American hunting controlled by quotas; energy production will continue under Threatened status

Sloth Bear

Numerous small populations faced with expanding human population; habitat diminishing rapidly due to human encroachment (declined 30 to 49 percent in last thirty years); found primarily in preserves; on IUCN Red List as Vulnerable; international trade regulated under CITES, Appendix I

Bangladesh: protected under Bangladesh Wild Life Preservation Act as Threatened; may now be extinct in Bangladesh

Bhutan: Threatened; hunting banned; declining

India: Threatened; Indian Wildlife Protection Act, Schedule I (no hunting); 174 "protected areas"; efforts to protect Bengal tigers and Asian elephants benefiting the sloth bear in shared habitat; vulnerable on the Indian subcontinent

Nepal: Threatened; not protected; limited habitat

Sri Lanka: Threatened; some protection under the Fauna and Flora Protection Ordinance of Sri Lanka; limited habitat

Sun Bear

One of the rarest tropical forest animals (probably always has been); numerous small populations competing for space with the fifth-largest (and expanding) human population; minimal government management or research; protection primarily in nature reserves; poaching prevails; listed under National Wildlife Protection Laws; on IUCN Red List as Vulnerable; international trade regulated by CITES, Appendix I; population declining approximately 1 percent each year; future bleak

Bangladesh: protected under Bangladesh Wild Life Preservation Act, 1974

Brunei Darussalam: minimal data available

Cambodia: protected, though poaching prevalent; specific data unavailable

China: survival in doubt; protected under Wildlife Protection Law of the People's Republic of China

India: totally protected under Wildlife Protection Act of 1972

Indonesia: completely protected under Wildlife Protection Ordinance of 1931; faces 231.6 million people

Laos: considered protected under Decree of the Council of Ministers in Relation to the Prohibition of Wildlife Trade; however, receives virtually no protection

Malaysia: listed as a game animal

Myanmar (Burma): protected under Burma (Myanmar) Wild Life Protection Act, 1936

Thailand: population stable; protected under Wild Animals Reservation and Protection Act; poaching and logging controlled

Vietnam: not protected

* Management status (protected, game species)
** Population status (stable, increasing, decreasing, unknown)

The grave of Old Ephraim, the last grizzly bear in Utah. A stone monument has since been erected in the general area to recognize the sadness in the destruction of these magnificent bears.
COURTESY THE FIVE HEIRS OF NEWELL J. CROOKSTON

THE LAST BEARS—EXTINCTION

The "last" is difficult to assess. The final black or grizzly bear of a population may have been an unreported or undocumented kill or may have died naturally without human awareness, and "rumors" always seemed to follow the last documentation. Some bear populations were eliminated, but a transient straggler from elsewhere may have passed through the subject area. The black bear populations of the East were the first to go. Then the grizzly bears of the plains vanished as the herds of bison, an important food and hide source, were eliminated.

Grizzly bears originally existed in seventeen states of the United States, four Mexican states, and nine Canadian provinces and territories. According to David Brown and John Murray in *The Last Grizzly*, the time frame of the grizzly bear's demise was, "from the arrival of Anglo-Americans in the 1820s to the present, thus spanning the period from 'Westerning Man's' initial encounters with the Great Bear to his eventual and absolute victory—a feat that, once attained, was never celebrated; only the conflict would be cherished.

Grizzly Bears in Colorado?

"And so the future of the grizzly in the Southwest hangs on the belief—one might say faith—that a few of the great beasts are holed up in some remote part of Mexico," notes David Brown in *The Grizzly in the Southwest*, "or that a couple of individuals still hang on in Colorado's San Juan Mountains."

Grizzly bears were once quite prevalent in Colorado, many occupying the rich bear habitat of the San Juan Mountains (southern part of the state and northern New Mexico), possibly the best habitat in the southwest United States. Does a grizzly bear population presently exist in this area?

- **Mid-1800s:** professional hunters/trappers/ranchers nearly eliminated grizzly bears
- **Mid-1800s to mid-1900s:** few observations
- **1950:** adult female grizzly killed; two cubs escaped; state of Colorado considered the grizzly bear "extinct"
- **1951:** two grizzlies killed; sightings and rumors continued
- **1954:** small grizzly killed
- **1956:** grizzly sow with cub sighted
- **1957:** grizzly tracks observed
- **1960s:** additional grizzly observations; skeptics considered the grizzly extinct
- **1979:** bow hunter killed a grizzly with a handheld arrow as it mauled him
- **1980–1982:** the state conducted an investigation, finding grizzly diggings and a partially collapsed grizzly den, and there was a possible sighting; the state concludes there is only "possible evidence" of grizzly bears
- **1990:** a bear-savvy rancher observed (with binoculars) a sow with cubs, claiming they were "definitely grizzlies"
- **1990:** Doug Peacock (author, grizzly bear expert) leads a team into the San Juans to determine if grizzlies exist; a 9-inch hind-paw track was located
- **1991:** a Peacock-led team (including a grizzly bear biologist) found a 9- x 5½-inch track and what appeared to be grizzly scat

- **1990s:** a San Juan, bear-savvy ranch hand observed a "grizzly" family and later checked the "very large" tracks
- **1995:** according to Rick Bass in *The Lost Grizzlies*, a man in the San Juan Mountains was charged by ". . . a large blond bear with stiff, dark-colored legs and long white claws. . . . The man dropped to the ground and curled up in the fetal position. . . . The bear . . . paced around him, circling, slamming its paws against the earth next to the man's body. . . . All the man could see was grizzly claws—over four inches long. The bear . . . blew slobber and hot breath on him. . . . Five times the bear stomped around the man. . . . Then the bear turned and walked off. . . ."

The San Juans are an enormous and rugged range of wildness that provides many secluded valleys and crannies of excellent bear habitat that could adequately hide grizzly bears. Rick Bass concludes, "They are still out there. We have not yet lost them. We stand only at the edge."

For now, any "extinct" designation for the grizzly bear in Colorado should have an asterisk*.

* *Extinction questionable*

LAST OBSERVED OR RECORDED BEARS	

AMERICAN BLACK BEAR

United States

Delaware	1700s
Illinois	Mid-1800s
Indiana	1888
Iowa	Approximately 1880 (recent transients)
Kansas	1880s (recent transients; one confirmed sighting per ten years)
Nebraska	1908 (recent transients)
Rhode Island	1880 (recent immigration from CT and MA)
South Dakota	Date undetermined; recent transients

Canada

Prince Edward Island	Shot by George (Geordie) and Bernard Leslie in 1927 with 12-gauge shotguns; killing shell had a ¾-inch ball bearing

Mexico

Nayarit	Date undetermined

GRIZZLY BEAR

United States

Arizona	Shot in Stray Horse Canyon, northeast of Clifton, by Dick Miller, September 13, 1935. Miller thought that a sow and cub may still have existed, but they were never observed.
	(A later but unconfirmed report: grizzly bear killed by B. B. Polk, U.S. government trapper in 1939, northwest slope of Mount Baldy in White Mountains, on the Fort Apache Indian Reservation)
California	Shot by Jesse B. Agnew (rancher), August 1922, in Horse Corral Meadow, Tulare County; evidence exists of "possible" observations in Sequoia National Park area until 1924
Colorado	Killed by Ed Wiseman (outfitter/hunting guide), September 23, 1979, with arrow in hand, while being mauled; San Juan Mountains* (see Grizzly Bears in Colorado, this chapter)
Kansas	Previously existed but minimal documentation; gone well before 1890, possibly about 1880
Nebraska	Previously existed but no documentation; gone well before 1890, possibly 1854
Nevada	No official record of previous existence—strange since large populations existed in surrounding states and some suitable habitat existed; one source (unconfirmed) describes a grizzly bear killed by Charles Foley in 1907 near Silver Creek
New Mexico	Shot by Tom Campbell, 1933, in the Jemez Mountains; however, a skull in the National Museum (Washington DC) from Magdalena Baldy, New Mexico, is dated 1935
North Dakota	Shot by Dave Warren, fall 1897, near Oakdale, eastern edge of Killdeer Mountains
Oklahoma	Previously existed but no documentation; gone well before 1890
Oregon	Killed by Evan Stoneman (government trapper), September 14, 1931, in Wallowa County; an unconfirmed report was recorded in 1933
South Dakota	Pre-1900, possibly about 1890; no official record
Texas	Shot by C. O. Finley and John Z. Means, October 1890; a pack of fifty-two dogs tracked down an 1,100-pound, very old male
Utah	Trapped and shot by Frank Clark (sheepherder) August 22, 1923, in northern Utah; 1,100-pound stock killer called Ephraim; Old Ephraim's memorial is of natural stone in Logan Canyon, a 9-foot, 11-inch, 9,000-pound monument with a plaque, erected in 1966 by local Boy Scouts, their parents, and other scouting program supporters

* Last (extinction) in Colorado questionable

GRIZZLY BEAR (continued)

Canada

Labrador	Extinct by 1927
Manitoba	Approximately 1825 but minimal documentation
Quebec	Extinct by 1927
Saskatchewan	Information unavailable

Mexico

Chihuahua	1928 and 1932: last grizzly bears killed in Colonia Garcia–Colonia Pacheco area
	1932: last-known grizzly bear killed in Sierra Madre, Chihuahua/Durango
	1954: grizzly bear in the Friar Mountains
	1957: grizzly bears killed in the Sierra del Nido in June and on October 4
	1957–1961: Starker Leopold investigated Sierra del Nido and estimated a population of thirty
	1960: John Nutt and Curtis Prock killed a large grizzly bear in Sierra del Nido
	1964 and 1967: grizzly bears killed in Sierra del Nido
	1969: last confirmed report of a grizzly bear in Sierra del Nido; biologist Dr. Carl Koford conducted a three-month survey; no grizzly bear evidence
	1982: David Brown (bear biologist) investigated the Sierra del Nido and found no evidence; a foreman of Rancho El Nido claimed that there had been no grizzly bears in "twenty years"
	1982: Tim Their and Jose Trevino investigated; no grizzly bear evidence
	1983: bear biologists Diana Doan-Crider and Charles Jonkel investigated in the del Nidos; no evidence of grizzly bears; eight black bears (many of cinnamon/blondish color, with longer hair than seen elsewhere in Mexico)
Coahuila	Information unavailable
Durango	Information unavailable
Sonora	1918; apparently in the Sierra de los Ajos

BROWN BEAR

Africa, Atlas Mountains	1891; an unverified report of a bear in the 1920s
Austria	Decreed extermination in 1788
Bavaria	1836
Denmark	1692 BC; approximately 3,700 years ago
Egypt	1500s
England	Eleventh century
French Alps	1937; recently reintroduced

BROWN BEAR (continued)

Germany (Eastern)	1770; recent unsuccessful attempts to reintroduce
Holland	300 years ago
Scotland	More than 900 years ago
Switzerland	1904
Most of Europe	By 1850 (Belgium, Ireland, Jordan, Luxembourg, Monaco, Netherlands, Tunisia, United Kingdom, and Vatican more than 500 years ago)

HUMAN IMPACTS ON BEARS

Conflicts between bears and people have occurred since the two species began sharing the same habitats. The bears were fine, until technology provided the repeating firearm. Early mortality was by direct killing, while in recent times the impacts in most areas are due more to the loss and degradation of bear habitat. Interaction with human activities is taking its toll on bear populations worldwide.

Early settlers in North America began eradicating bears as they cut forests, thereby eliminating bear habitat, and intensely hunted the American black bear for subsistence and as a pest. Grizzly bears were killed out of fear and for sport, as well as for food. Eurasians killed bears for subsistence and out of fear.

Whalers provided the first major human impact on polar bears when they shot and trapped the bears for the hide trade. They also provided the Eskimos with rifles, which improved the hunting ability of these arctic residents. "It was in the seventeenth century, when whalers first penetrated the Norwegian and Russian sectors of the Arctic, that their [polar bears'] survival as a species began to be threatened." Today the polar bears are imperiled, not because of firearms but by climate change.

Today's Worldwide Impacts on Bears

We are a "resource-intense society," and our world population is rapidly increasing. The impacts and pressures affecting all bear species, as well as other wildlife, are varied, intertwined, and severe. Many are interrelated, such as agricultural activities that are eliminating bear habitat with increased cultivation and at the same time dispersing fertilizers and other chemicals harmful to bears (and humans). Often human activities (agriculture, subsistence, recreation, etc.) bring people and bears into conflict.

Many bear populations worldwide are at risk due, in varying degrees, to a multitude of impacts, with the most concern in South America and Asia. Dense human populations in Asia are eliminating bears from many areas, including entire countries. "In a country [China] with one [1.3] billion people the demand for agricultural land, timber, and other resources is so great that the panda's wilderness home continues to shrink," notes George Schaller et al. in *The Giant Pandas of Wolong*.

Major Concerns

Habitat Loss

Habitat loss includes numerous elements that cause the degradation and destruction of bear habitat, all resulting in the displacement of bears and the fragmentation of bear populations that is a precursor to extinction. Bear habitat is shrinking as humans physically occupy the land, as well as displace bears with their related activities in adjacent areas. Bears are forced into areas that have inadequate food, small isolated ranges, and conflict with humans. Habitat loss is considered the most serious threat to 86 percent of the "threatened" mammals of the world.

Agricultural Activities

Land is removed from bear habitat and cultivated as farms, ranches, and plantations. Crops and livestock become attractants with resulting human/bear conflicts. Numerous Asian farmers are killed while protecting their crops, normally without a firearm, and many bears are killed as well. Bears become "pests," and negative opinion grows. Agricultural fertilizers and other chemicals are introduced into the bears' food chain.

Climate Change

Polar bear habitat is diminishing due to loss of the arctic ice pack, and the denning, available foods, and distribution of other species is being altered.

Fire (Human Caused)

Habitat is altered or destroyed with fires set by humans to "improve" the land for cultivation of crops; careless use of fire also contributes to the loss of bear habitat.

Power line installation in bear habitat of Alaska
©2008 PATRICK ENDRES/
ALASKASTOCK.COM

Clear-cut logging operation
©2008 JOHN HYDE/ALASKASTOCK.COM

Forestry Activities

Harvest of timber directly eliminates bear habitat, while associated road construction, helicopter use, settlements/camps, and other related activities displace bears. Eurasian firewood gatherers displace bears as well as engage in direct conflict.

Human Population (Increasing)

Worldwide populations are rapidly increasing, requiring more land to raise food; to build homes, businesses, and infrastructure; and to develop all related activities.

World Population

January 2009: 6.7 billion people

The root of all human/bear conflict is close association (crowding) between the two species. As the world population increases, more land—often bear habitat—is required to reside and raise food. In general, more people result in more human activity conflicting with bears. Some species of bears are competing for space to survive in countries with *extremely* dense human populations:

Bangladesh	2,675 people per square mile (ppsm); Asiatic black bear, brown bear; sun bear already extinct?
China	351 ppsm; Asiatic black bear, brown bear, giant panda; sun bear already extinct?
India	860 ppsm; Asiatic black bear, brown bear (rare), sloth bear; sun bear already extinct?
South Korea	1,229 ppsm; Asiatic black bear, brown bear (uncommon)
Sri Lanka	809 ppsm; sloth bear
Vietnam	650 ppsm; Asiatic black bear, sun bear

Oil, Gas, and Mineral Development

Seismic, drilling, mining, and transportation activities, on the surface as well as underground, degrades bear habitat and provides bear-displacement activities (settlements/camps, equipment, roads, pipelines, helicopters, noise, oil and chemical spills, etc.).

Recreational Activities/Bear Viewing

Most outdoor recreational activities (hunting, fishing, hiking, camping, four-wheeling, bicycling, horseback riding, etc.) are conducted in undeveloped areas where bear habitat may exist.

Reservoir Construction

Bear habitat is lost as countries worldwide inundate vast areas with the construction of hydroelectric dams and the accompanying facilities to meet the electrical power demands of a rapidly increasing human population.

Road Construction

As human populations and related activities increase, there is a corresponding need for more roads. Roads degrade bear habitat and displace bears.

Urban/Suburban Sprawl

Urban and suburban areas are expanding, spreading into rural and remote areas. Many people are now seeking smaller towns and cities away from high-density living, and those small towns are now "sprawling" into bear habitat with roads, utilities, homes, public buildings, and commercial developments. Once-remote forest and wild areas are becoming dotted with "wilderness" homes and in some cases full subdivisions. Bears are being displaced, as well as coming into direct conflict with human activities, resulting in the related human injuries, property damage, and bear deaths.

Direct Impacts on Bears

Chemical Pollution

Harmful chemicals are accumulating in the food chain worldwide. Pollutants are found in the air, soil, and waters, and most, if not all, bear populations are being affected.

The arctic is of most concern, where marine mammals, polar bears, and humans test positive for high degrees of industrial pollutants. According to Christian Sonne, Danish wildlife veterinarian and toxicologist, "It is a huge cocktail. . . . There are several thousand different contaminants in polar bears."

A sample of worldwide pollutants found in bears:

- Pesticides
- Heavy metals
- Ethylene glycol (antifreeze)
- PCBs (organohalogens)
- Other classes of organohalogens
- Brominated fire retardant
- Petroleum products
- Commercial fertilizers

Harmful effects of chemical pollution observed in bear populations:

- Birth rates decreasing (decline in fertility)
- Cub survival reduced
- Insulation value of bear's fur decreasing (polar bear)
- Size of genitals decreasing (polar bear)
- Deformity of paws (grizzly bear)
- Decrease in immunity to diseases
- Bears with both male and female sexual organs (polar bears; a black bear in New Mexico)
- Bear weights decreasing
- Decrease in insect populations (important bear food)

Food Shortage

Some bear species face a shortage of a specific food. Giant pandas suffer from a bamboo die-off, which occurs several times a century. Other species (deer, wild boar) are degrading bear habitats and competing for foods. Mountain pine beetles and blister rust (tree disease) in North America are killing whitebark pines, whose seeds are an extremely important fall food for grizzly bears. Polar bears have fewer available seals as the arctic ice cap recedes, resulting in less hunting area.

Ocean Toxins

Domoic acid poisoning (also known as the red tide) is accumulating in the ocean food chain. Polar bears are showing evidence of this poisoning.

Poaching

Bears are killed when they directly conflict with human activities and livelihoods, and they are also taken as trophies and for their market value. Asian families can poach and sell a bear (or its parts) for multiple times their normal annual income.

Poisoning

Bears are directly poisoned as pests, but they also consume poisons set for rodents and other animals.

Shipping Disturbance

As the arctic ice pack diminishes, shipping lanes become available in polar bear habitat, and the potential for shipping-related chemical and petroleum spills increases.

Sport and Subsistence Hunting

Hunting is a valuable wildlife management tool but is detrimental to bear populations worldwide when not regulated. Hunting also results in unintended bear/human conflicts.

Struck by Vehicle

Every year an increasing number of bears are struck and killed by vehicles on highways (see Bear Mortality, this chapter).

Use of Bears and Their Parts (Food, Medicine, as Pets)

The trade in bears and bear parts continues at a high level, with illegal killing, shipping, and sales (see The Use of Bears and Bear Parts, Chapter 7)

General Concerns

Climate Change

The world's climate is changing as the earth's surface temperature gradually increases. Our atmosphere is overloaded with a concentration of greenhouse gases, primarily carbon dioxide, which trap solar heat within our environment.

Robert H. Busch writes in *The Grizzly Almanac*, "One pervasive threat to all living things is global warming. *Global warming* is loosely defined as the warming effect of carbon dioxide and other gases that are accumulating above the Earth and acting as an insulating blanket, keeping heat in and raising atmospheric temperatures."

The change in our climate is adversely altering the lives of bears, especially polar bears, and is impacting the human world as well. The arctic region is experiencing the warmest air temperatures in four centuries, and the sea ice is decreasing. According to James Graff (*Time* magazine, October 2007), ". . . for the first time in recorded history, the Northwest Passage was ice-free all the way from the Pacific to the Atlantic. . . . melting this year [2007] was 10 times the recent annual average. . . ."

Polar bears depend on the ice pack for hunting, mating, and denning. Most significantly, they are losing their hunting grounds as the arctic ice cap melts, receding from land, thinning, and otherwise diminishing. Polar bears cannot catch their prey (seals) in open water but take them at breathing holes in the ice.

Other situations are developing:

- Bears overheating (even in cold weather)
- Shortened winter hunting season
- Diminishing hunting grounds
- Bears must swim greater distances for food.
- Evidence of bears drowning
- Evidence of starvation
- Evidence of cannibalism (males killing sows and cubs)
- Physical condition of bears diminishing
  Polar bears in western Hudson Bay weigh about 15 percent less than thirty years ago (Stirling 1988).
  Polar bears in southern Hudson Bay weigh about 15 percent less than twenty years ago (Government of Ontario).
- Reproductive parameters diminishing
- Denning locations altered

U.S. Geological Survey researcher Steven Amstrup in an Associated Press article stated, "There is a definite link between changes in the sea ice and the welfare of polar bears. . . . *As the sea ice goes, so goes the polar bear.*"

Climate warming impacts are being observed, not only in the arctic but worldwide. Bears are denning for considerably shorter periods where temperatures have been 10 degrees Fahrenheit above average. Some bears have emerged from their dens several months earlier than normal. Grizzly bears have been observed in more north-

erly areas. Natural bear foods (berries, pine nuts, corms, other vegetation, fish populations) have failed.

The reduction of greenhouse-gas (carbon dioxide) emissions is the primary and manageable solution to this global impact upon all living things.

Competition with Other Species
In China, deer and wild boar compete with the endangered giant panda for bamboo as well as overall habitat.

Habitat Loss
Habitat loss is the displacement of bears from their habitat, degradation of habitat quality, and total elimination of the habitat.

Most North American state and provincial wildlife-management agencies evaluate the level of habitat loss.

High Mortality
Many bear populations worldwide are decreasing, and the human ability to reverse this trend is questionable.

Human Attitudes
Attitudes range from the lack of appreciation of bears and their value in the wild, considering them dangerous animals competing with people for space and in some situations food, to those who see a commercial value—the sale of bears and parts.

Insufficient Research and Management
There is a lack of adequate bear management and research worldwide, as appropriate and nec-

BEAR HABITAT LOSS

United States	Serious	Not Serious		Serious	Not Serious
Alabama	X		Nevada	X	
Alaska		X	New Hampshire	X	
Arizona	X		New Mexico		X
Arkansas	X		New York		X
California		X	North Carolina	X	
Colorado	X		Ohio	X	
Florida	X		Oklahoma		X
Georgia	X		Pennsylvania		X
Kentucky		X	Rhode Island		X (b)
Maine		X	South Carolina	X	
Maryland	X		Tennessee	X	
Massachusetts	X		Texas	X	
Michigan		X	Utah		X
Minnesota		X	Vermont	X	
Mississippi		X	Virginia	X	
Montana	X (a)		West Virginia	X	
Nevada	X		Wisconsin		X

Canada	Serious	Not Serious		Serious	Not Serious
British Columbia	X		Nova Scotia	X	
Manitoba	X (c)		Nunavut	X (c)	X (d)
New Brunswick	X (e)		Ontario	X (c)	X (d)
New Foundland/Labrador	X (c)		Quebec	X (c)	X (d)
Northwest Territories	X (c)		Yukon		X

Mexico	Serious	Not Serious
Mexico	X (f)	

(a) Of concern
(b) Potentially serious
(c) Polar bear
(d) American black bear and brown/grizzly bear
(e) Habitat increasing as farmland is abandoned
(f) Due to urban sprawl; rural regions improving due to termination of communal land system

Polar bear sow and cub in diminishing habitat
©2008 AMANDA BYRD/ALASKA STOCK.COM

essary bear management is a low priority in many countries. A lack of cooperation exists between government jurisdictions; more research funding and resource-planning programs are necessary, especially in South America and Eurasia; sport and subsistence hunting is poorly managed; laws are inadequate or poorly enforced in many countries and states. Additional preserves are necessary.

Livestock Depredation

As livestock grazing (with related forest clearing) expands into bear habitat worldwide, bears are displaced. They are also considered a threat to cattle, sheep, yaks, goats, llamas, livestock herders, and others and are directly killed.

Low Numbers

Populations have declined to such low numbers in many countries, due to displacement, fragmentation, and direct deaths, that recovery is questionable.

Population Fragmentation

A small number of bears confined to small pockets of undisturbed habitat threaten population viability. Genetic variability is lacking in small populations, which leads to inbreeding problems and a decline in the health and numbers of that population of bears.

War

War has historically been highly detrimental to bear populations due to habitat destruction, displacement, and direct bear deaths.

BEAR MORTALITY

Bears die from a variety of natural and human-related causes. Naturally caused deaths are understandable, but most human-influenced deaths are preventable.

Bear Deaths (Natural Causes)

Natural deaths are obviously difficult to determine, as humans are normally not witness to the event. Bears are able to remain in balance with natural mortality, but when humans interfere, natural compensation is often inadequate to maintain populations.

Age

Death from "old age" catches up with bears as well as humans.

Asphyxiation

Bears have been found dead (suffocated) in hot-spring areas (Yellowstone National Park) when they entered a draw or other depression in which carbon dioxide had displaced the oxygen.

Avalanches and Rockfalls

Bears are caught in these natural phenomena or are simply crushed by a rolling boulder.

Crushing

A sow crushes the cubs; dens collapse on bears (asphyxiation may be associated with this cause).

Disease

Bears are susceptible to numerous systemic infections, though death due to disease is uncommon (see Diseases and Parasites, Chapter 3).

Drowning

Bear cubs drown while attempting to cross streams, especially in the spring when water levels are high and cubs are small.

Enemies

Other animals—occasionally other bears—inflict mortal wounds.

Falls

In Italy a biologist witnessed a brown bear stumble and fall over a thousand-foot cliff. A small American black bear fell to its death while scrambling on the ledges next to Yellowstone Falls. Paul Schullery in *Yellowstone Bear Tales* (park ranger F. T. Johnston's description): ". . . climb up to a point even with the top of the falls. Here he slipped when a rock came loose, and slid and fell back into the canyon, and then down into the river under the falls." James Jonkel in his article "Animal Accidents and Deaths" notes, ". . . an adult polar bear dead in the Northwest Territories that had broken its back while sliding down a snowfield."

Fire (Natural and Human Causes)

Fires, ignited by lightning or human activities (including prescribed management fires), may have similar results. Bears normally manage to elude the flames but occasionally are caught within the fire, suffering burns or death (from flames or smoke inhalation).

Freezing

A bear may die in its den due to inadequate fat reserves or exceptionally low temperatures with minimal snow cover (which acts as insulation).

Internal Hemorrhage

A grizzly bear died while digging for prey under a rock and was found with its head in a pool of blood, according to Andy Russell in *Grizzly Country*.

Parasites

Internal and external parasites weaken a bear, leading to death by other causes.

Predation

Male bears kill cubs. Brown and grizzly bears occasionally prey on smaller bears of other species.

Starvation

Bears ill prepared for hibernation may die in their dens due to inadequate fat reserves. They may also be unable to chew the necessary foods because of worn and abscessed teeth, and adequate nutrition is no longer possible. Cubs die from malnutrition.

Thermal Areas

Bears have broken through the thin surface crust of thermal areas, fallen into extremely hot water, and succumbed to the near-boiling water and/or drowned.

Unknown

Disappearance; bears radio-collared for research purposes occasionally disappear.

Bear Deaths (Human Causes)

Most bear deaths caused by human attitudes and activities are avoidable. However, in a predominantly human world, bears are most often on the losing end of the conflicts when vying for space and food. Thomas McNamee in *The Grizzly Bear* notes, ". . . some folks, of course, kill grizzly bears just for the sheer rawhided hell of it."

Electrocution

Coming into contact with fallen power lines or exploring high-power junction boxes that are left open has electrocuted bears.

Fire

Refer to Bear Deaths (Natural Causes), Fire.

Hunting

Hunting is a major element in bear management, helping to control the size of populations and eliminating problem bears. Some countries allow indiscriminate hunting, and many prohibit hunting but are unable to control the illegal taking of bears. Ernest Thompson Seton in *The Biography of a Grizzly* wrote, "There was nothing that really frightened him [a bear] but that horrible odor of man, iron, and guns. . . ."

Management/Nuisance

Bears are often destroyed as nuisances, or they die during other management and research actions due to immobilization problems.

Poaching

Poaching of bears originally was synonymous with family subsistence but now is controlled and influenced to a major extent by commercial operations. The illegal taking of wildlife is prevalent around the world and is a significant cause of bear mortality in many countries. International bear-poaching rings are impacting bear populations in Eurasia and North America. Some Asian market figures and North American law-enforcement records indicate approximately 40,000 American black bears are illegally killed annually. Poaching of bears is rampant and extremely difficult to control. The loss of entire populations threatens wildlife diversity throughout North America and around the world. In Eurasia, as bears are forced into isolated pockets, poachers find these well-defined populations easy shooting. "We talked with a researcher who witnessed hunters carrying a poached bear back to camp inside Thailand's Khao Yai National Park," relate Judy Mills and Christopher Servheen, "home to nearly 60 poacher camps at the time. . . ."

Poisoning

Bears die from poisons intended for them or other animals or from eating the carrion of poisoned animals.

Self–defense

Bears are often shot when threatening a person with a firearm.

Trapping

Trapping and killing bears is legal in some jurisdictions but also occurs illegally. Traps set for other animal species are the second-largest cause of giant panda deaths.

Vehicles

In North America, increasing numbers of bears are killed by vehicles as they cross roads, including interstate highways. Here are statistics for average numbers of recorded bear kills by vehicles in a year for a few states and one Canadian territory:

Florida	125
Georgia	25–30
Maine	90
Massachusetts	10
Minnesota	25
Nevada	28
New Hampshire	28
New Jersey	55
North Carolina	126
Ohio	1–2*
Virginia	25
Yukon	13

* Significant number when total state bear population is only 50–100

A Few Vehicle/Bear Notes

- Nevada: Of 114 road-killed bears (of known age) during 1997–2007, fifty-seven (50 percent) were one year old or younger (the sows, leading their cubs, manage to safely cross the highways ahead of their young?).
- North Carolina: 97 percent of bear mortality is by vehicles.
- Sweden: 5 percent of bear mortality is by vehicles.
- United States: Vehicles may account for more bear deaths than hunting in some states.
- Bear/vehicle incidents result not only in the death of the bear but in major property damage and sometimes human death.

Wildlife Crossings

Several states and a Canadian province are providing wildlife crossings on major highways. Overpasses and culvert underpasses with fences to guide the bears and other wildlife to the safe crossings are being constructed. Florida has more than thirty-six crossings at a cost of $20-plus million. Alberta, Canada; California; Montana; Massachusetts; Washington; and other states have crossings. The measures are quite successful for wildlife, though bears, being good climbers, are at times going over the fences onto the highways.

Bears and Trains

Trains strike bears that are using railroad rights-of-way. Corn spills from derailed train cars in Montana have attracted bears that were subsequently killed by passing trains, as well as by cars and trucks driving along the adjacent roads.

A Bear and an "Old Vehicle" (Stagecoach)

A grizzly bear caused a "vehicular" accident in 1881 near Virginia City, Montana. A stagecoach was traveling rapidly around a curve when the horses observed a bear on the road ahead. The spooked horses turned sharply and rolled the stage off the road, resulting in a tangle of injured horses and passengers and a damaged stagecoach. The unharmed bear departed the scene. Stagecoach driver James McCabe became known as "Grizzly" McCabe.

War

Bear habitat is lost or bears directly die during international and civil wars from any of the following causes:

- Artillery
- Bombing
- Contamination of air, land, and water by toxic chemicals
- Destruction (physical) of habitat
- Displacement of bears
- Gunshots
- Land-mine explosions (a postwar hazard)
- Poaching (subsistence killing by war refugees)
- Unexploded artillery shells (also a future hazard)

BEAR MANAGEMENT IN NORTH AMERICA

The management of bears is actually people/bear management—providing a situation whereby humans and bears can coexist in the same locations. Management is also directed by cooperation—the mutual and cooperative efforts of the involved agencies, conservation organizations, private landowners, residents, and general public.

A "bear management" program has six basic elements:

1. Awareness

Every effort is made to educate those who live, travel, and visit bear country about their actions when in this realm that is shared with the bear. We must understand bears, appreciate them, and know how to preserve and maintain wild populations. Agencies and others accomplish awareness by disseminating information in the form of publications, verbal messages, television, and signs.

2. Reduction of Unnatural Bear-Human Contacts

Encounters and conflicts are detrimental to people and bears and must be minimized, if not eliminated. The sources of conflict have been previously addressed. We prevent bears from obtaining nonnatural foods (human, pet, stock, and garbage) by proper storage. Bears should not be fed.

3. Bear-Management Areas

Bear-management areas are identified and established to reduce human-related impacts on bears in important bear habitat and to provide for human safety. Human activities are limited or eliminated in these areas; thus bears are provided opportunities to pursue natural behavior patterns and activities (feeding, breeding, resting, and traveling) free from human disturbance.

4. Control Nuisance Bears

Bears that become habituated and are unafraid of people are conditioned to nonnatural foods, and even those that seek natural foods in developed areas are relocated or removed from the population.

Managing human/bear conflicts is costly. The province of Manitoba's expenditures over a five-year period (2002–2006) are shown below:

- Average costs per year $120,000
- Range of costs $91,300–194,000
- Average number of personnel hours per year   5,050
- Range of personnel hours   3,800–7,900

5. Enforcement of Regulations

Appropriate regulations must be in place to provide guidance for people to properly conduct themselves in bear country. These regulations and laws must be enforced, and the courts must address violations with penalties that are strong deterrents.

6. Research

Appropriate research—research that addresses management needs—is necessary. Bear management must be based on valid research. However, on occasion certain drastic actions, prior to achieving research results, may be necessary to protect bears.

A translocation release of a nuisance grizzly bear, captured in another area, is made with hopes it will remain out of trouble.
©GARY BROWN

BEAR RESEARCH

Bear research may be described as "getting to know bears better" and is critical to the management of all bears. Credible knowledge of the species provides the necessary direction for managers to balance the requirements of humans and bears. "Research on bears, especially their space and habitat needs," observe Paul Shepard and Barry Sanders in *The Sacred Paw*, "is essential in order to provide for their survival in a world of competing land uses."

Bear research has progressively increased in North America during the past fifty years and is now progressing and improving worldwide. Current research is designed to meet management requirements and more recently is centered on the plight of bear species. International and local conservation organizations are leading the way in Eurasia and South America to develop bear-research programs.

All species of bears are quite difficult to study in the wild, as they are shy, cautious, and in many instances scarce. A myriad of ongoing bear studies focus on varying topics, such as anatomy, physiology, ecology, and behavior, with strong emphasis on reproduction and survivorship, sex and age structure of populations, and bear-habitat characterization and utilization (including feeding and nutrition). Population studies focus on bear distribution, movements (interrelationships between populations), densities, and ranges. Studies also address bear/human activities, interactions, and management methods. Bear evolution, hibernation, and genetics receive considerable attention. These studies are only a few of a multitude of bear-research projects that are approached by dedicated researchers in the field, amidst the bears. Erwin Bauer in *Bear in Their World* provides this description of Lynn Rogers (Wildlife Research Institute, Ely, Minnesota), black bear research scientist, author, and dedicated American black bear authority: "Since his college days at Michigan State, Rogers has tracked black bears from trucks, canoes, snowmobiles, cross-country skis, aircraft, afoot, and sometimes on hands and knees [into occupied bear dens]."

DNA

DNA analysis is the research tool that provides an insight into a multitude of long-existing questions about bears. Mitochondrial DNA is the DNA of the mitochondrial chromosome, which is in each of our cells and is inherited from the female. Each cell has stored the information about each individual living organism. We most often see and read of the use of DNA in solving criminal cases (hair or blood is matched to the crime scene, and the criminal is apprehended). However, this genetic fingerprinting has provided wildlife science a major tool as well. Lance Craighead in *Bears of the World* writes: "Mitochondrial DNA has helped us learn about the differences that have been found between bear species, which bears came first, which bears evolved from other bears, and approximately how long ago two bear species diverged from a common ancestor." He adds, "Nuclear DNA contains the blueprint for the individual animal. Studying nuclear DNA can tell us about differences between individuals and between populations."

Information Gathered from DNA Analysis

- Species identification
- Genetic diversity
- Species and subspecies differences*
- Individual identification
- Gender (female? male?)
- Population size
- Population distribution
- Population fragmentation
- Habitat use
- Evidence of inbreeding
- Mortality rates
- Population trends
- Necessary protection (conservation requirements)
- Home ranges of bears (individual movements)
- Recent history of an individual or population
- Evolutionary history of species and populations
- Evidence of illegal taking/sales (captive-bred parents or wild)
- Population health
- Population viability

* Craighead: "Deciding how much of a genetic difference is sufficient to define a subspecies is still basically a subjective decision."

DNA Collection

Material for DNA analysis is collected by several methods:

Hair

- "Snag stations" (small, nonconfining corrals with single-strand, shoulder-high barbed wire, where bears may freely enter for an attractant, leaving snagged hair on the wire)
- Rub trees (natural sap; applied tar)
- Clipped during capture (management actions)
- Clipped from dead bears (management deaths, highway kills, harvests, etc.)
- Removed from feces

Blood, Skin Tissue, Muscle Tissue

- Collected during management actions (capture, deaths)
- Collected from dead animals (dried carcasses, highway kills, hunting harvests)

The Laboratory for Ecological and Conservation Genetics (University of Idaho, Moscow, Idaho) and Wildlife Genetics International laboratory (Nelson, British Columbia) are two of a few facilities in North America that analyze DNA (genetic information taken from animals, e.g., hair, bone, blood, and feces) for wildlife managers.

Satellite Monitoring

Bears are fitted with collars that transmit radio signals to a satellite, thereby pinpointing the location of the individual bear. Global positioning system (GPS) technology has become a major tool in bear research. According to C. Schwartz, et al. in their article "Grizzly Bear," ". . . advances [GPS] . . . are providing insight into bear movements, home range analyses, habitat use, and other spatial statistics not obtainable via conventional telemetry. . . . Satellite telemetry enables the collection of thousands of locations during the life of a transmitter, thus reducing the need to put collars on numerous individuals."

THE FUTURE OF BEARS

"Conservation of bears requires human intervention in the competitive interaction between man and bear to assure resource availability for both species to the exclusion of neither," notes Servheen (1989).

Conservation Measures

Bear managers in all countries need to balance bear and human needs, addressing bear biology and human economic requirements and social concerns.

Bear researcher applying radio telemetry collar for satellite monitoring, Alaska
©2008 JOHN WARDEN/ALASKASTOCK.COM

- Develop and maintain a strategy that addresses the needs of bears but also focuses more on human social, economic, and cultural issues, whereby people are not hindered nor burdened with hardships due to bear conservation. The keys are education and values, with humans developing an understanding of bears and their positive value and importance in the world as wild animals.
- Address social questions, targeting the people who live with bears—providing incentives for them to change and balance the risks of this dual occupancy. The local people must support the long-term maintenance of the various species, developing an economic value for bears that is an alternative to killing them and where the degradation of bear habitat is not necessary for humans to survive. Presently (in 2008) the basic annual income of many Asian families is less than US$400, while they can illegally kill and sell a bear for US$4,000 to $5,000.
- Manage social issues in a manner beneficial to bears as well as people.
- Provide compensation payments for bear-caused losses.
- Adjust the present management of people and bear relationships utilizing experimental management concepts.
- Improve land-use planning, including the implementation of proactive measures and the enhancement of cooperative planning and management between governments (counties, states, provinces, cities, and countries).
- Balance the consumptive and nonconsumptive uses of land, move and resettle people (this is critical in Asia), and control human access into important bear areas.

- Take measures to deter bears from developments, protecting people and property.
- Provide for research that addresses efficient bear management, including proper compatibility of people and bears; initiate, enhance, and refocus such research, directing it to management problems, especially social and economic concerns.
- Initiate, continue, or enhance the broad spectrum of research and management measures that addresses the survival of all species of bears.
- Protect bear habitat, with the reduction or elimination of human activities in critical habitat, and with habitat quality optimized and degraded areas restored.
- Increase the number of reserves for bears, with existing areas enlarged and buffer zones provided where necessary.
- Provide contiguous lands for bears, with continuity between populations (eliminate population fragmentation and prevent future fragmentation).
- Develop strategies to protect bears on private lands.
- Provide compatibility between bear-hunting programs and bear populations and habitat.
- Improve hunters' knowledge and understanding of bears, especially concerning identification of species.
- Control the exportation, importation, and sales of bears and bear parts.
- Enhance and strictly enforce regulations and laws that provide protection for bears and their habitat.
- Courts and judges must apply appropriate fines and jail terms, considering not only punitive measures, but the value of preventing other detrimental impacts on bears.

Future of the Species

American black bear	Species survival ensured; some populations increasing; others endangered by fragmentation
Andean bear	Population declining (projected 30 percent in a thirty-year period); inaccessibility of remaining habitat may protect them for many years, but population fragmentation may have already doomed the species
Asiatic black bear	Uncertain future; population highly fragmented and declining; world's human population will double by 2025, with most of the growth in the habitat of this species (Southeast Asia)
Brown bear	Species survival ensured; large and widely distributed worldwide population with minimal decline; small European populations threatened; grizzly bears tenuous in United States (Lower 48)
Giant panda	Rare; survival outside preserves doubtful; highly fragmented population; according to George Schaller et al. in *The Giant Pandas of Wolong,* "The panda provides a living blueprint for extinction. We face now the scientific and moral challenge of producing a blueprint for its survival."
Polar bear	Species overall threatened; rapidly losing habitat (arctic ice) due to global warming; projected 30 percent population loss by 2050
Sloth bear	Habitat diminishing rapidly; survival outside parks doubtful
Sun bear	Highly uncertain future; small isolated populations; overall population rapidly declining (more than 40 percent in past thirty years and will continue at this rate); possibly extinct in some areas

Epilogue

MARVELOUS CREATURES, bears have long been extremely important components in our lives—mythical, religious, exciting, and humanlike. The many aspects of bears are related and intertwined, not only within the world of the bears but within the human world as well. Bears provide subsistence, sport, excitement, death, comfort, and values. They reach us nearly daily with names, images, art, literature, the heavens, foods, parks, flags, financial markets, festivals, religion, conflicts, and so much more. Bears have carried forth historical traditions to our "modern" world. And they are unquestionably in nature and wilderness—*they belong*.

A pair of grizzly bears feeding on berries in Denali National Park, Alaska
©JOHNNY JOHNSON

Bears were on the earth before us but today cling to shrinking habitats around the world as human technology, population growth, and certain philosophies challenge their ability to survive. We could someday be without bears, except in zoos and other captive situations, as is already the situation with several animal species of the world.

Bears, worldwide, evolved in wilderness—a natural, expansive, diverse, and precarious region, unsettled and in an untamed state. "They [bears] represent a natural world without controls, the dangerous side of nature," writes David Rockwell in *Giving Voice to Bear*.

"Nature has few creations like the great bear to enforce respect for the order she has wrought," explains Douglas Chadwick in *A Beast the Color of Winter*, "few remaining works whose very spoor, once seen, can make the mountains suddenly higher, the valleys wider, the wind louder as it bends around a rise."

Bears require undisturbed expanses for survival, and humans, whether we know it or not, also need wilderness, time away from the ever-increasing chaos of our everyday lives. "Knowing that we are in the presence of bears adds spice to the outdoor adventure," notes George Laycock in *The Wild Bears*. "Whenever we go where the wild bear lives, we feel a keen sharpening of the senses, an unforgettable level of alertness."

Bears *are* wilderness—the element that must be there in order to have a complete natural scheme. It would not be wild without them. But during the last 200 years, bears worldwide have been reduced in numbers, slowly at first, but now more drastically, as species are eliminated from areas and threatened with extinction, primarily due to the reduction of their habitat—isolated and undisturbed areas. The world's human population is rapidly increasing, and the associated urban and suburban sprawl eliminates bears.

"There seems to be a tacit assumption," wrote Aldo Leopold in *A Sand County Almanac*, "that if grizzlies survive in Canada and Alaska, that is good enough. It is not good enough for me. Relegating grizzlies to Alaska is about like relegating happiness to heaven; one may never get there."

We should be able to coexist with and enjoy bears, but we happen to have the technology to be the dominant species. We do not have to *like* bears but should respect them for what they are. View and experience this longtime symbol of our culture, and enjoy them as that and as wild animals, an important ingredient of our lives and our world. Humans are challenged to be creative and to address the worldwide social situations that are necessary to assist and support bears.

This "bear almanac" is not all inclusive, and hopefully the cast of characters and facts have intrigued the reader—perhaps enticed you to investigate, to have a *bearlike curiosity*, and to learn more about these remarkable animals that are in some manner part of our everyday lives.

If you gain but a single thing from this book, it should be an understanding and appreciation for the bears of the world—a world big enough for bears and people.

> *It would be fitting, I think, if among the last man-made tracks on earth could be found the huge footprints of the great brown bear.*
>
> E. J. Fleming, 1958
> (As quoted in *The Grizzlies of Mount McKinley*, by Adolph Murie)

Appendix A

Stratigraphic Periods

Era	Period/Epoch	Duration (Years Ago*)
Cenozoic Era (63,000,000 years ago to present)	Tertiary Period	63,000,000 to 2,000,000 to 500,000
	—Oligocene Epoch	63,000,000 to 25,000,000
	—Miocene Epoch	25,000,000 to 13,000,000
	—Pliocene Epoch	13,000,000 to 2,000,000 to 500,000
	Quaternary Period	2,000,000 to 500,000 to present
	—Pleistocene Epoch	2,000,000 to 500,000 to 11,000
	—Holocene Epoch	11,000 to present

There are no definitive beginnings or endings for some periods or epochs due to the enormous amount of time considered, as well as different dating methods utilized around the world.

Appendix B

International Conservation Organizations

Convention on International Trade in Endangered Species of Wild Fauna and Flora (CITES)

The Convention on International Trade in Endangered Species of Wild Fauna and Flora (1973) serves as an oversight body and regulates, to some degree, the international trade in most bear species (although individual countries must be parties to CITES).

Appendix I of CITES includes those species threatened with extinction. Any legal trade of these species requires exceptional circumstances to be permitted. Trade in specimens of these species must be subject to particularly strict regulation in order not to further endanger their survival and must only be authorized in exceptional circumstances.

Appendix II includes those species that are not threatened with extinction; however, they must be protected with strict trade regulation in order to provide for their survival.

Appendix III includes species protected in countries requesting CITES assistance in trade control.

Several bear-trade countries are not parties to CITES, and among those that are, many do not have laws to enforce trade restrictions. Where laws do exist, enforcement is often negligible.

International Union for Conservation of Nature and Natural Resources (IUCN)

The world's largest conservation organization, with its headquarters located in Gland, Switzerland, consists of eighty-four states, 108 government agencies, more than 800 nongovernment organizations, and more than 10,000 scientists from 147 countries.

IUCN maintains a Red List (a worldwide listing of species of concern and their status). The organization does not have enforcement powers but identifies, lobbies, and promotes protection and conservation of all threatened species of plants and animals.

IUCN Bear Specialist Group: Consists of teams of experts that address the respective species/subspecies of bears, plus captive bears and the bear-parts trade.

The Bear Specialist Group represents fifty-five countries and is comprised of 130 members.

International Association for Bear Research & Management (IBA)

IBA promotes the restoration and conservation of all bear species worldwide, utilizing science-based education, research, and management. The IBA is active in over fifty countries and consists of more than 550 members (biologists, managers, and others).

Public Conservation Organizations

Hundreds of conservation organizations exist worldwide (a list too unwieldy for this almanac). Some are bear organizations, some focus primarily on bears, others address bears within their myriad of concerns and projects. All are highly important to the conservation of bear species worldwide.

Glossary

alimentary canal: the mucous-membrane-lined tube of the digestive system

anthropomorphism: (1) the attribution of human feelings to nonhuman beings, (2) a being or object having or suggesting human traits

aphrodisiac: a substance that stimulates or intensifies sexual desire

arboreal: (1) living in trees, (2) an animal that spends the majority of its time in trees

bearcat: panda; one who fights with ferocity

bile: bitter, alkaline secretion of the liver, stored in the gallbladder; also aids digestion

binocular vision: when both eyes are used at the same time and have the same movement and direction

bipedal: walking on two feet as opposed to four (quadpedal)

BP: before the present

bromeliad: a plant, such as an orchid or fern, that grows on other plants for mechanical support rather than nutrition

bunodont: refers to the molar teeth of bears; flat cusps, broad and grinding type of teeth

carnivore: an animal that is predominantly a flesh eater; belongs to the classification order Carnivora

carrion: dead and decaying flesh; refers to dead animals available as food

cloud forest: mountains shrouded in heavy clouds nearly all year, with torrential rains

COSEWIC: Committee on the Status of Endangered Wildlife in Canada

crepuscular: active at twilight or a period just prior to sunrise

dressed: refers to a dead animal that is gutted and cleaned; intestines removed; hunting term

embryogenesis: growth and development of an embryo

estrus: period of ovulation and sexual activity in female mammals; in "heat"

extant: exists; not destroyed

femur: upper leg bone

game animal: an animal managed by fish and game departments for the purpose of hunting harvest

gram: 0.0353 ounce

habitat: the area or environment in which a bear or other animal normally lives

herbivore: an animal that eats mostly vegetation

humerus: upper arm bone

invertebrate: an animal without a backbone or spinal column

kilo: 2.2 pounds

league: 3 miles

New World: the western hemisphere; North and South America and adjacent islands

nictitating membrane: inner eyelid in numerous animals; thin membrane

Old World: the eastern hemisphere; Eurasia, Africa; commonly refers to Europe

olfactory: contributing to, or of, the sense of smell

omnivore: an animal whose diet consists of a balance of flesh and vegetation

pelage: fur, hair; soft covering of a mammal

plantigrade: walking with the entire sole surface of the paw on the ground

protrusile: extendable; able to push forth

pseudobulbs: (1) false bulbs; bulbs similar to true bulbs, (2) a bear food

rain forest: tropical, evergreen forest with high annual precipitation

shambling: a "wide" stance, straddling-like walk

spyhop: marine mammals' (primarily whales') act of vertically rising in the water to better observe their above-water surroundings

tattoo: military pageant; outdoor display

temperate: zones of moderate climate; two middle-latitude zones of the earth

translocation: bear-management term; capturing a bear in one area and releasing it in another location

ungulate: a hoofed animal (mammal)

vertebrate: an animal with a backbone or spinal column

vestigial tooth: a degenerate, nonfunctioning, and unnecessary tooth

Bibliography

Books

Adams, Ramon F. *Western Words*. Norman: University of Oklahoma Press, 1968 & 1981.

Ambrose, Stephen E. *Undaunted Courage*. New York: Simon & Schuster, 1997.

Armstrong, Richard B., and Mary Willems Armstrong. *The Movie List Book*. Jefferson, Carolina: McFarland & Company, Inc., Publishers, 1990.

Auel, Jean M. *The Clan of the Cave Bear*. New York: Bantam Books, 1980.

Bakeless, John. *Lewis and Clark: Partners in Discovery*. New York: William Morrow & Co., 1947.

Banfield, A. W. F. *The Mammals of Canada*. Toronto: University of Toronto Press, 1974.

Bass, Rick. *The Lost Grizzlies*. Boston: Houghton Mifflin Company, 1995.

Bassett, W. *History of the Town of Richmond, Cheshire County, New Hampshire*. Boston: C. W. Calkins Company, 1884.

Bauer, Erwin. *Bear in Their World*. New York: Outdoor Life Books, 1985.

————. *Bears—Behavior/Ecology/Conservation*. Stillwater, MN: Voyageur *Press*, Inc., 1996.

Beecham, John, and Jeff Rohlman. *A Shadow in the Forest*. Moscow: University of Idaho Press, 1994.

Blevins, Win. *Dictionary of the American West*. Seattle, WA: Sasquatch Books, 2001.

Bright, Michael. *Intelligence in Animals*. London: The Readers Digest Association Limited, 1997.

Brown, David E. *The Grizzly in the Southwest*. Norman: University of Oklahoma Press, 1985.

Brown, David E., and John Murray. *The Last Grizzly*. Tucson: The University of Arizona Press, 1988.

Brown, Gary. *Outwitting Bears*. New York: The Lyons Press, 2001.

————. *Safe Travel in Bear Country*. New York: Lyons & Burford, Publishers, 1996.

Buffalo Horn Man, Gary, and Sherry Firedancer. *Animal Energies*. Lexington, KY: Dancing Otter Press, 1992.

Bull, Peter. *The Teddy Bear Book*. New York: Random House, 1970.

Burnaby, A. *Travels through the Middle Settlements in North America in the Years 1759 and 1760*. Ithaca, NY: Cornell University Press, 1968.

Burton, Maurice. *Systematic Dictionary of Mammals of the World*. New York: Thomas Y. Crowell Company, 1962.

Busch, Robert H. *The Grizzly Almanac*. New York: The Lyons Press, 2000.

Cahalane, Victor H. *Mammals of North America*. New York: The Macmillan Company, 1947.

Caras, Roger A. *North American Mammals*. New York: Galahad Books, 1967.

Cardoza, James E. *The Black Bear in Massachusetts*. Westborough: Massachusetts Division of Fisheries & Wildlife, 1976.

Carleton, Mary Tennent. *The Byrnes of Berkeley*, from letters of Mary Tanner Byrne and other sources.

Chadwick, Douglas H. *A Beast the Color of Winter*. San Francisco: Sierra Club Books, 1983.

———. *True Grizz*. San Francisco: Sierra Club Books, 2003.

Chartrand, Mark R., and Helmut K. Wimmer. *Skyguide, a Field Guide to the Heavens*. Racine, WI: Western Publishing Company, 1982.

Chatwin, Bruce. *The Songlines*. New York: Viking Penguin Inc., 1987.

Cheek, Roland. *Learning to Talk Bear*. Columbia Falls, MT: Skyline Publishing, 1997.

Cherr, Pat. *The Bear in Fact and in Fiction*. New York: Harlin Quest, Inc., 1967.

Chuinard, E. G. *Only One Man Died*. Glendale, CA: The Arthur H. Clark Company, 1979.

Clarkson, Peter, and Linda Sutterlin. *Bear Essentials*. Missoula, MT: School of Forestry, University of Montana, 1984.

Cline, Dave, and Tim Richardson, eds. *Kodiak Bears & The Exxon Valdez*. Kodiak, AK: Kodiak Brown Bear Trust, 2002.

Clutton, Cecil, Paul Bird, and Anthony Harding. *The Vintage Car Guide*. New York: Doubleday & Co., 1976.

Coffin, Tristram Potter, and Henning Cohen. *The Parade of Heroes*. Garden City, NY: Anchor Press/Doubleday, 1978.

Colcord, Willard Allen, ed. *Animal Land*. Philadelphia: The Judson Press, 1925.

Craighead, Frank C., Jr. *Track of the Grizzly*. San Francisco: Sierra Club Books, 1979.

Craighead, Karen. *Large Mammals of Yellowstone and Grand Teton National Parks*. Karen Craighead, 1978.

Craighead, Lance. *Bears of the World*. Stillwater, MN: Voyageur Press, Inc., 2000.

Craighead-George, Jean. *Beasty Inventions*. New York: David McKay Company, Inc., 1970.

Cramond, Mike. *Killer Bears*. New York: Charles Scribner's Sons, 1981.

———. *Of Bears and Man*. Norman: University of Oklahoma Press, 1986.

Crampton, William. *Flags of the United States*. New York: W. H. Smith Publishers, Inc., 1989.

———. *Flags of the World*. New York: Dorset Press, 1990.

Crofton, Ian (compiler). *Brewer's Curious Titles*. London, England: Cassell, 2002.

Crookston, Newell J. *The Story of Old Ephraim*. North Logan, UT: Newell J. Crookston, 1959.

Cummins, John. *The Hound and the Hawk*. New York: St. Martin's Press, 1988.

Cushing, Frank Hamilton. *Zuni Fetishes*. Las Vegas: KC Publications, 1990.

Darwin, Charles. *The Origin of Species*. New York: The New American Library of World Literature, Inc., 1958.

Dary, David A. *The Buffalo Book*. New York: Avon Books, 1974.

Davis, W. H. *Sixty Years in California*. San Francisco: 1889.

Day, Beth. *Grizzlies in Their Backyard*. Surrey, BC: Heritage House Publishing Co. Ltd., 1994.

DeHart, Don. *All about Bears*. Boulder, CO: Johnson Publishing Co., 1971.

Dellenbaugh, Frederick S. *A Canyon Voyage, The Narrative of the Second Powell Expedition*. Tucson: University of Arizona Press, 1988.

Dewey, Donald. *Bears*. New York: Michael Friedman Publishing Group, Inc., 1991.

Dillon, Richard H. *The Legend of Grizzly Adams*. Reno: University of Nevada Press, 1966.

Domico, Terry, and Mark Newman. *Bears of the World*. New York: Facts on File, 1988.

Drimmer, Frederick. *The Animal Kingdom*, Vol. 1. New York: Greystone Press, 1954.

Dufresne, Frank. *No Room for Bears*. New York: Holt, Rinehart and Winston, Inc., 1965.

East, Ben. *Bears*. New York: Outdoor Life Books, 1977.

———. *The Ben East Hunting Book*. New York: Harper & Row, 1974.

Eberhart, George M. *Mysterious Creatures*. Santa Barbara, CA: ABC-CLIO, Inc., 2002.

Elman, Robert. *Bears, Rulers of the Wilderness*. Stamford, CT: Longmeadow Press, 1992.

Evans, Ivor H., ed. *Brewer's Dictionary of Phrase and Fable*. New York: Harper & Row, 1959.

Farnham, T. J. *Life, Adventures and Travels in California*. New York: Nafis and Cornish, 1849.

Feazel, Charles T. *White Bear*. New York: Henry Holt Company, 1990.

Finnerty, Edward W. *Trappers, Traps, and Trapping*. New York: A. S. Barnes and Company, 1976.

Flint, Richard Foster. *Glacial and Quaternary Geology*. New York: John Wiley & Sons, Inc., 1971.

Fox-Davies, A. C. *A Complete Guide to Heraldry*. New York: Skyhorse Publishing Co., 2007.

Funk, Charles Earle. *A Hog on Ice*. New York: Harper & Row, 1948.

———. *Horsefeathers*. New York: Harper & Row, 1958.

———. *Thereby Hangs a Tale*. New York: Harper & Row, 1950.

Gard, Wayne. *The Great Buffalo Hunt*. Lincoln: University of Nebraska Press, 1959.

Gilchrist, Duncan. *All about Bears*. Hamilton, MT: Outdoor Expeditions and Books, 1989.

Gowans, Fred R. *Mountain Man & Grizzly*. Orem, UT: Mountain Grizzly Publications, 1986.

Greener, W. W. *The Gun and Its Development*. Secaucus, NJ: Chartwell Books Inc., 1988.

Griggs, Robert F. *The Valley of Ten Thousand Smokes*. Washington, DC: The National Geographic Society, 1922.

Grosswirth, Marvin. *The Heraldry Book*. Garden City, NY: Doubleday & Co., 1981.

Grzimek, H. C. Bernard, ed. and contributor. *Grzimek's Animal Life Encyclopedia*, Vol. 12, Vol. 14. Farmington Hills, MI: Gale, 2004.

————. *Grzimek's Encyclopedia of Mammals*, Vol. 3. New York: McGraw-Hill Publishing Company, 1990.

Halfpenny, James. *A Field Guide to Mammal Tracking in Western America*. Boulder, CO: Johnson Publishing Company, 1986.

————. *Yellowstone Bears in the Wild*. Helena, MT: Riverbend Publishing, 2007.

Hanna, Warren L. *The Grizzlies of Glacier*. Missoula, MT: Mountain Press Publishing Co., 1978.

Haynes, Bessie D., and Edgar Haynes. *The Grizzly Bear*. Norman: University of Oklahoma Press, 1966.

Herrero, Stephen. *Bear Attacks: Their Causes and Avoidance*. Guilford, CT: The Lyons Press, 2002 (1985).

Hill, W. W. *An Ethnography of Santa Clara Pueblo, New Mexico*. Albuquerque: University of New Mexico Press, 1982.

Hillary, Sir Edmund, and Desmond Doig. *High in the Thin Cold Air*. Garden City, NY: Doubleday & Company, Inc., 1962.

Hoh, LaVahn G., and William H. Rough. *Step Right Up!: The Adventures of Circus in America*. Crozet, VA: Betterway Publications, Inc., 1990.

Hornaday, William T. *The American Natural History*. New York: Charles Scribner's Sons, 1904.

————. *Camp-Fires in the Canadian Rockies*. New York: Charles Scribner's Sons, 1907.

Hoyt, Olga. *Witches*. New York: Abelard-Schuman Ltd., 1969.

Hubbard, W. P., and Seale Harris. *Notorious Grizzly Bears*. Chicago: The Swallow Press Inc., 1960.

Ingles, Lloyd Glenn. *Mammals of California*. Stanford, CA: Stanford University Press, 1947.

Jamieson, David, and Sandy Davidson. *The Colorful World of the Circus*. London: Octopus Books Limited, 1980.

Kanes, Joseph Nathan. *Famous First Facts*. New York: The H. W. Wilson Company, 1950.

Kaniut, Larry. *Alaska Bear Tales*. Anchorage: Alaska Northwest Publishing Company, 1983.

————. *More Alaska Bear Tales*. Anchorage: Alaska Northwest Books, 1989.

Kevles, Bettyann. *Females of the Species*. Cambridge, MA: Harvard University Press, 1986.

Koch, Thomas J. *The Year of the Polar Bear*. New York: The Bobbs-Merrill Company, Inc., 1975.

Kurten, Bjorn. *Pleistocene Mammals of Europe*. Chicago: Aldine Publishing Company, 1968.

Kurten, Bjorn, and Elaine Anderson. *Pleistocene Mammals of North America*. New York: Columbia University Press, 1980.

Laycock, George. *The Wild Bears*. New York: Outdoor Life Books, 1986.

————. *Wild Hunters*. New York: David McKay Company, Inc., 1978.

————. *Wilderness Legend—Grizzly*. Minocqua, WI: Northwood Press, 1997.

Lehner, Ernst. *Symbols, Signs & Signets*. New York: Dover Publications, Inc., 1950.

Lekagul, Boonsong, and Jefrey A. McNeely. *Mammals of Thailand*. Bangkok, Thailand: Sahakarnbhat Company, 1977.

Leonard, Rhoda. *Arctos the Grizzly*. Sacramento: California State Department of Education, 1969.

Leopold, Aldo. *A Sand County Almanac*. New York: Oxford University Press, 1949.

Long, Ben. *Great Montana Bear Stories*. Helena, MT: Riverbend Publishing, 2002.

Lopez, Barry. *Arctic Dreams*. New York: Charles Scribner's Sons, 1986.

MacDonald, Margaret Read. *The Folklore of the World Holidays*. Detroit, MI: Gale Research, Inc., 1992.

Marty, Sid. *Men for the Mountains*. New York: Vanguard Press, Inc., 1979.

Matteucci, Marco. *History of the Motor Car*. New York: Crown Publishers, 1970.

Matthiessen, Peter. *The Snow Leopard*. New York: The Viking Press, 1978.

McCoy, J. J. *Wild Enemies*. New York: Hawthorn Books, Inc., 1974.

McCracken, Harold. *The Beast That Walks Like Man*. Garden City, NY: The Garden City Press, 1955.

McGuire, Bob. *Black Bears*. Blountville, TN: Bowhunting Productions, 1983.

McIntyre, Rick. *Grizzly Cub*. Anchorage: Alaska Northwest Books, 1990.

McNamee, Thomas. *The Grizzly Bear*. New York: Alfred A. Knopf, 1984.

McNeely, Jeffrey, and Paul S. Wachtel. *Soul of the Tiger*. New York: Doubleday & Co., 1988.

Medawar, P. B., and J. S. Medaware. *Aristotle to Zoos*. Cambridge, MA: Harvard University Press, 1983.

Menzel, Donald H. *A Field Guide to the Stars and Planets*. Boston: Houghton Mifflin, 1964.

Miles, Alfred H. *The Universal Natural History*. New York: Dodd, Mead & Co., 1895.

Mills, Enos A. *The Grizzly—Our Greatest Wild Animal*. Boston: Houghton Mifflin, 1919.

————. *The Spell of the Rockies*. Lincoln: University of Nebraska Press, 1989 (Originally Houghton Mifflin, 1911).

————. *Wild Life on the Rockies*. Lincoln: University of Nebraska Press, 1988 (Originally Houghton Mifflin, 1909).

Morris, Desmond, and Ramona Morris. *The Mammals*. New York: Harper & Row, 1965.

————. *Men and Pandas*. New York: McGraw-Hill Book Company, 1966.

Muir, John. *The Mountains of California*. New York: Dorsett Press, 1988.

————. *Our National Parks*. New York: Houghton Mifflin, 1901.

————. *Trails of Wonder, Writings on Nature and Man*. Edited by Peter Seymour. Kansas City, MO: Hallmark Cards, Inc., 1972.

————. *Wilderness Essays*. Salt Lake City, UT: Peregrine Smith, Inc., 1980.

Murie, Adolph. *A Naturalist in Alaska*. New York: The Devin-Adair Company, 1961.

————. *Ecology of the Coyote in Yellowstone*. Fauna Series No. 4. Washington, DC: United States Government Printing Office, 1940.

———. *The Grizzlies of Mount McKinley*. Washington, DC: United States Department of the Interior, 1981.

Murie, Olaus J. *A Field Guide to Animal Tracks*. Boston: Houghton Mifflin, 1954.

Napier, John. *Bigfoot*. New York: E. P. Dutton & Company, Inc., 1972.

National Geographic. *Atlas of the World*. Washington, DC: NGS, 2007.

Nielsen, Leon, and Robert D. Brown, eds. *The Translocation of Wild Animals*. Milwaukee: Wisconsin Humane Society, Inc., 1988.

Ormand, Clyde. *Bear*. Harrisburg, PA: The Stackpole Company, 1961.

———. *Complete Book of Hunting*. New York: Outdoor Life Books, 1962.

Osteen, Phyllis. *Bears around the World*. New York: Coward-McCann, 1966.

Paradiso, John L. *Mammals of the World*. Baltimore: Johns Hopkins University Press, 1975.

Partridge, Eric. *A Dictionary of Slang and Unconventional English*. New York: Macmillan Publishing Co., Inc., 1976.

Peacock, Doug. *Grizzly Years*. New York: Henry Holt & Company, 1990.

Peacock, Doug, and Andrea Peacock. *In the Presence of Grizzlies*. Guilford, CT: The Lyons Press, 2006.

Perry, Richard. *Bears*. New York: Arco Publishing Company, Inc., 1970.

———. *The World of the Giant Panda*. New York: Bantam Books, Inc., 1969.

Peterson, Thomas Carl. *Heaven and Earth*. New York: Prentice Hall Press, Inc., 1986.

Prodgers, Jeanette. *The Only Good Bear Is a Dead Bear*. Helena, MT: Falcon Press Publishing Company, 1986.

Quammen, David. *Monster of God*. New York: W. W. Norton & Company, 2003.

Rennicke, Jeff. *Bears of Alaska in Life and Legend*. Boulder, CO: Roberts Rinehart, Inc. Publishers, 1987.

Revkin, Andrew C. *The North Pole*. Boston: Houghton Mifflin Company, 2006.

Riley, William, and Laura Riley. *Guide to the National Wildlife Refuges*. Garden City, NY: Anchor Press/Doubleday, 1979.

Rockwell, David. *Giving Voice to Bear*. Niwot, CO: Roberts Rinehart, Inc., 1991.

Room, Adrian. *Brewer's Dictionary of Phrase & Fable*. New York: HarperCollins Publishers, 1999.

Roosevelt, Theodore. *The Works of Theodore Roosevelt* (Elkhorn Edition). New York: G. P. Putnam's Sons, 1893.

Roots, Clive. *The Bamboo Bears*. Winnepeg, Manitoba, Canada: Hyperion Press Limited, 1989.

Russell, Andy. *Grizzly Country*. New York: Lyons and Burford, Publishers, 1984.

Russell, Carl P. *Firearms, Traps, & Tools of the Mountain Men*. Albuquerque: University of New Mexico Press, 1967.

Russell, Osborne. *Journal of a Trapper*. Lincoln: University of Nebraska Press, 1955.

Salisbury, Albert, and Jane Salisbury. *Two Captains West*. New York: Bramhall House, 1950.

Samson, Jack. *The Bear Book*. Clinton, NJ: The Amwell Press, 1979.

————. *The Grizzly Book*. Clinton, NJ: The Amwell Press, 1982.

Savage, Candace. *Grizzly Bears*. San Francisco: Sierra Club Books, 1990.

Schaller, George B. *The Last Panda*. Chicago: The University of Chicago Press, 1993.

Schaller, George B., Hu Jinchu, Pan Wenshi, and Zhu Jing. *The Giant Pandas of Wolong*. Chicago: The University of Chicago Press, 1985.

Schneider, Bill. *Where the Grizzly Walks*. Missoula, MT: Mountain Press Publishing Company, 1977.

Schullery, Paul. *American Bears: Selections from the Writings of Theodore Roosevelt*. Boulder: Colorado Associated University Press, 1983.

————. *The Bear Hunter's Century*. New York: Dodd, Mead & Co., 1988.

————. *The Bears of Yellowstone*. Niwot, CO: Roberts Rinehart, Inc., 1986.

————. *Lewis and Clark among the Grizzlies*. Guilford, CT: Falcon (Globe Pequot Press), 2002.

————. *Mountain Time*. New York: Lyons & Burford, Publishers, 1984.

————. *Pregnant Bears and Crawdad Eyes*. Seattle, WA: The Mountaineers, 1991.

————. *Yellowstone Bear Tales*. Niwot, CO: Roberts Rinehart, Inc., 1991.

————, ed. *American Bears*. Boulder: Colorado Associated University Press, 1983.

Scott, M. Douglas, and Suvi A. Scott. *Heritage from the Wild*. Bozeman, MT: Northwest Panorama Publishing, Inc., 1985.

Seidensticker, John, and Susan Lumpkin. *Giant Pandas*. New York: HarperCollins Publishers, 2007.

Service, Robert W. *Ballads of a Bohemian*. New York: Barse & Hopkins, 1921.

Seton, Ernest Thompson. *The Biography of a Grizzly*. New York: Grosset & Dunlap, 1919.

————. *Lives of Game Animals*. Garden City, NY: Doubleday, 1925-27.

————. *Monarch the Big Bear*. New York: Charles Scribner's Sons, 1904.

Sheldon, Charles. *The Wilderness of Denali*. New York: Charles Scribner's Sons, 1930.

Shepard, Paul, and Barry Sanders. *The Sacred Paw*. New York: Viking Penguin Inc., 1985.

Silverstone, Paul. *U.S. Warships of World War I*. Garden City, NY: Doubleday & Co., 1970.

Skinner, M. P. *Bears in the Yellowstone*. Chicago: A. C. McClurg & Company, 1932.

Smith, F. Dumont. *Book of a Hundred Bears*. Chicago: Rand McNally & Company, 1909.

Speaight, George. *A History of the Circus*. San Diego, CA: A. S. Barnes & Co., 1980.

Stefansson, Vilhjalmur. *Arctic Manual*. New York: The Macmillan Company, 1944.

————. *Hunters of the Great North*. New York: Harcourt, Brace & Co., 1922.

Stein, Ralph. *The World of the Automobile*. New York: Random House, 1973.

Stevens, Montague. *Meet Mr. Grizzly*. San Lorenzo, NM: High-Lonesome Books, 1987.

Stewart, George R. *Ordeal by Hunger*. New York: Pocket Books, Simon & Schuster, 1974.

Stimpson, George. *A Book about a Thousand Things*. New York: Harper & Brothers, 1946.

Stirling, Ian. *Polar Bears*. Ann Arbor: University of Michigan Press, 1988.

Stone, Irving. *Men to Match My Mountains*. Garden City, NY: Doubleday & Co., 1956.

Storer, Tracy I., and Lloyd P. Tevis, Jr. *California Grizzly*. Berkeley: University of California Press, 1955.

Talocci, Mauro. *Guide to the Flags of the World*. New York: William Morrow & Co., 1982.

Teale, Edwin Way. *The Wilderness World of John Muir*. Boston: Houghton Mifflin Company, 1954.

Thwaites, Reuben Gold, ed. *Original Journals of the Lewis and Clark Expedition 1804–1806*. New York: Dodd, Mead & Company, 1904.

Tomkins, William. *Universal Indian Sign Language*. San Diego, CA: William Tomkins, 1926.

Topsell, Edward. *The History of Four-Footed Beasts*. London: William Jaggard, 1607.

Tracy, Jack. *Scherlockiana, the Encyclopedia*. New York: Avenel Books, 1977.

Van Wormer, Joe. *The World of the Black Bear*. New York: J. B. Lippincott Company, 1966.

Walker, Ernest P. *Mammals of the World*. Volume II. Baltimore: The Johns Hopkins Press, 1968.

Walker, Tom. *The Way of the Grizzly*. Stillwater, MN: Voyageur Press, Inc., 1993.

———. *We Live in the Alaskan Bush*. Anchorage: Alaska Northwest Publishing Co., 1977.

Wasserman, Paul, and Edmond L. Applebaum. *Festivals Sourcebook*. Detroit, MI: Gale Research Company, 1984.

Wells, H. G. *The Outline of History*, vol. 2. Garden City, NY: Doubleday & Co., Inc., 1920.

Whittlesey, Lee H. *Death in Yellowstone*. Boulder, CO: Roberts Rinehart, Inc. Publishers, 1995.

Wilson, Herbert Earl. *The Lore and the Lure of Yosemite*. San Francisco: Sunset Press, 1923.

Woodcock, Thomas, and John Martin Robinson. *The Oxford Guide to Heraldry*. Oxford: Oxford University Press, 1988.

Wright, Banton. *Kachinas, A Hopi Artist's Documentary*. Flagstaff, AZ: Northland Press, 1973.

Wright, William H. *The Black Bear*. New York: Charles Scribner's Sons, 1910.

———. *The Grizzly Bear*. Lincoln: University of Nebraska Press, 1977.

Young, Robert. *Analytical Concordance to the Bible*. Grand Rapids, MI: Wm. B. Erdmans Publishing Company, 1972.

Yukon Wildlife Branch. *The Bear Facts*. The Government of the Yukon Territory.

Zappler, Lisbeth. *Nature's Oddballs*. Garden City, NY: Doubleday & Co., 1978.

Zhi, Lu. *Giant Pandas in the Wild*. New York: Aperture Foundation, 2002.

Articles, Bulletins, Papers, Reports

Amstrup, Steven. Climate Change article; Associated Press, Washington, DC. *Billings Gazette* (Montana), September 2007.

Banci, Vivian. "The Status of the Grizzly Bear in Canada in 1990." A COSEWIC Status Report. Governments of Alberta, British Columbia, and Yukon, 1991.

Barnes, Victor G., and Olin E. Bray. "Population Characteristics and Activities of Black Bears in Yellowstone National Park," A Final Report. Fort Collins: Colorado Cooperative Wildlife Research Unit, 1967.

"Bears and Bear-Hunting," *Harper's New Monthly Magazine*, Vol. XI, No. IXV, October 1855.

Bell, W. B. "Hunting Down Stock-Killers," Yearbook of Agriculture for 1920, Washington, DC: U.S. Government Printing Office, 1921.

Benedetti-Cecchi, Lisandro, Iacopo Bertocci, Stefano Vaselli, and Elena Maggi, "Temporal Variance Reverses the Impact of High Mean Intensity of Stress in Climate Change Experiments," *Ecology*, October 2006.

Blanchard, Bonnie M., and Richard R. Knight. "Reactions of Yellowstone Grizzly Bears, *Ursus arctos horribilus*, to Wildfire in Yellowstone National Park," *The Canadian Field-Naturalist* 104 (1990).

Bolgiano, Chris. "Do Appalachia's Bears Have a Future?" *Defenders of Wildlife*, November/December 1987.

California (state of). "Final Environmental Document, Bear Hunting." Sacramento, CA: Department of Fish and Game, 1991.

———. "A Plan for Black Bear in California." Sacramento, CA: Department of Fish and Game, 1987.

Ceballos-G., Gerardo. "The Importance of Riparian Habitats for Conservation of Endangered Mammals in Mexico." Paper read at First North American Riparian Conference at University of Arizona, 1985.

Craighead, J. J., and F. C. Craighead, Jr. "Grizzly Bear–Man Relationships in Yellowstone National Park," a report in *Bears—Their Biology and Management*, IUCN, 1972.

Dalquest, Walter W., and O. Mooser. "Arctodus Pristinus Leidy in the Pleistocene of Aguascalientes, Mexico," *Journal of Mammalogy* 61, no. 4 (November 1980).

Demaster, Douglas P., and Ian Stirling. *"Ursus Maritimus," Mammalian Species*, no. 145. The American Society of Mammalogists, The Johns Hopkins University Press, 1981.

Dye, Lee. *Good Nappers*. ABC News Release, 2004.

Emmons, E. "Reports on the herbaceous plants and on the quadrupeds of Massachusetts." Cambridge, MA: Folsom, Wells & Thurston, 1840.

Erdbrink, D. P. "A Review of Fossil and Recent Bears of the Old World." Paper. Deventer, Netherlands, 1953.

Graff, James. "Fight for the Top of the World." *Time* magazine, October 2007.

Hall, E. Raymond. "Geographic Variation Among Brown and Grizzly Bears in North America." Lawrence: University of Kansas Museum of Natural History, 1984.

Hamann, Andreas, and Tongli Wang. "Potential Effects of Climate Change on Ecosystem and Tree Species Distribution in British Columbia," *Ecology*, November 2006.

Harlow, Richard F. "Characteristics and Status of Florida Black Bear." From proceedings at 26th North American Wildlife and Natural Resources Conference. Washington, DC: Wildlife Management Institute, 1961.

Herrick, B. F. "Grade-School Grizzly," *California Historical Society Quarterly*, 1946.

Hintz, Martin. "Animals Inside the Earth," *American Archeology*, Spring 1997.

Home, W. S. "Color Change in a Growing Black Bear," *The Murrelet*, Winter 1977.

Jonkel, C., and I. McTaggert Cowan. "The Black Bear in the Spruce-fir Forest," *Wildlife Monograph* no. 27 (1971).

Jonkel, James J. "Animal Accidents and Deaths," *Outdoor Life Magazine*, January 1987.

Kiliaan, H. P. L., and Ian Stirling. "Observations on Overwintering Walruses in the Canadian High Arctic," *Journal of Mammalogy* 59, no. 1 (1978).

Knight, Richard R., Bonnie M. Blanchard, and David J. Mattson. "Yellowstone Grizzly Bear Investigations," Annual Report of the Interagency Grizzly Bear Study Team, Bozeman, MT, 1991.

Kurten, Bjorn. "The Evolution of the Polar Bear, Ursus Maritimus Phipps." Acta Zoologica Fennica 108. Helsinki, Finland: Institute of Zoology and Institute of Geology and Paleontology of the University, Helsingfors, 1964.

Kurten, Bjorn, and Elaine Anderson. "Association of *Ursus arctos* and *Arctodus simus* in the Late Pleistocene of Wyoming." Abstract in the periodical *Breviora*, no. 426. Cambridge, MA: Museum of Comparative Zoology, 1974.

Laurie, Andrew, and John Seidensticker. "Behavioural Ecology of the Sloth Bear," *Journal of Zoology* (1977).

LeCount, Albert. "Causes of Black Bear Mortality." Arizona Game and Fish Department, 1986.

Lentfer, Jack W. "Polar Bear." Article in *Wild Mammals of North America*, edited by Joseph A. Chapman and George A. Feldhamer. Baltimore: Johns Hopkins University Press, 1982.

Lindzey, Frederick G., and E. Charles Meslow. "Population Characteristics on an Island in Washington." *Journal of Wildlife Management* (1977).

———. "Winter Dormancy in Black Bears in Southwestern Washington." *Journal of Wildlife Management* 41 (3) (1976).

Linnel, John D. C., Daniel Steuer, John Odden, Petra Kaczensky, and Jon E. Swenson. "European Brown Bear Compendium." Safari Club International Foundation, 2002.

Mattson, David J. "An Evolutionary and Ecological Interpretation of the Life Histories and Distributions of Northern Bears." Unpublished paper for Interagency Grizzly Bear Study Team, Bozeman, MT, 1991.

———. "Human Impacts on Bear Habitat Use." Paper presented at the 8th International Conference on Bear Research and Management, Victoria, British Columbia, 1988.

McIntyre, Thomas. "American History—Grizzly," *Sports Afield*, September 1983.

Meagher, Mary, and Sandi Fowler. "The Consequences of Protecting Problem Grizzly Bears." Paper presented at Bear-People Conflicts Symposium, Yellowknife, Northwest Territories, 1987.

Merriam, C. H. "Review of the Grizzly and Big Brown Bears of North America." *North America Fauna* 41 (1918). Washington, DC: United States Department of Agriculture, Biological Survey.

Mills, Judy A., and Christopher Servheen. "The Asian Trade in Bears and Bear Parts." A project report. Washington, DC: World Wildlife Fund. Inc., 1991.

Paque, Bernard. Bear hunting article. *Wall Street Journal*, 1991.

Pelton, Michael R. "The Black Bear in the Southern Appalachian Mountains: An Overview." Excerpts from a paper presented at conference, Is There a Future for the Southern Appalachian Black Bear? Asheville, NC, 1987.

Poilker, Richard J., and Harry D. Hartwell. "Black Bear of Washington." Biological Bulletin no. 14, 1973. Washington State Game Department.

Reiss, Marguerite. "How to Be Safe in Bear Country," *Outdoor Life*, 1987.

Revenko, Igor A. "Brown Bear Reaction on Man on Kamchatka." Paper presented at Ninth International Bear Conference on Bear Research and Management, Missoula, MT, 1992.

Rogers, Lynn. "Effects of Mast and Berry Crop Failures on Survival, Growth, and Reproductive Success of Black Bears." Paper read at 41st North American Wildlife and Natural Resources Conference, Wildlife Management Institute, Washington, DC, 1976.

———. "Shedding of Footpads by Black Bears during Denning," *Journal of Mammalogy* 55, no. 3 (1974).

Rozell, Ned. "Debunking the Myth of Polar Bear Hair," Article #1390, Alaska Science Forum, 1998.

———. "Farthest North Grizzlies Among Alaska's Most Adaptable," Article #1350, Alaska Science Forum, 1997.

Schullery, Paul. "Bear Myths." *Field and Stream*, December 1984.

Schwartz, C. C., S. D. Miller, and M. A. Haroldson. "Grizzly Bear." *Wild Mammals of North America: Biology, Management, and Conservation.* 2nd ed. Baltimore: The Johns Hopkins University Press, 2003.

Schwartz, C. C., M. A. Haroldson, Gary C. White, et al. "Temporal, Spatial, and Environmental Influences on the Demographics of Grizzly Bears in the Greater Yellowstone Ecosystem. Wildlife Monographs (supplement to *The Journal of Wildlife Management*), 2006.

Servheen, Christopher. "The Status and Conservation of Bears of the World." Paper read at 8th International Conference on Bear Research and Management, Victoria, British Columbia, 1989.

Stirling, Ian. "Sleeping Giants." *Natural History*, January 1989.

Stone, Ian R., and Andrew E. Derocher. "An Incident of Polar Bear Infanticide and Cannibalism on Phipsoya, Svalbard." *Cambridge Journals (Polar Record)*, March 2007.

Urquhart, D. R., and R. E. Schweinsburg. "Polar Bear, Life History and Known Distribution of Polar Bear in the Northwest Territories up to 1981." Yellowknife, Northwest Territories: Department of Renewable Resources, Northwest Territories, 1984.

Voorhies, M. R., and R. George Corner. "Ice Age Superpredators." Museum notes, University of Nebraska State Museum, 1982.

Other References

The American Heritage Dictionary of the English Language. New York: American Heritage Publishing Co., Inc., 1975.

The Book of Mormon. Salt Lake City, UT: The Church of Jesus Christ of Latter-day Saints, 1981.

The Holy Bible. King James Version. New York: Thomas Nelson & Sons.

Webster's New Collegiate Dictionary. Springfield, MA: G. & C. Merriam Co., 1953.

The World Book Encyclopedia. Chicago: Field Enterprise Educational Corporation, 1969.

Web Sites

The author retrieved information from several hundred Web sites (too many to list), nearly all with the keyword *bear*.

Index

Italicized page references indicate illustrations.

hearing, 84
height and weight
    averages, 61
hibernation, 153, 154,
    155, 157
historical observations of, 44
human injuries and deaths
    due to, 251, 271
hunting harvest statistics, 239
intelligence, 99
interactions with
    humans, 268
as largest, 62–63
longevity records, 94
motherhood, 149, 150, 151
names of, historical and
    contemporary, 16, 28, 185
national parks and refuges
    with, 42, 43
navigation capabilities,
    125, 126
odor, 87, 157
parasites common to, 91
paws (feet), 74, 76
populations, 30, 32, 36
postage stamps featuring, 216
range distances, 165
reproduction, 135, 138,
    139, 140
skulls, 63, 71, *71*
smell, sense of, 86
social behaviors, 101
status of, 284–85, 291, 308
subspecies of, 21
swimming abilities, 127, *127*
tails, 81
teeth, 73
thermoregulation, 88
tracks, 79
vocalizations, 102, 104
weight, 57, 60
in zoos, 231

pollution, chemical, 294
Pope, Samuel, 249
populations, 29–36
porcupines, 109, 114, 178
postage stamps, *214*, 214–16,
    215, 235
posturing, 105, *105*
predation, 99, 116–18,
    175, 300
pronghorn antelopes, 114
property damage, 273
protection efforts, 23–24,
    281–83, 306–7
Protursus, 7

raccoons, 178
range distances, 164–65
red pandas, 52
religions and cults, 191–97,
    198–99, 219
reproduction, 106, 107,
    134–41, 203
research, 296, 298,
    303–6, 306
respiration, 89, 159
rhinoceros, 61, 114
Romans, 223, 235
Roosevelt, Theodore, 112, 175,
    219, 233, *234*, 242, 246
routes, 120
running, 123–25, *124*

saddles, beartrap, 218
safety precautions and
    tips, 34, 274–78
saints, 196, 216
salt licks, 175–76
Samuel, James, 249
Sasquatch, 203
satellite monitoring, 306, *306*
Savin's bears, 7
scat (feces), 90, *90*, 253

scenting, 81, 106–8, *107*, *108*
"school" bears, 34
Schoppert, James: "Sea
    Bear," 204
sea-bear, 178
"Sea Bear" (Schoppert), *204*
seals, 114
Sergius of Radonezh,
    Saint, 196
Service, Robert, 208
shamans, 191, 193–94
she-bears, defined, 28
shedding, 64
Sherlock Holmes books, 205
ships, names of, *213*, 213–14
short-faced bears, 2, 8, *8*, 9
size, 56–63, 71
skeletons, 2–3, 10, 48, *74*, 182.
    See also skulls
skulls
of ancient bears, 8, 10
    as bear part commodity,
        255, 261
    comparative sizes of, 63
    for hunting records scoring,
        242–43
    overview and species
        descriptions, 71, *71*
skunks, 114
slang, 187
sleuth, defined, 28
sloth, defined, 28
sloth bears
    activity periods, 177
    animal interactions, 113
    attack behaviors, 117, 263
    bipedal standing and
        walking, 123
    classification, 13, 17, *17*
    claws, 77
    climbing capabilities, 130
    coloration, 55, 66, 70

About the Author

Gary Brown is retired from the National Park Service following a thirty-seven-year career in a variety of park ranger positions at seven western national parks. He was involved in bear-management thirty of those years, and his assignments included Chief Ranger at Denali and Rocky Mountain National Parks, and Assistant Chief Ranger at Point Reyes National Seashore and Yellowstone National Park. He was Bear-Management Specialist at Yellowstone for ten years.

Gary lives near Bozeman, Montana, where he has a natural resource consulting business, specializing in park and bear conservation and management. He is author of *Safe Travel in Bear Country* (Lyons & Burford) and *Outwitting Bears: The Essential Handbook for Living with Bears* (The Lyons Press).